MIDLOTHIAN, TEXAS
THROUGH TIME

KAREN KAY ESBERGER

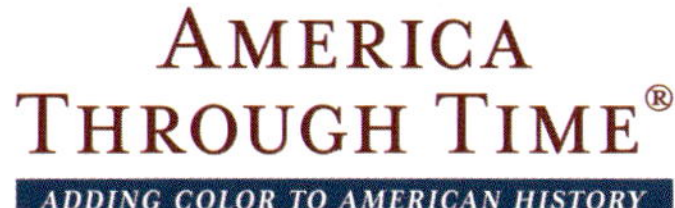

For my sons, Doug and Jim,
Jim's wife, Melany,
and their children, Elizabeth and Gabriel.
For my parents, Phama Duke and James T. Kay, Jr.

America Through Time is an imprint of Fonthill Media LLC
www.through-time.com
office@through-time.com

Published by Arcadia Publishing by arrangement with Fonthill Media LLC
For all general information, please contact Arcadia Publishing:
Telephone: 843-853-2070
Fax: 843-853-0044
E-mail: sales@arcadiapublishing.com
For customer service and orders:
Toll-Free 1-888-313-2665

www.arcadiapublishing.com

First published 2019

ISBN 978-1-63500-088-7

Typeset in Mrs Eaves XL Serif Narrow
Printed and bound in England

Introduction

Before Anglo settlement, the area that would become Midlothian was covered with tall prairie grasses, interspersed with cool springs arising from the underlying Balcones Escarpment, a high limestone ridge. The springs gave rise to Waxahachie Creek, and many settlers chose land near its headwaters, including the Hawkins, Hinckley, Garvin, Kelley, Jenkins, and Witherspoon families. The villages of Barker, Lebanon, and Midlothian would begin near those headwaters. If a family did not live on the creek or at a spring, good water was available via a well.

Native Americans moved freely about the area. The tribes of Tonkawa, Waco, Bidais, Anadarko, and Kickapoo were frequent visitors. In the 1840s, Anglos, such as fur traders, were in the area. After Sam Houston finalized a treaty with the Native Americans in 1843, Anglo settlement began in earnest. Even before the treaty, Peters' Colony, out of Louisville, KY, held an "Empresario Land Grant" contract from the Republic of Texas to bring settlers to Texas. Most of the early settlers to this area came under its auspices. Under their contract, a married man could receive 640 acres, while a single man could obtain 320 acres. However, the Empresarios could keep a large portion of that as payment for services rendered.

By 1850, a village called Lebanon had arisen near a good spring on the land of B. F. Hawkins. A floorless log cabin served as both church and school. When it burned in 1855, another cabin was put up in its place. Concurrently, the mail was delivered once weekly to the home of Rev. Charles Barker who lived nearby. So, the area began to be called "Barker" or "Barkersville."

When Ellis County was formed in 1850, many men from the Midlothian area were elected to the new offices. William A. Hawkins became Chief Justice, and his son, Benjamin Franklin Hawkins, was County Clerk. Larkin Newton was a commissioner. Benjamin G. Garvin was the presiding officer for elections in Precinct Four, and Charles H. Barker was District Clerk.

As early as June 3, 1881, the *Waxahachie Enterprise* referred to this community as Midlothian, thus discounting the common story about a train conductor naming it for his home in Scotland on the day of the land sale, May 10, 1883. The newspaper reported on May 19, 1882 that a petition had been signed and sent to "Washington City" to "change the name of our post from Barker" to Midlothian.

PUBLIC SALE OF TOWN LOTS

IN THE TOWN OF

MIDLOTHIAN

ON THE

CLEBURNE AND DALLAS BRANCH

OF THE

Gulf, Colorado & Santa Fe R. R.

ON

THURSDAY, MAY 10, 1883.

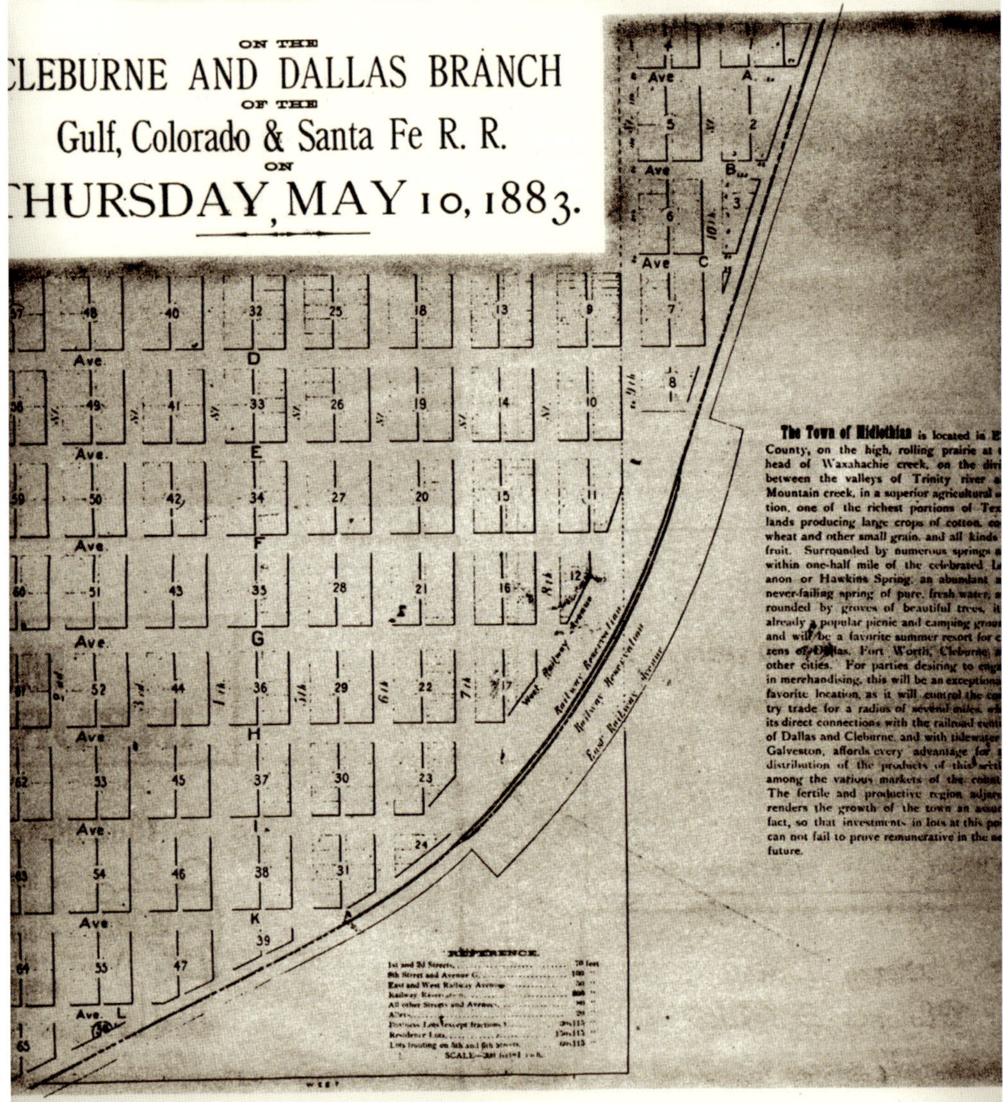

HALF FARE FROM ALL STATIONS,

In the May 4 edition of the *Waxahachie Enterprise*, the Gulf, Colorado and Santa Fe Railroad ran an article announcing the details of a public sale of town lots in Midlothian to be held on Thursday, May 10. Soon after the sale, the company built a stock yard below the depot. By late May, there were 2,500 head of cattle in the yard awaiting shipment to the north.

Railroads directly led to the establishment of Midlothian. The establishment of the Gulf, Colorado & Santa Fe Railway (GC&SF) led to businesses in the Lebanon and Barker area moving the mile or two to the railroad tracks. Houses began to be erected. At the land sale, GC&SF had donated land to the new town for churches and schools. The GC&SF was crossed by the Fort Worth and New Orleans Railroad (FW&NO) in 1886, but it promptly sold out to Houston and Texas Central Railroad (H&TC). The old FW &NO then ended up being part of the Southern Pacific system.

Thus, the town was located at a prominent crossroads. The residents voted to incorporate Midlothian in 1888 and elected a mayor and city council.

The Memorial and Biographical History of Ellis County, Texas, was published in 1892. At that time, the town boasted two gins, two general stores, one drugstore, one hardware and agricultural implement establishment, one livery stable, one saddle and harness shop, one millinery shop, one confectionary, one furniture store, three grocery stores, one hotel, one bakery, one barbershop, one blacksmith and wagon repair shop, and one newspaper, along with a population between 700 and 800.

Only two brick buildings had been erected in the "downtown" area, 100 block of North 8th Street, before a major fire destroyed all the wooden business buildings on November 25, 1893. Before the end of the year, businessmen began constructing brick buildings. By the time the Sanborn fire map was drawn in 1898, over half of the brick business houses that were to be located in the town were already in place. These were mostly located in the 200 block of West Avenue F and on the west side of the 100 block of North 8th Street. Construction on the east side of 8th followed soon, as the last major brick business building in downtown is dated 1913.

Ellis County was a top cotton producer during the 1890s and early twentieth century due to experiencing heavy immigration from the Old South, people who already knew how to grow cotton. The land was abundant, and several gins were built to prepare the cotton for shipping. Cotton was in such high demand that Ellis County farmers did not diversify their crops. Unfortunately, their relatively high standard of living dropped when the Great Depression brought a rapid decrease in the demand for cotton.

Trades Days on Saturdays were common, as were yearly horse and mule shows, fairs, and rodeos. The merchants stayed open late on Saturday nights to accommodate the rural residents who had come to town to shop and visit.

Many villages were only 3 to 5 miles from Midlothian. They contributed to the economy and participated in social activities. Midlothian was the commercial center for buying goods that one could not grow on a farm and for selling the items that the farm did produce. People from the surrounding areas sent their students to Polytechnic Institute, a boarding school in Midlothian, while one-room country schools were closer to most homes.

People appeared to prefer burying their dead in the Midlothian Cemetery. There are few family cemeteries in the area, the exceptions being Newton, and Krantz which was begun by the Garvin family. The Mount Zion Cumberland Presbyterian Church had a burying ground beside its church, about 2 miles east of town. Mountain Peak, an older community about 6 miles south of town, had a large cemetery.

World War II brought many changes to town. Volunteers and draftees quickly departed. The women rallied to handle traditional men's jobs, and many commuted to the metroplex defense plants to become Rosie the Riveters. Some held more than one job in order to take up the slack created by a diminished labor force.

After the war, the returning servicemen eagerly took up a normal life with their families and worked hard to better the town and the quality of life for everyone. Social clubs carried out plans for improvement. Although many farmers remained in Midlothian, many men and women began commuting to various metroplex businesses and industries to earn their livings.

The villages surrounding Midlothian gradually disappeared as schools were consolidated with Midlothian, men took other jobs besides farming, and the automobile made it easier to connect with folks in town. Such villages as Auger Hole, Christian Chapel, Onward, Long Branch, Plainview, Walnut Grove, and Wyatt now exist only in memories or books.

Today, the chalk and shale of the Balcones Escarpment provide materials for the manufacture of cement, with three cement plants located in Midlothian.

There is one survivor that people watch rather closely and lovingly. One can only document the existence of this mesquite tree back to 1920, but it is a beloved landmark to people who travel up and down FM 663 every day.

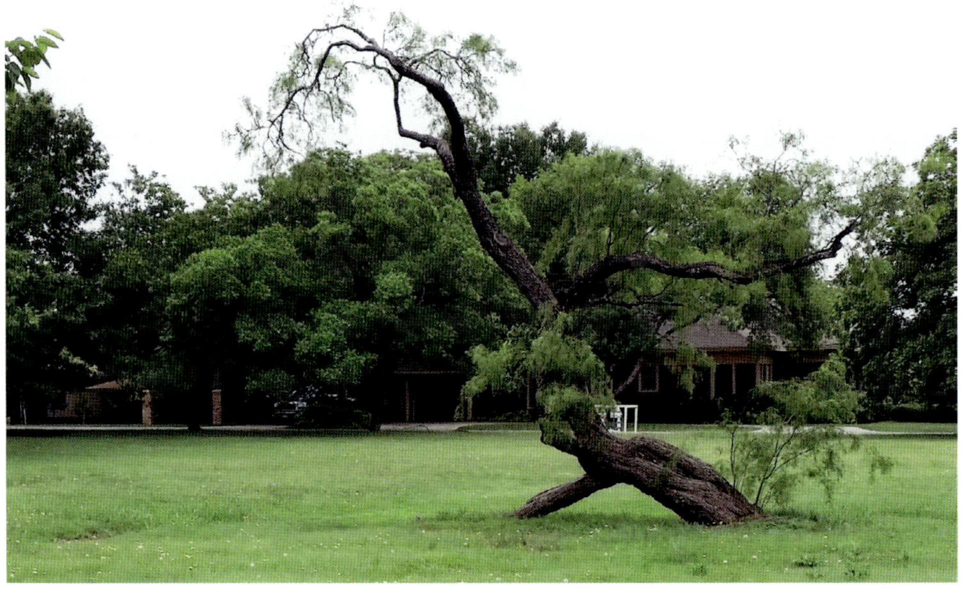

Contents

Acknowledgments

I am so grateful to these people for their assistance in answering questions and providing photographs for this effort. They love their native hometown as much, if not more, as I do and like to see its information preserved. They are Beverly Sink, Mark Countryman, Moe Holland, Grant Pryor, Linda Munden Love, Carolyn Burleson Meacham, Kevin Blankenship, Stuart Pryor, Judith Ralston Howard, Allison Greenburg, Dr. Charles R. Williams, Cherry F. Williams, Kathy McElroy Robinson, Wayne Ray, and Patricia Few Stinson.

1

FOUNDING

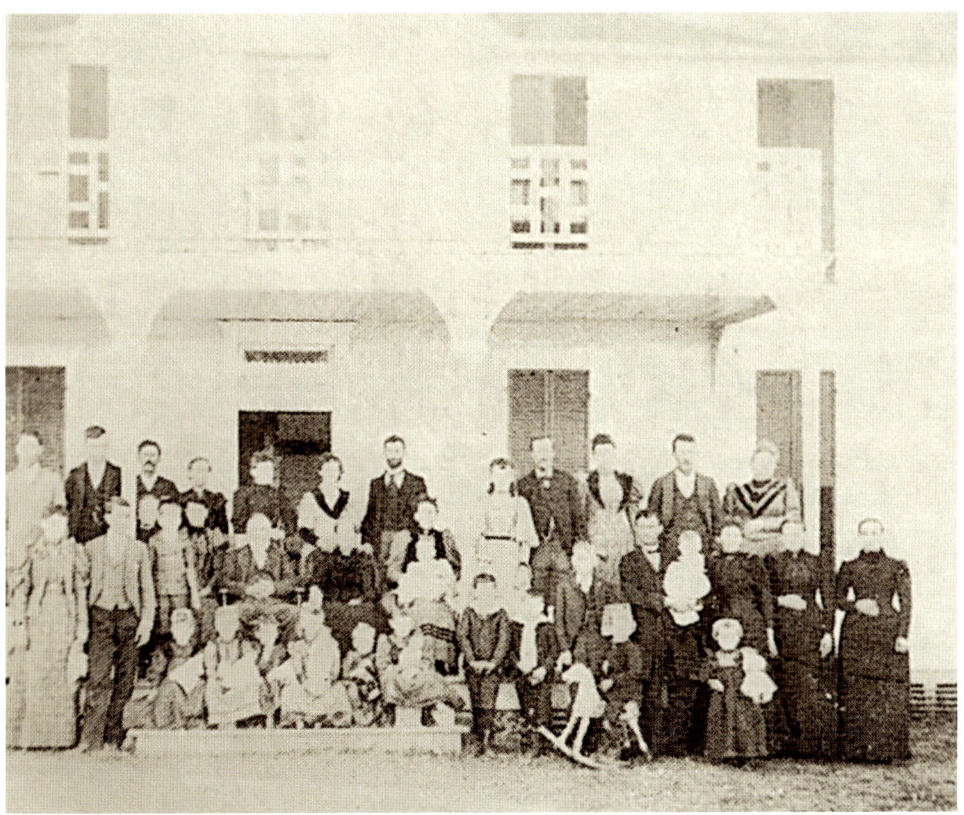

Marcellus Tolbert Hawkins came from Indiana in 1848. Marcellus received 320 acres of land where he built a cabin immediately, so he could keep the improved land and begin farming right away. His Hereford cattle were healthy and numerous, and his crops kept threshers busy. In 1850, he married Amanda Newton, daughter of Larkin & Mary Anne Wilson Newton.

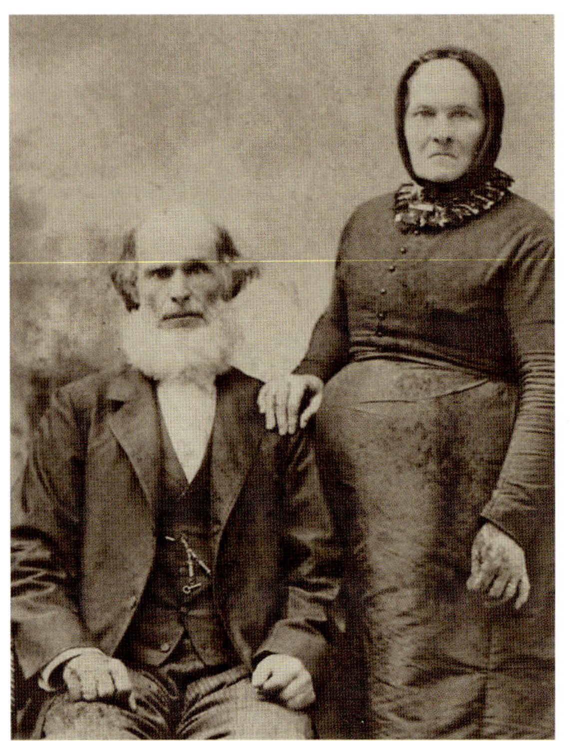

EARLY SETTLERS AND SUMMER KITCHEN: Joseph Munden, Jr., came to Texas from Indiana in 1846 by horseback. In 1847, he married Elizabeth Ann Baggett in Dallas County. The couple and their first three children moved to Ellis County about 1853, where they had six more children. Besides constructing their cabin and other needed buildings, they built this summer kitchen, which still stands as of 2018. Food being prepared outside the main house prevented the possibility of fire destroying the whole house. These kitchens were doubly useful in the summer when cooking there would prevent the kitchen from overheating.

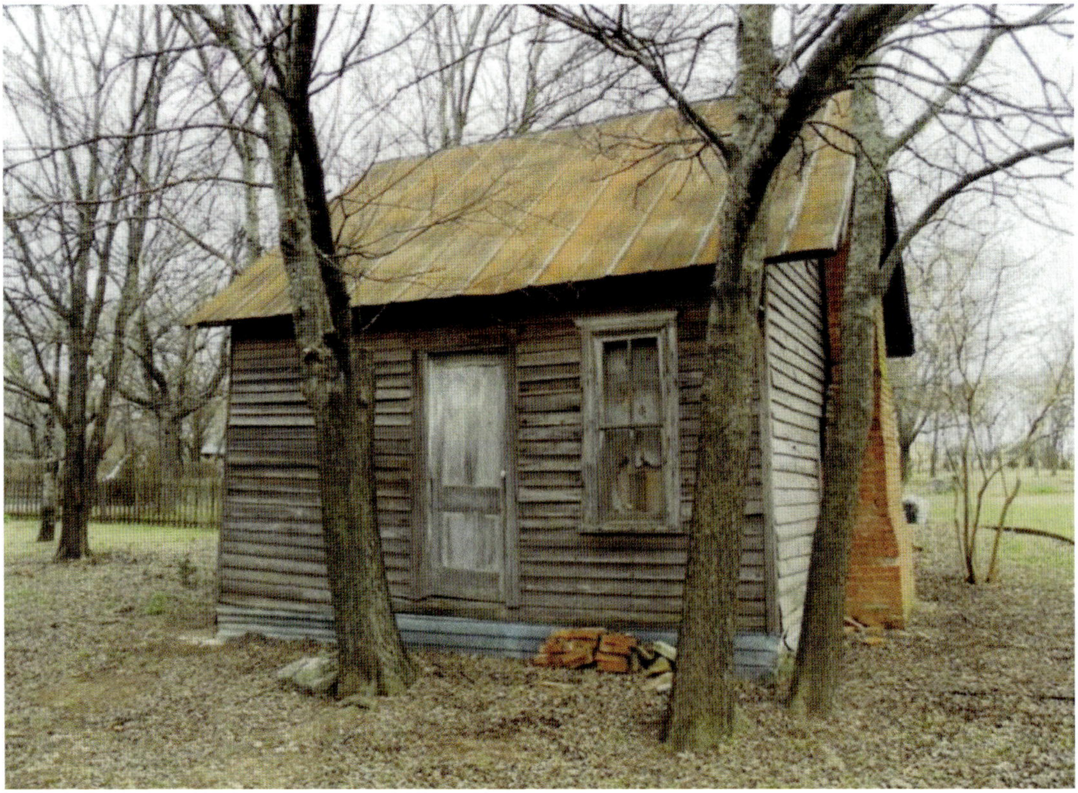

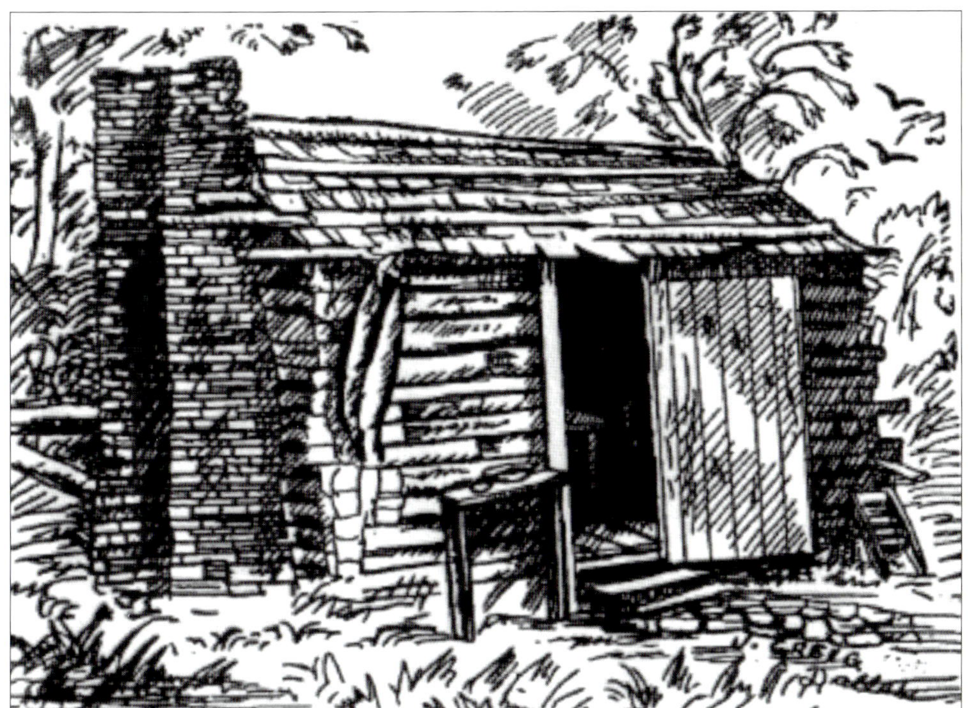

FIRST CEMETERY: Benjamin Franklin Hawkins and his wife, Mary A. Pinnell, came from Indiana with his family in 1848. He received 640 acres of land where he built this cabin. The village of Lebanon began on a hill on his property, seen in the background behind the cemetery. Because the church was there, he donated land for a burying ground. He became the first County Clerk when Ellis County was formed, serving 1850–1869 and 1875–1891.

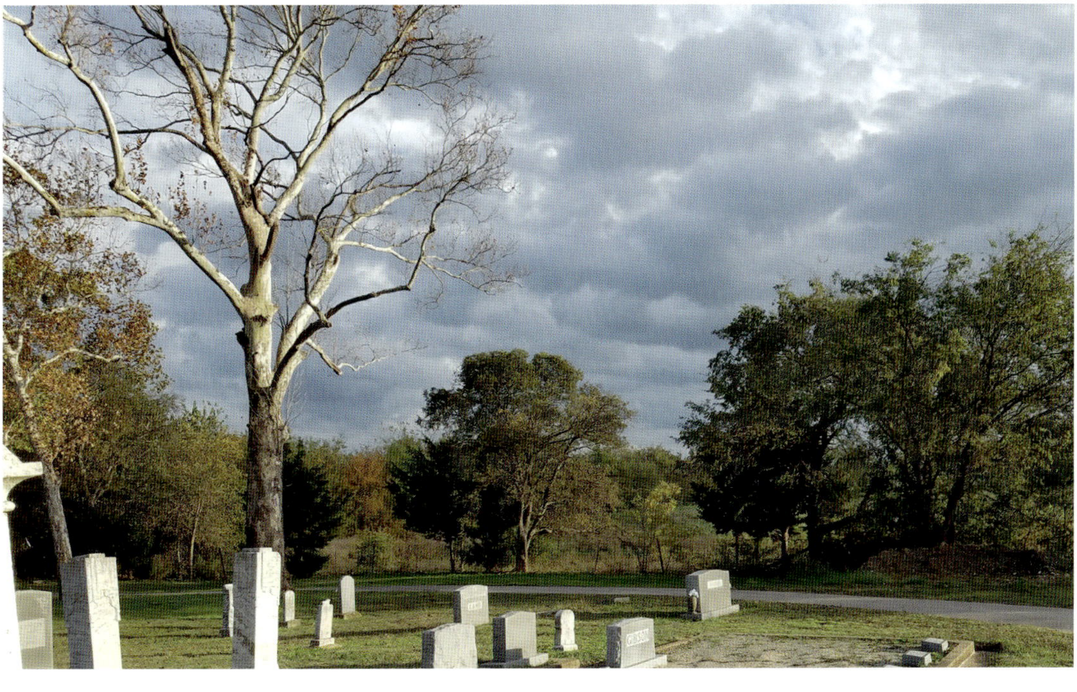

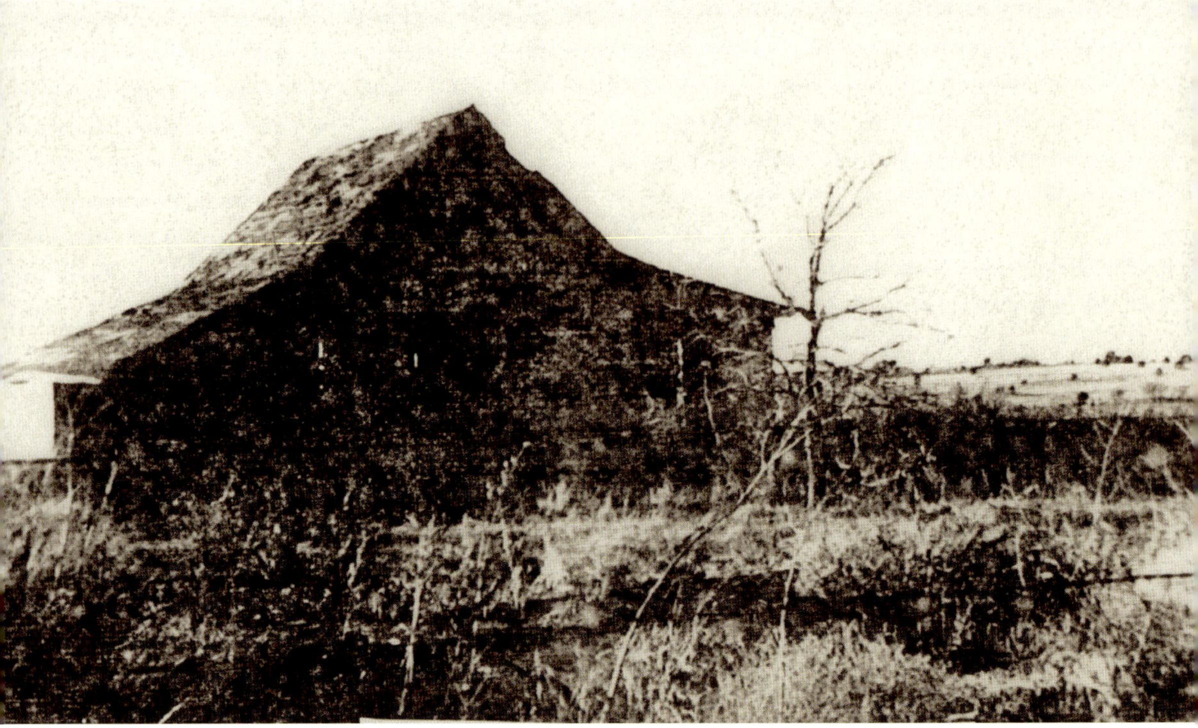

Extended Family Comes: Evan and Sarah Morgan lived in this cabin, built 1853. They were accompanied to Texas by his cousins, brothers Jefferson and William Martin Morgan. Jefferson constructed chairs and traded them for staples, books, and dry goods at a nearby general store. He and his wife, Amanda Sportsman, had two daughters, one son, and another daughter born during the War Between the States. Their son, Hugh Martin Morgan, later occupied the two-story home. William Martin Morgan and his wife, Delisa Sportsman, moved on to Eastland County, TX, after the war.

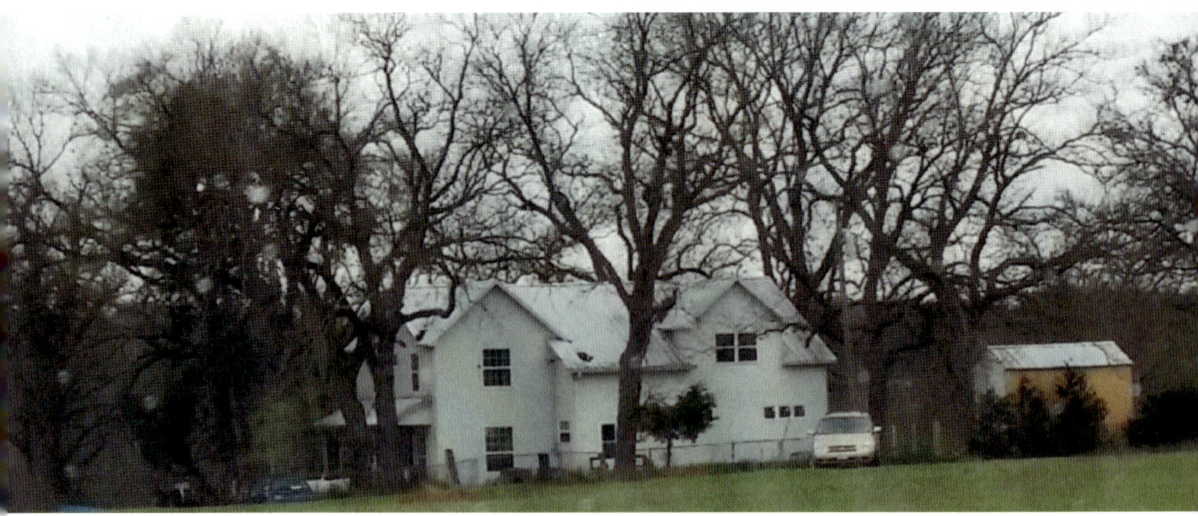

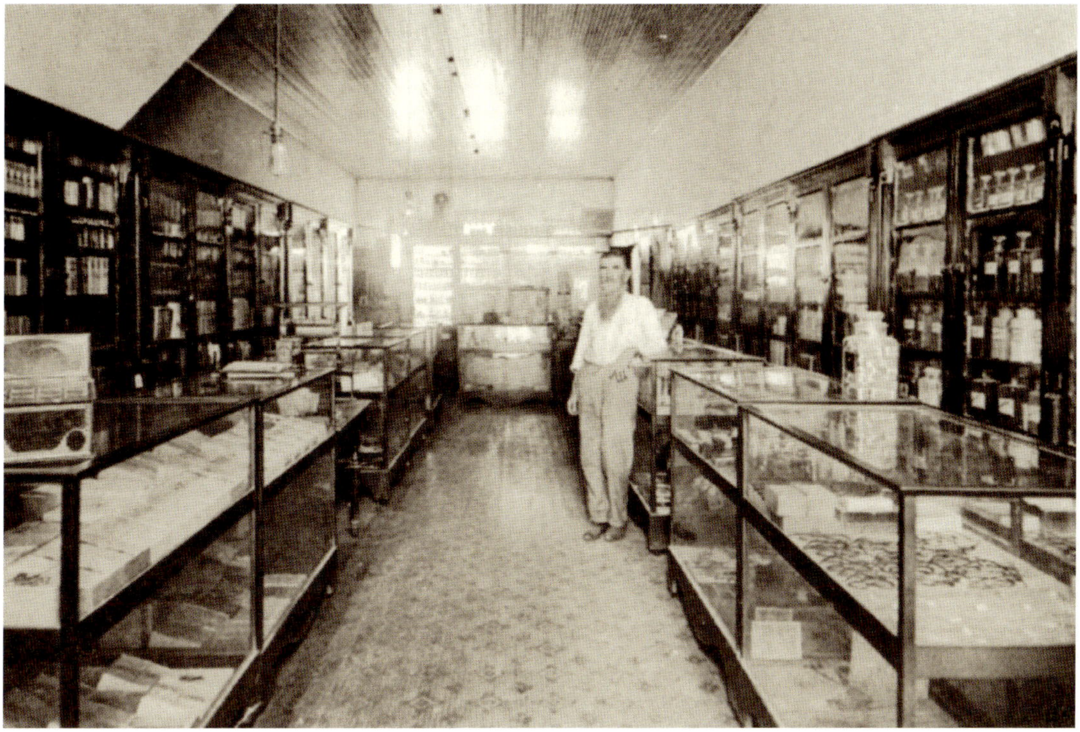

First House, Second Store: Evan and Sarah had several sons fighting for the Confederacy. Those soldiers were David Jonah, John, Robert, and William. Cousins William Martin and Jefferson enlisted. Jefferson, as well as Evan's son, John, died in Louisiana. Evan's son, Thomas Adams Morgan, was the first man to build a house in Midlothian. He owned the second store, a drugstore, which he moved in from the village of Lebanon. Four of the second generation had a portrait made together about 1900. *From left to right*: Hugh Martin (son of Jefferson), John Madison (son of William), Robert and Tom (sons of Evan).

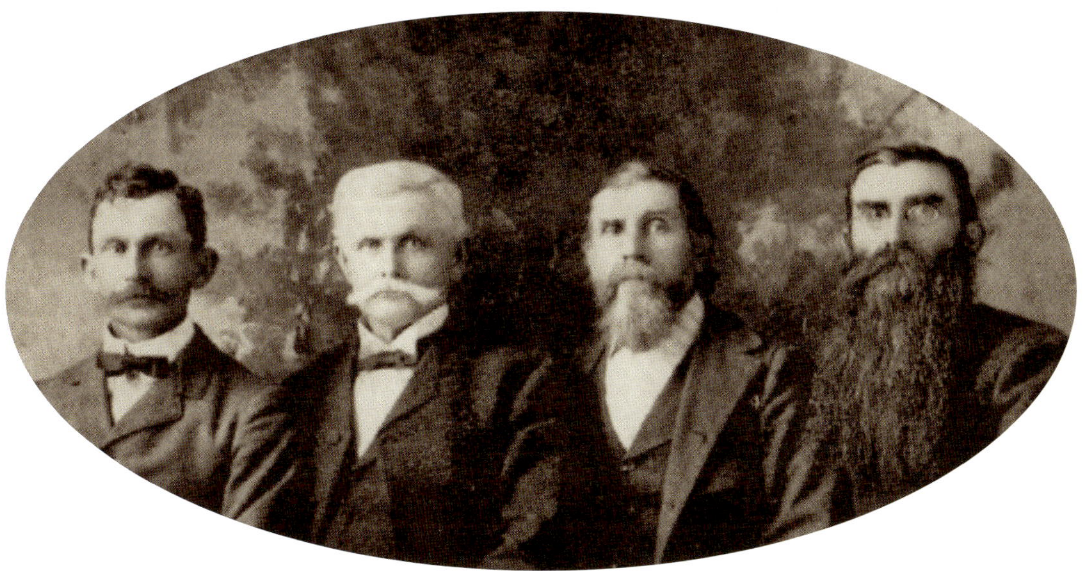

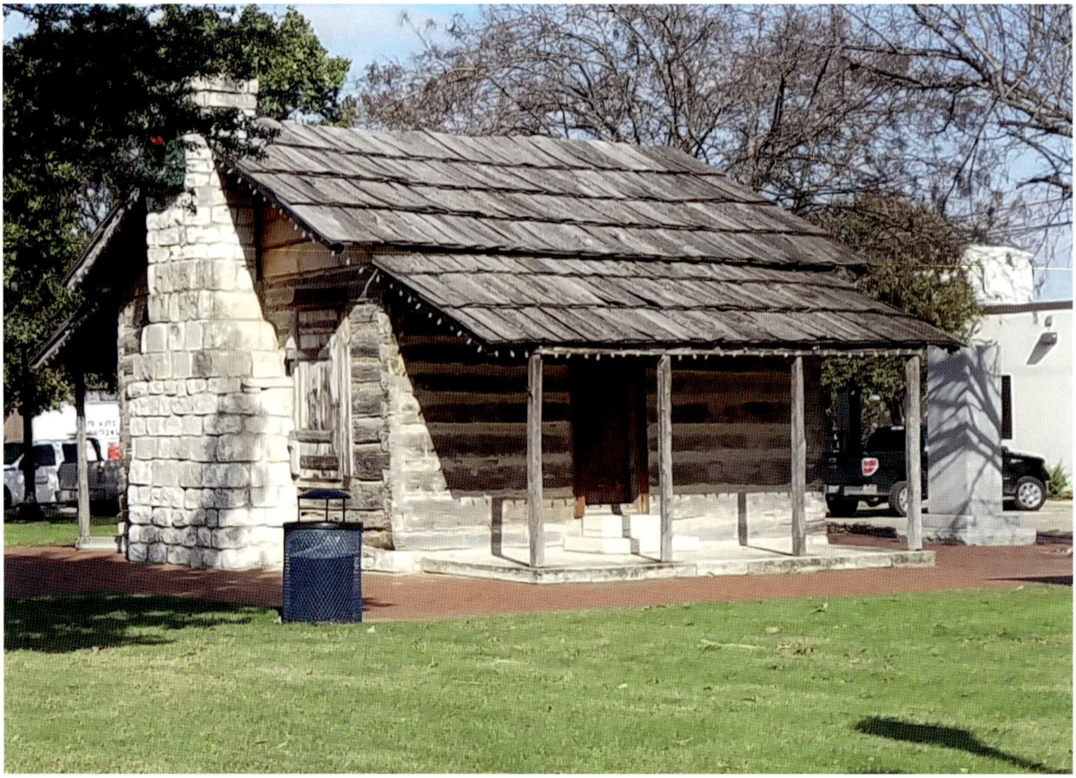

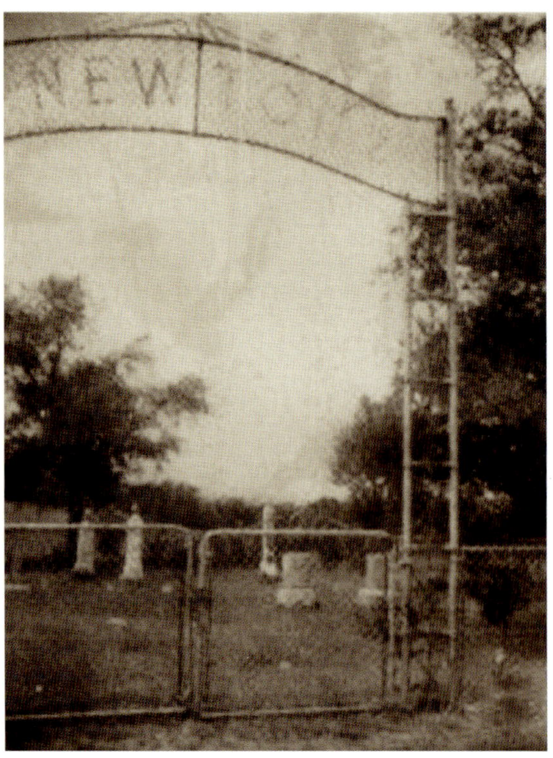

Cabin Restored: Upon arrival in Texas in 1848, Larkin Newton constructed this log house for his family. He and his wife, Mary Anne Wilson, brought nine children from Missouri and had two more after arrival. The house was moved from its original location to the Anderson farm and then to downtown Midlothian where it has been restored. The Newton Cemetery was begun in 1858 near the original location of the house.

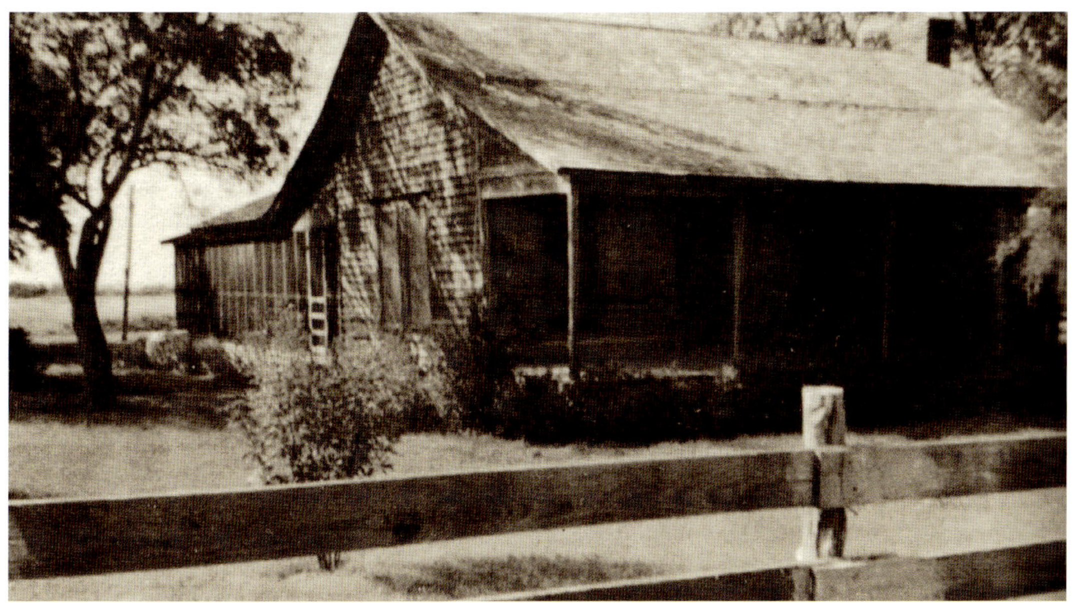

CEMENT COMPANY USES LIMESTONE: Three miles north of Midlothian, Benjamin and Sally Bedford received a land patent in 1855. Their daughter, Letitia (Milton), inherited and had this home built. In 1965, Gifford Hill Cement Company began buying large acreages north of Midlothian because of the native limestone being a major component of cement. That company purchased the Milton, Anderson, and many surrounding farms.

About 1985, the white area showed how limestone had already been quarried on the Milton land and adjacent farms. The Anderson home and buildings in the lower part of the image were removed in 2017, so that quarrying can begin in that area.

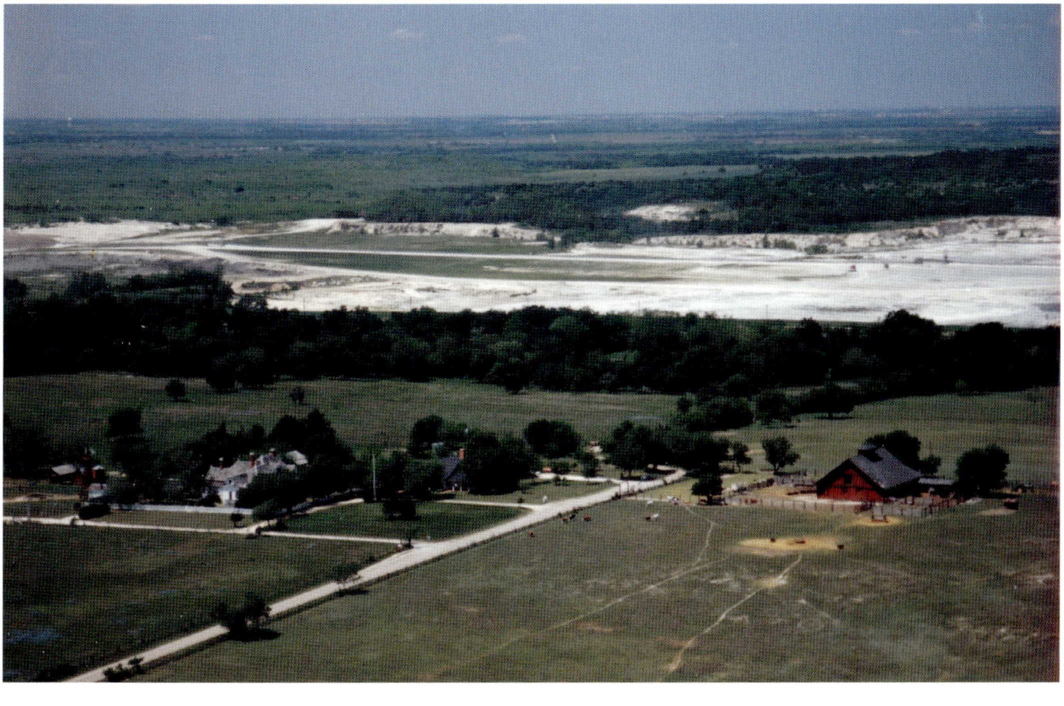

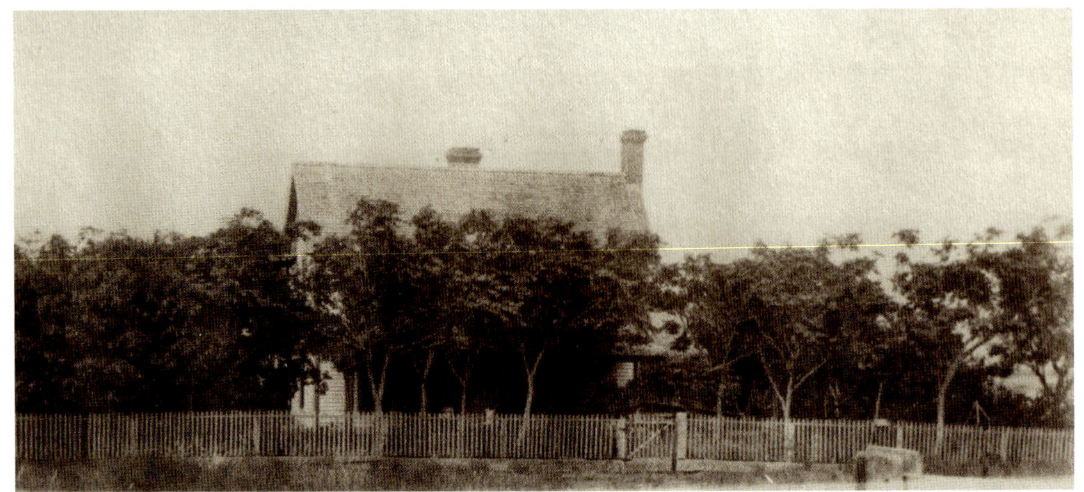

LARGE FARM FAMILY: Elgin Kossuth Ward married Mary Frances Evans in Leon County in 1874, before moving to Ellis County. The family eventually included the following. *From left to right, back row*: Royal Aubry, Joseph Evans, Charles Edward, and Herman Levi. *From left to right, second row*: Mary Elizabeth (Isbell), Lilla Kidd (Wallace), Laura Etta (Few), Alice May (Burleson), Sarah Josephine (Wallace), and Frances Raine (Hays). *From left to right, front row*: Isabella, Dad E. K. Ward, Sr., mother Mary Frances, and E. K. Ward, Jr. Cousin C. Turner is seated in front. Later, the home was unoccupied and burned about 1966.

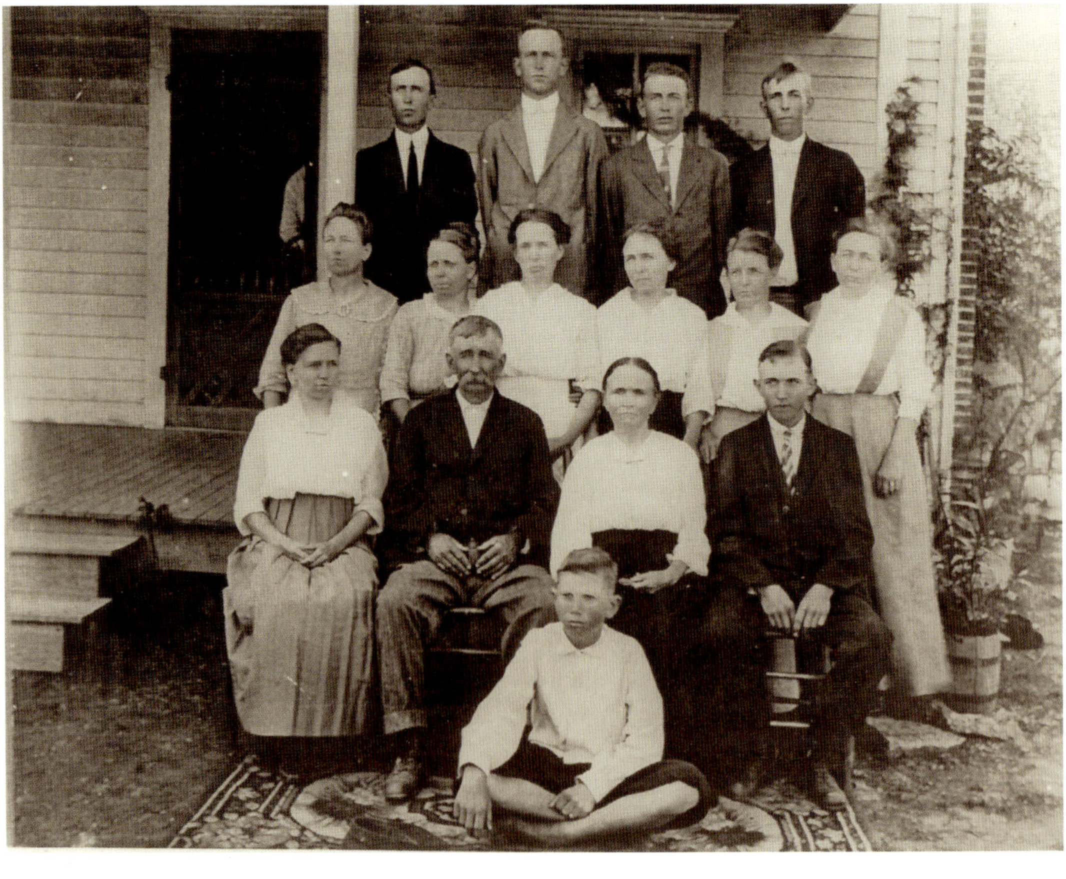

FARM PETS: Daughters of David and Malvina Smith, Minnie (left) and Myrtle, posed with their pet about 1905. Minnie married Isaac Burton Goodwin in 1923. They maintained this family farm until the late 1950s when they retired and moved into a new home in town. Myrtle married, also in 1923, Louis B. Eskridge, a farmer. Their daughter Lucille's husband, Philip Baxter, was the builder who developed North Ridge, the first housing addition to modern-day Midlothian. This aerial of the farm was made in the 1950s. The farm is much smaller in 2018, since housing additions have been built around it.

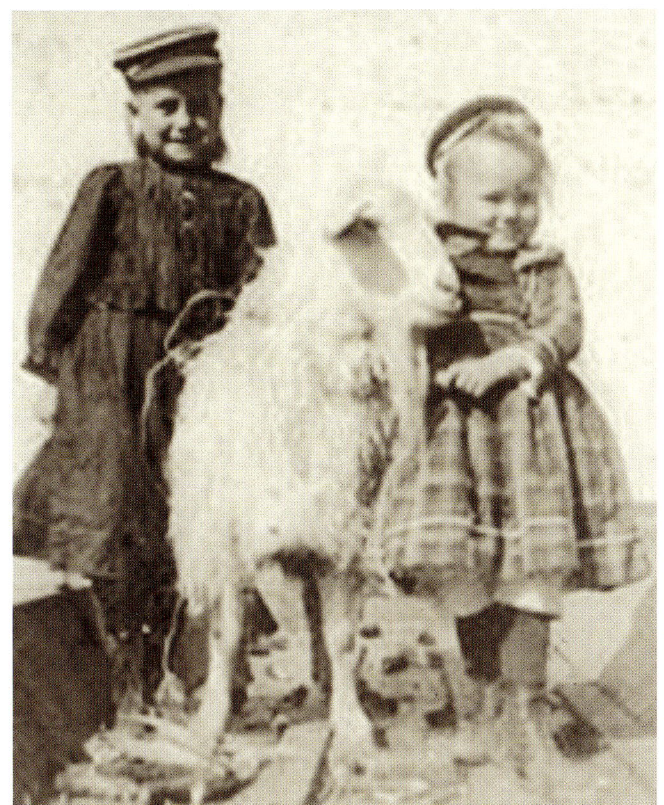

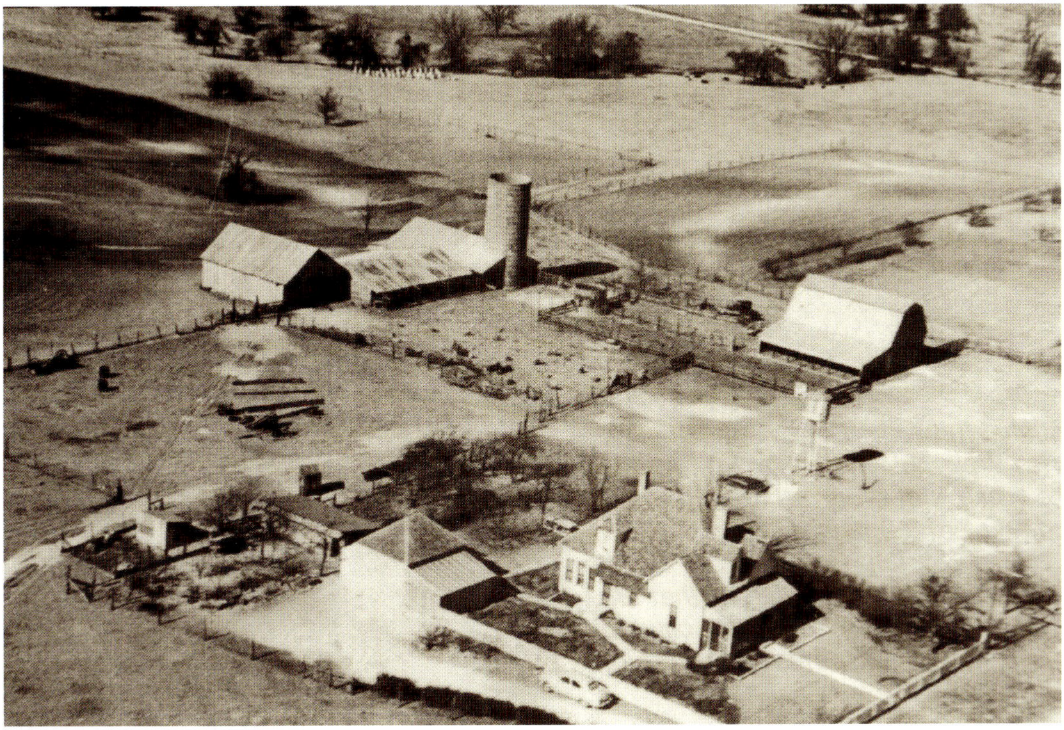

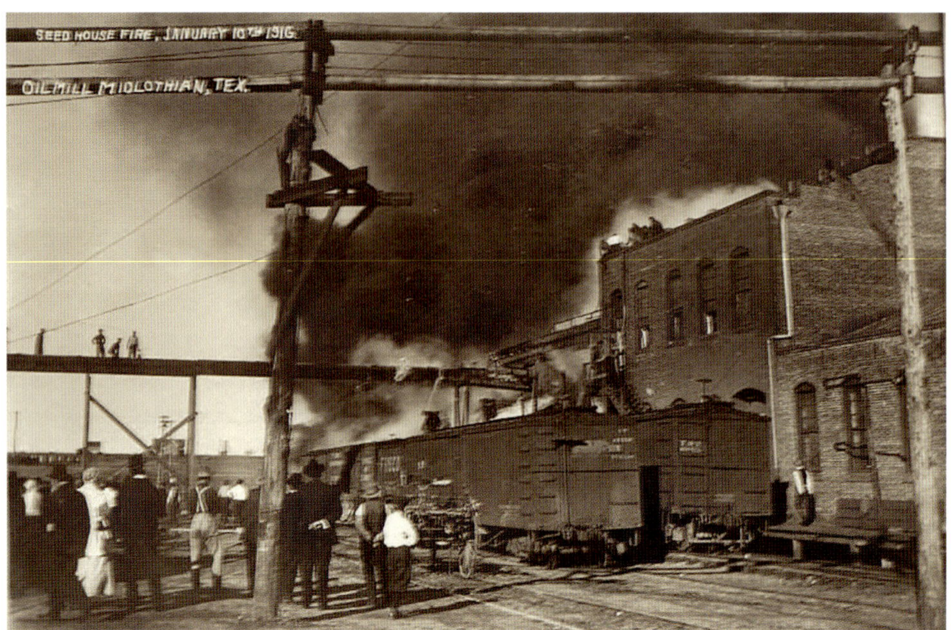

GINS AND FIRE TRUCK: By 1882, there were already two gins in town, Witherspoon's and Chamberlain's. The Midlothian Oil and Gin Company, established 1898, lost its seed house and 3,000 tons of cottonseed, worth $100,000 on January 10, 1916. The Midlothian Fire Department had no mechanized equipment, but the Waxahachie Department responded and helped limit loss. The Oil Mill was entirely covered by C. R. Rea & Brother, a local insurance company established in 1895.

The city purchased a 1918 Ford Howe Model T Fire Truck and completed the first Fire Hall in 1920. The 1918 truck was compared to a 2013 model in the lower photo.

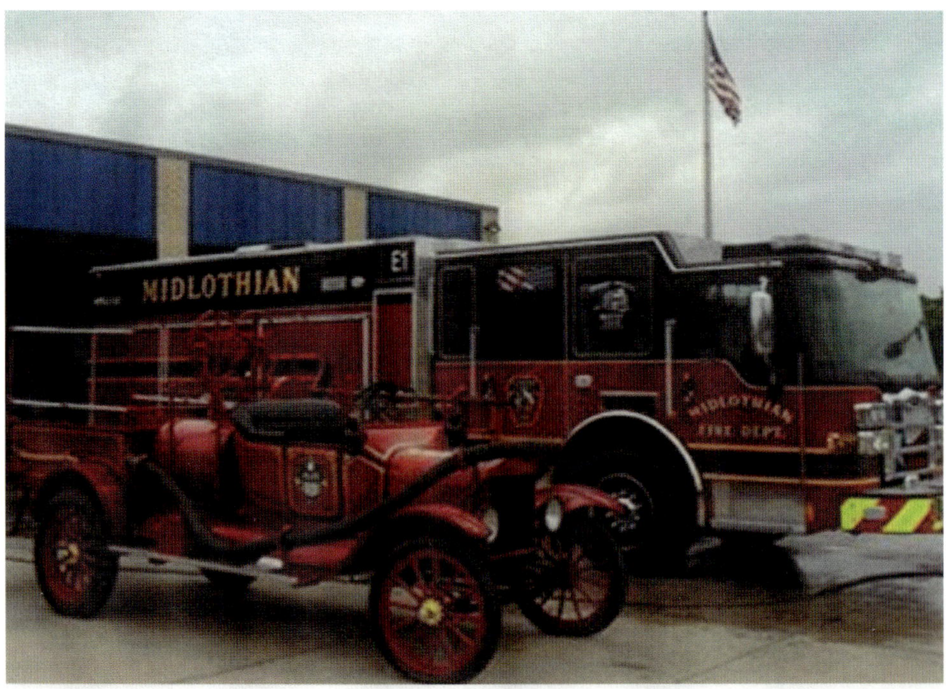

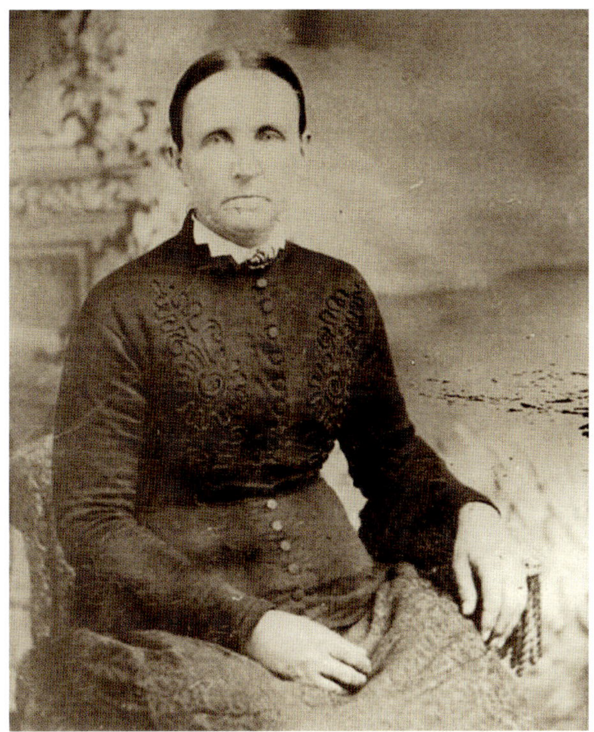

WORKING THE LAND: Flora Newton arrived here in 1848 with her parents, Mary Anne and Larkin Newton, who immediately built a log home about 3 miles west of Lebanon. As her dad received 640 acres and had only two sons, aged fifteen and six, he needed hired help badly. One of the men he hired was William Barnett, aged twenty, from Tennessee, who married Flora in 1854. Their children were as follows. *From left to right, back row*: John William, George L., James R., Henry C., and Thomas Larkin, MD. *From left to right, front row*: Tennessee (Owens), Texanna (Embry), and Mary.

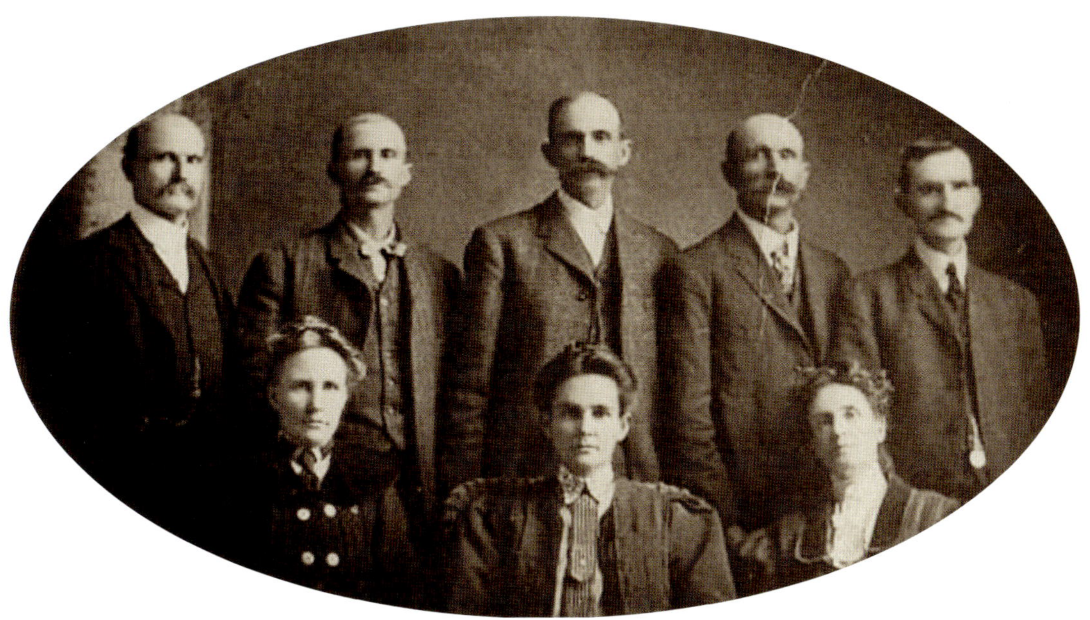

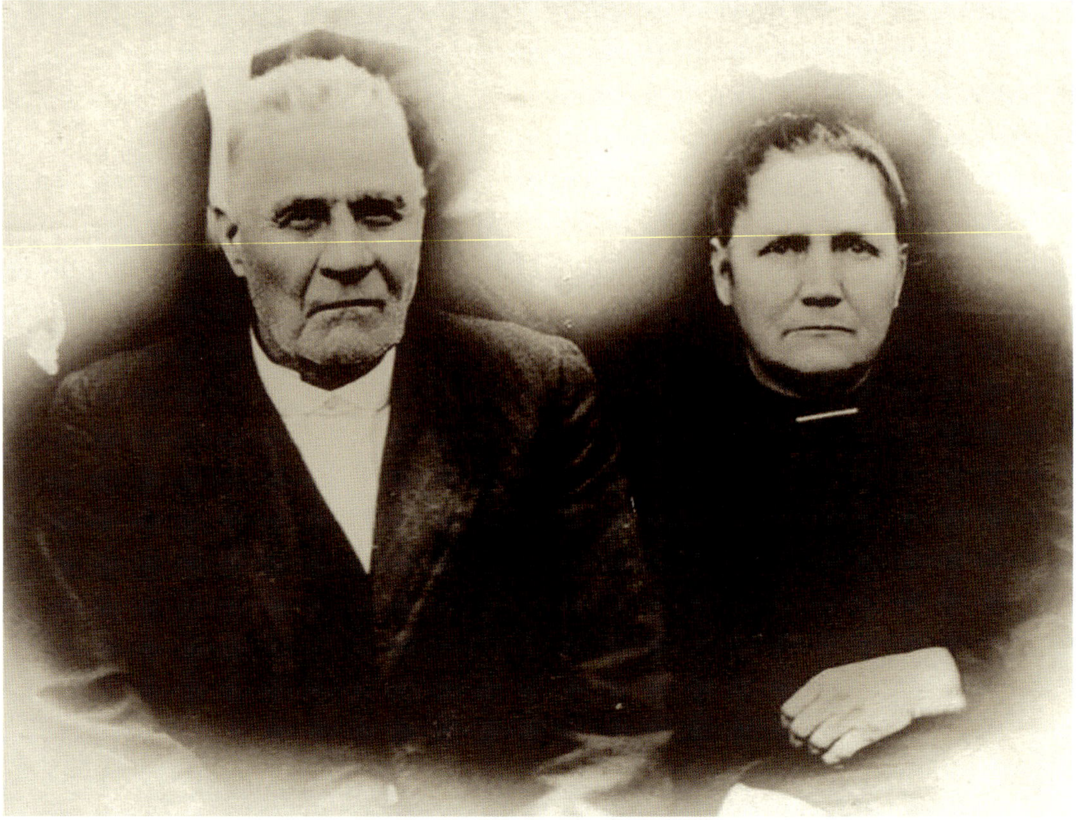

FIRST MAYOR: William Andrew and Helen Brundage brought their family to this area in 1877. He was a carpenter, building several local houses, including one for his brother, Daniel, which still stood in 2018. He also ran a furniture and undertaking business. Upon Midlothian's incorporation in 1888, William was elected Mayor and again in 1891. He was a member of the International Order of Oddfellows and a charter member of the Midlothian Masonic Lodge No. 584. The snow-covered Brundage home was photographed in 1917 but is no longer standing.

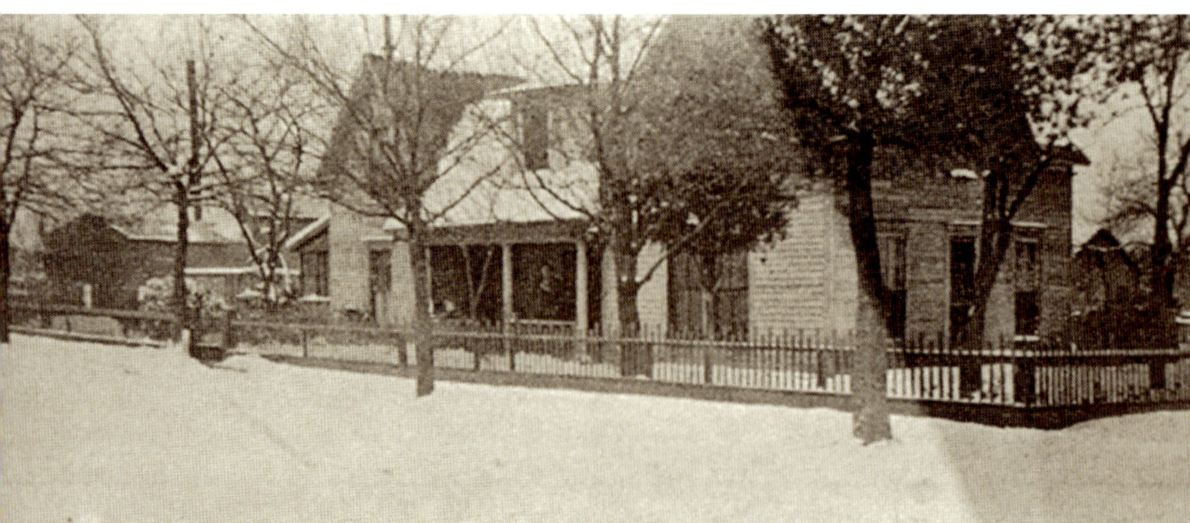

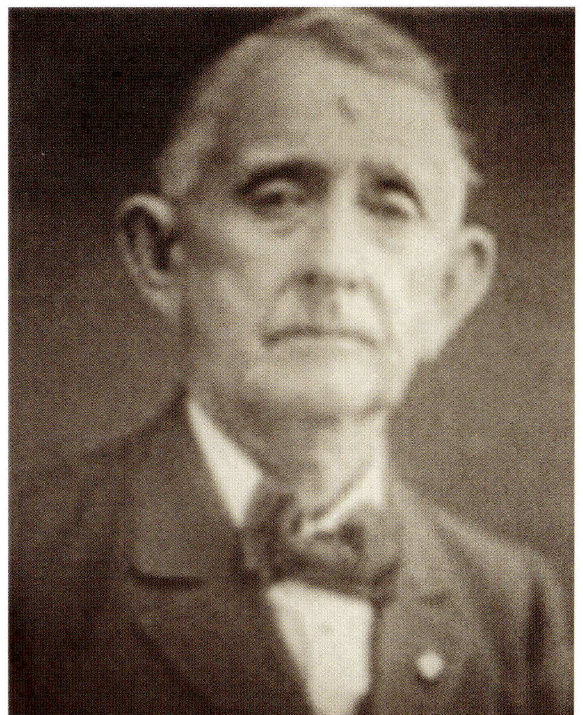

FIRST CITY COUNCIL: William Franklin Beck was born in Illinois. He married Amanda Louise Harp in 1882, and they soon moved to Midlothian where he was elected to the first City Council in 1888. Mr. Beck owned a business in Midlothian and was a member of the IOOF (International Order of Odd Fellows) Lodge No. 296, serving as treasurer in 1893. He was a member the Methodist Church.

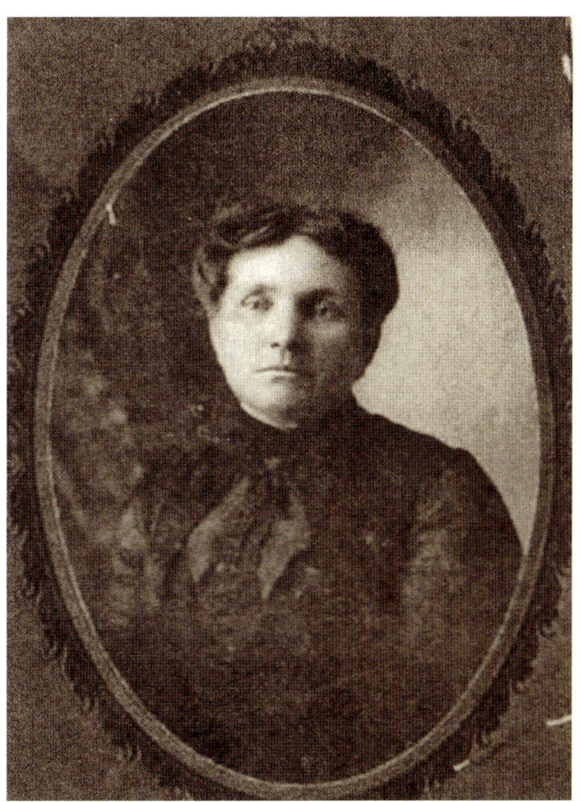

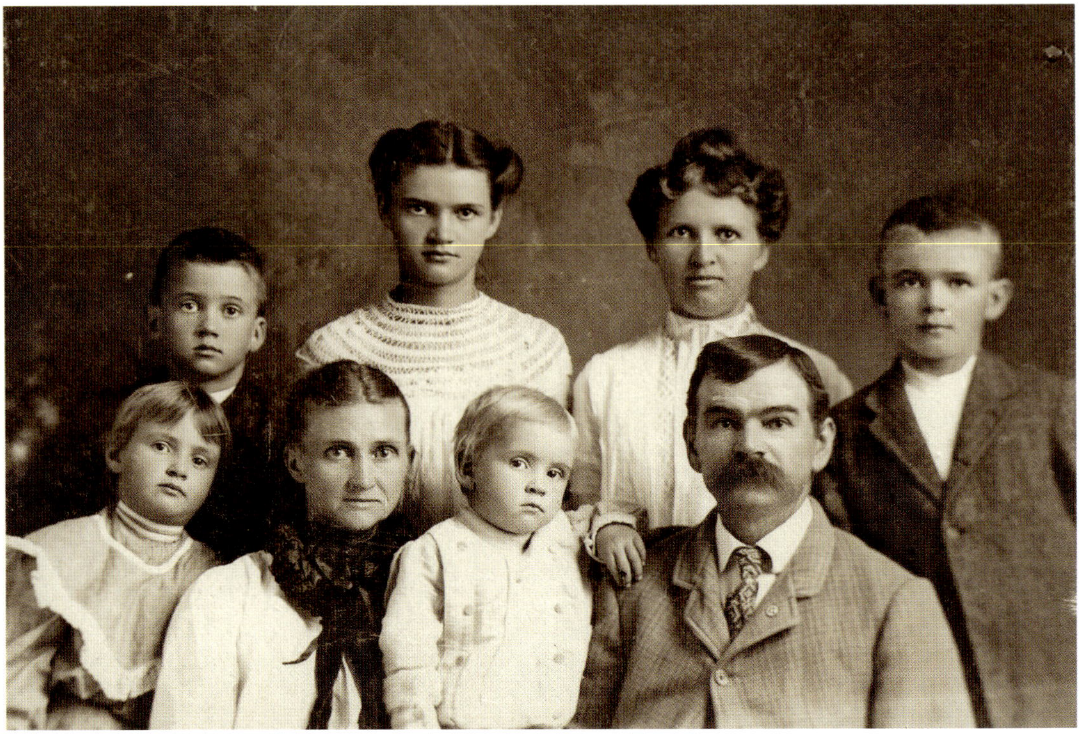

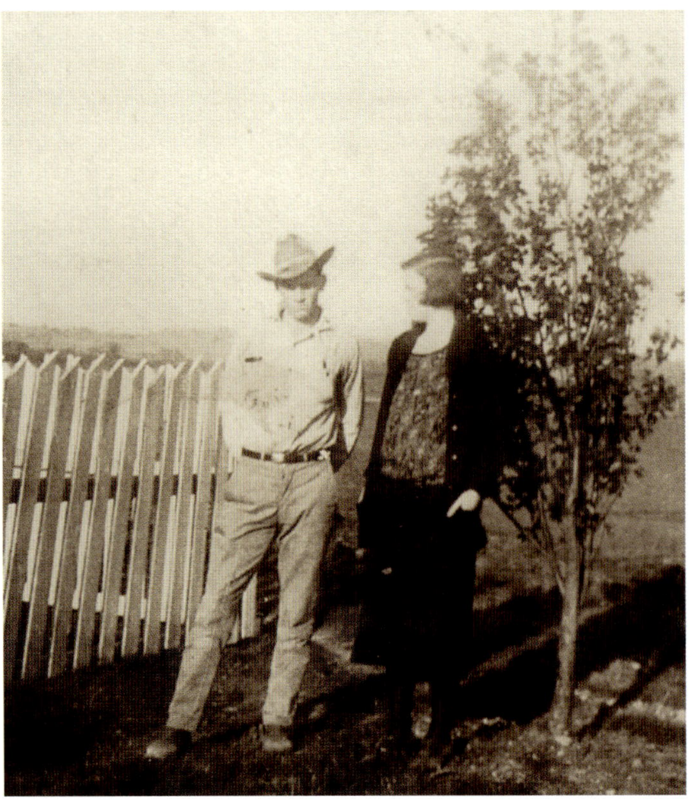

Tornadoes in Area: While John David and Johnnie Etta Tribble Duke lived in Rockett, a tornado struck their home killing their newborn son. Soon, John bought land near Midlothian and moved his family to their new home. As that baby was the second son the family had lost, they soon planned a family portrait. *From left to right, back row*: Dewey Lee, Etta Beatrice, Lula Sophronia, and Blanton Dunkin. *From left to right, front row*: Maude May, Johnnie Etta, Vernon Merrill, and John David. The two older sons, riding horseback to the studio, did not arrive on time. About 1925, Vernon posed with his younger sister, Phama, the only child born after the storm.

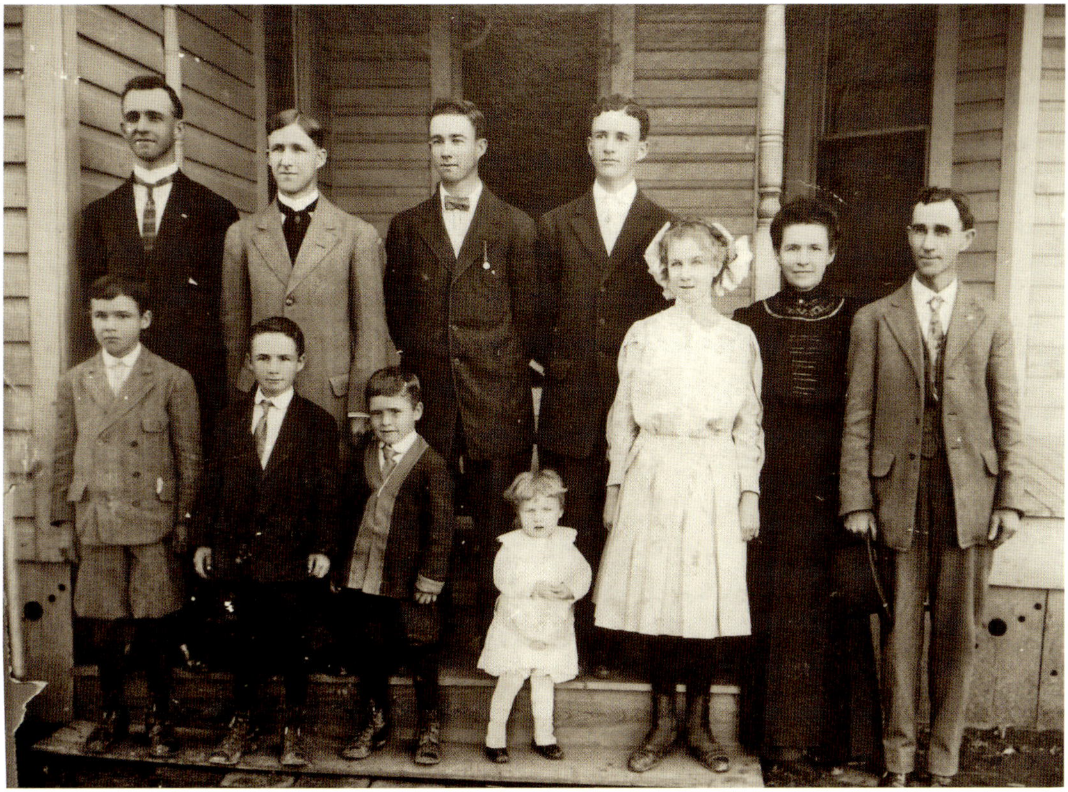

DRY GOODS MERCHANT: David Bunch Holland, Sr., bought a dry goods store from W. W. Major in 1894. In 1911, he and his wife stood with their children. *From left to right, back row*: William, Harve, C. B., and Herbert "Hub." *From left to right, front row*: Ned, Moe, Berin "Abie," D. B., Jr., Loneta, and parents Elizabeth Scythia Baker Holland & D. B., Sr. In 1940, D. B. and son Ned stood in front of the store where his business had been located since 1905, the Martin-Hendricks Building. Later known as the "Blue Jean Factory," the Martin-Hendricks Building was torched in 1964. Their home was replaced by a newer one about 1961.

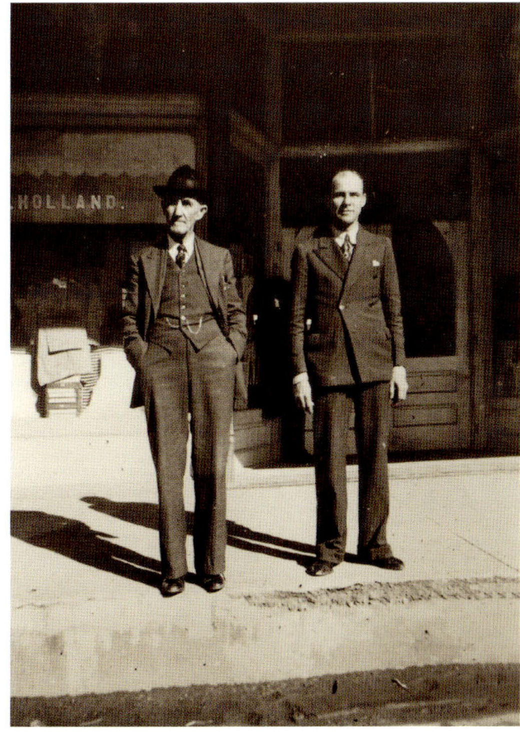

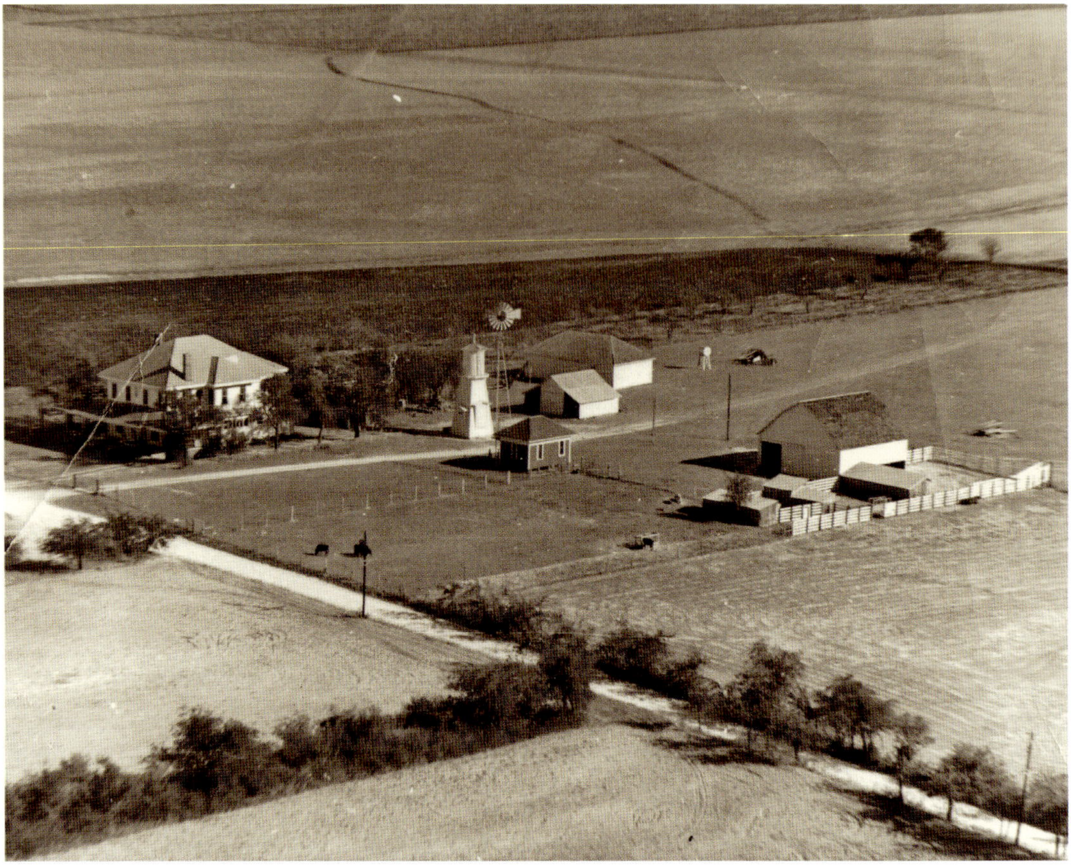

FARMS BECOME SMALLER: B. F. Stiles had this house built in 1906 on the very south edge of town, enlarging and remodeling by 1916. In 1954, a small shop was built near the east side of the home where the wife ran a florist. The business no longer existed in 1956, and the family let the Girl Scouts use it for meetings. In 2018, one finds that most of the various barns and other outbuildings have been torn down with the home now surrounded by housing additions.

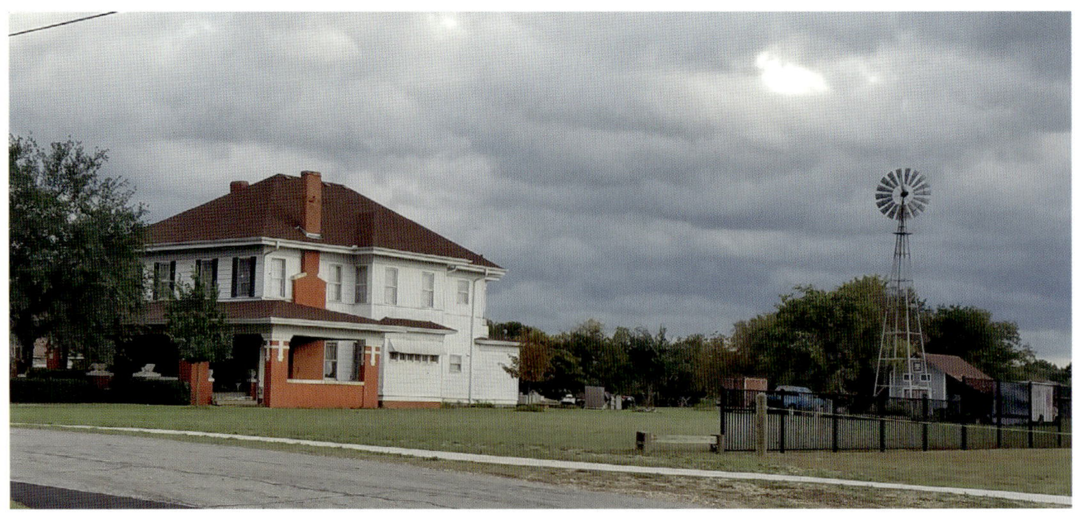

2

Businesses

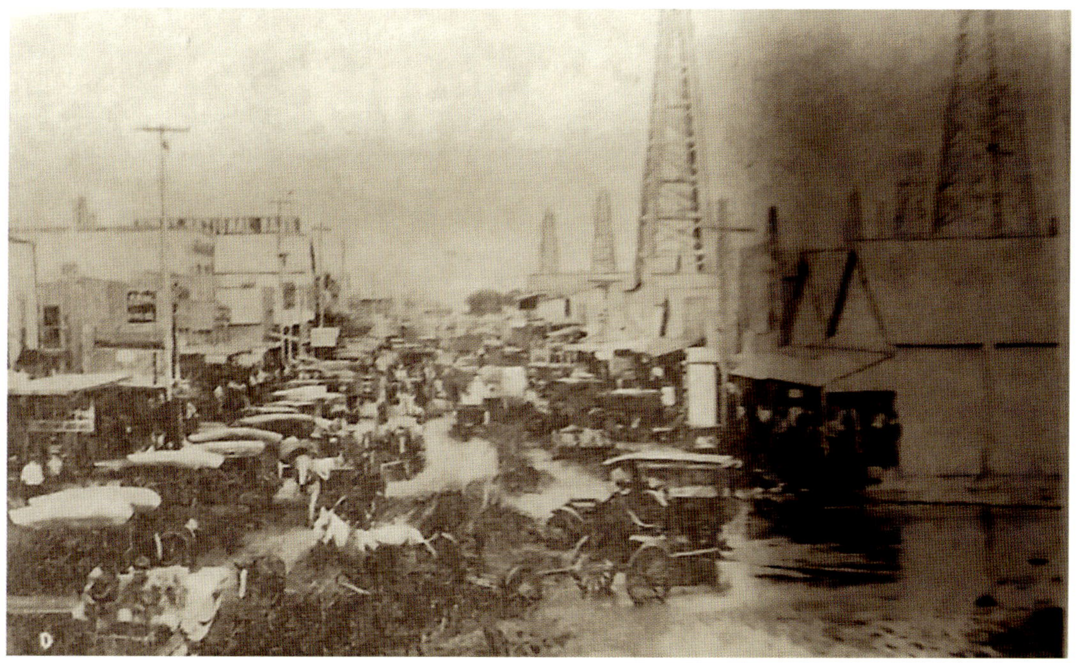

In 1918, Tom Moore Dees, local banker and businessman, learned of a "showing" of oil on Hog Creek, in Eastland County. He secured a lease to drill on Joe Duke's land. Tom's friends in Midlothian, hearing about the situation, wanted in on the action. So Tom formed the Hog Creek Oil Company and sold shares for $100 each. When the first gusher came in in September 1918, the value of each share rose to $10,250.

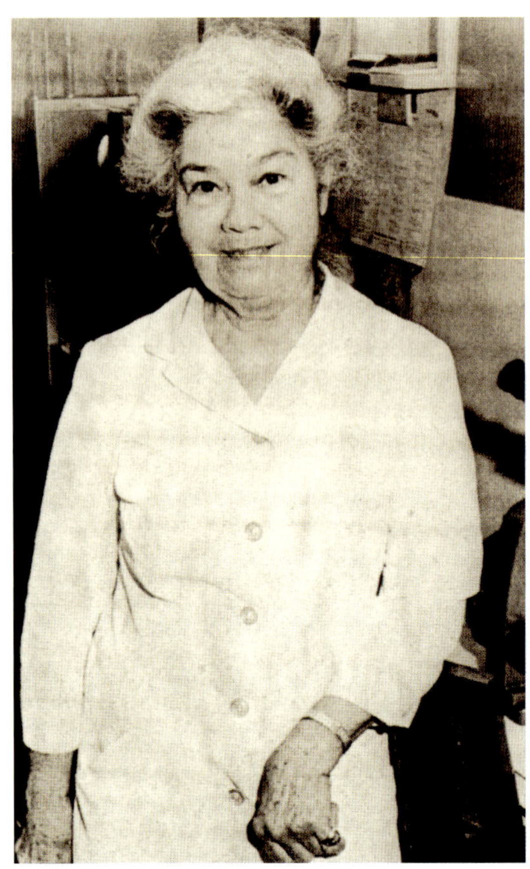

NURSES & PHYSICIANS: Gladys Loraine Bell Anderson served as office nurse for several Midlothian physicians, 1935–1971. She was really a "Girl Friday," acting as bookkeeper, lab technician, doctor's general assistant, accompanying doctors on hospital visits, and participating in public health activities. This sweet lady passed away in 1980. Gerald John Kochevar, M.D., was the beloved family doctor in Midlothian, 1948–1964. He was born on February 13, 1918 in MN where he attended medical school. After serving as a captain in 313 Station Medical Group during World War II, he located in Midlothian as a general practitioner and surgeon.

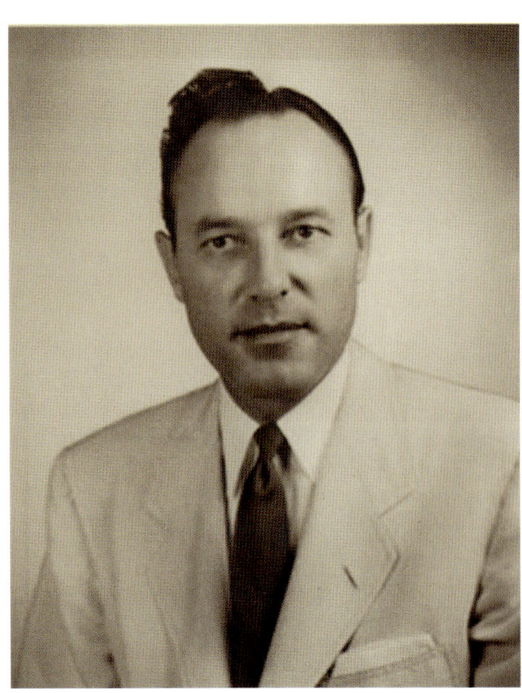

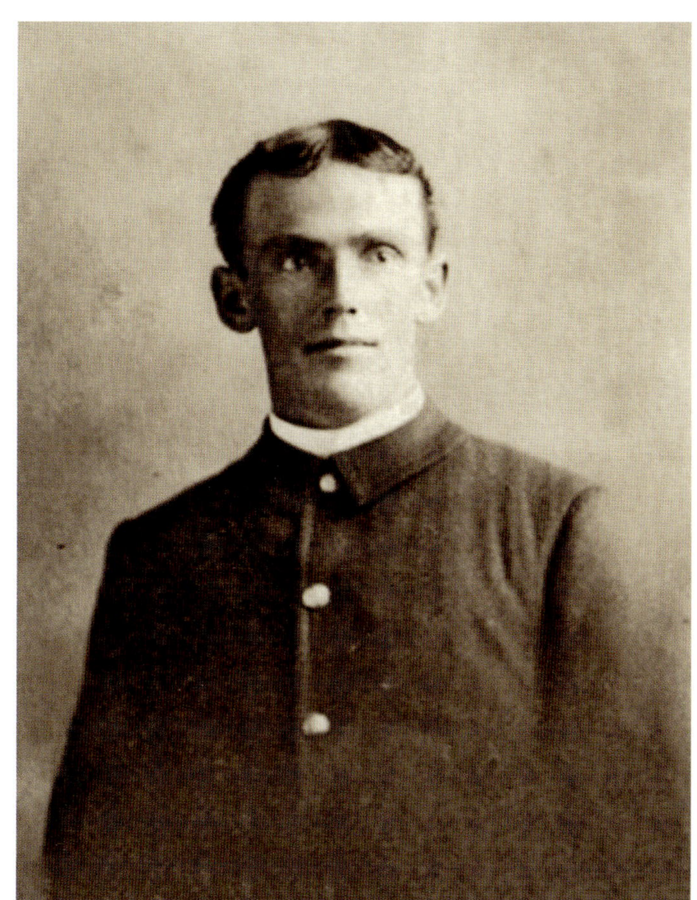

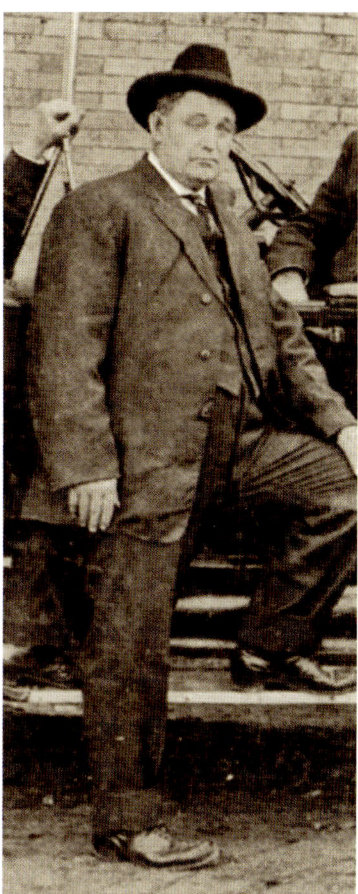

Mercantile Store: William Houston "Hugh" Page (to the left), born 1879, married Ethel Hurt on September 31, 1909. They had three sons: William Hurt, born 1912, John Hugh 1915, and Eugene Augusta, 1920. In 1907, Hugh entered the mercantile business with his cousin, Rufus Henry Morton, under the firm name of R. H. Morton & Co., which continued until Rufus died in 1929. Rufus married Katie Alice Morris in 1884. They had eight children.

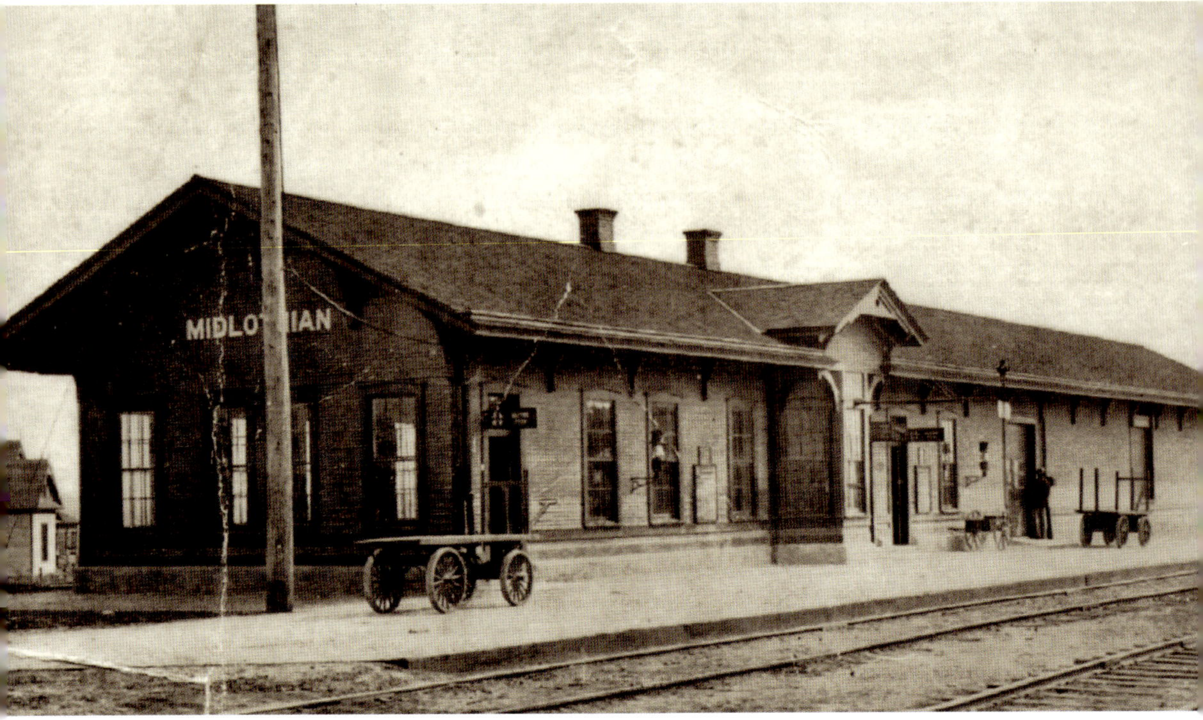

First Railroad Arrives: By January 1883, the Gulf, Colorado, & Santa Fe tracks were completed to Cleburne and passenger trains were running. A depot, 50 by 120 feet, was constructed in April and photographed in 1908. On May 4, the GC&SF announced the details of a public sale of town lots in Midlothian to be held on Thursday, May 10. The Santa Fe train is shown coming up from "the valley" in a 1937 snow scene. B. F. Stiles's home and windmill stand out in the background.

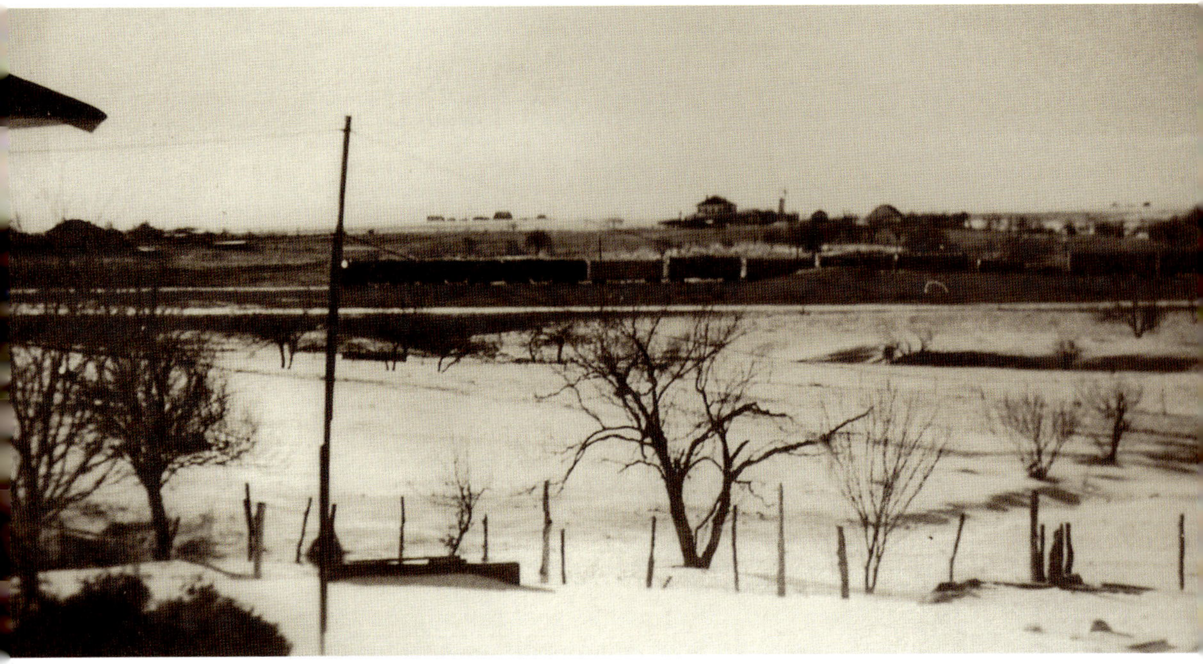

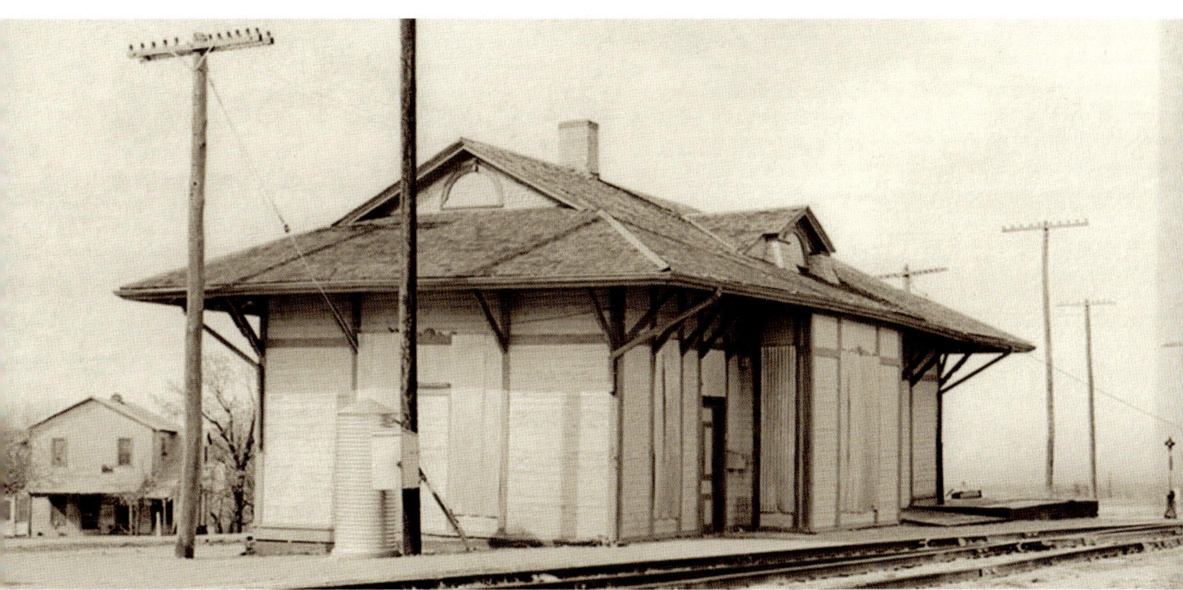

SECOND RAILWAY CROSSES: The Fort Worth and New Orleans Railway, chartered in June 1885, first wanted to connect with the Central Texas and Northwestern Railway, built 1879, in Waxahachie. The 42 miles of track from Fort Worth to Waxahachie, passing through Midlothian, was begun in September 1885 and completed the next year. The FW&NO was acquired by the Houston and Texas Central in December 1886. The depot was already boarded up by 1961 when photographed. In the left-hand background, one sees the two-story grocery and hotel run by T. P. Turner. By 2018, the entire area had been cleared off.

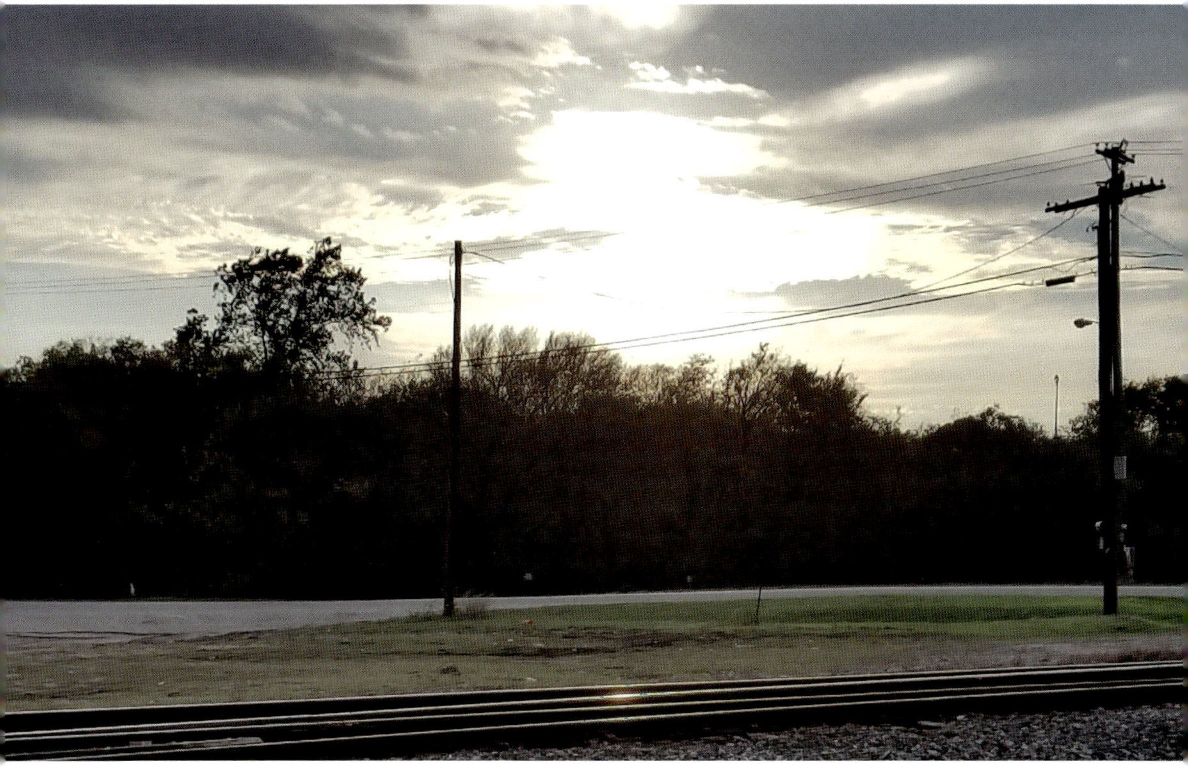

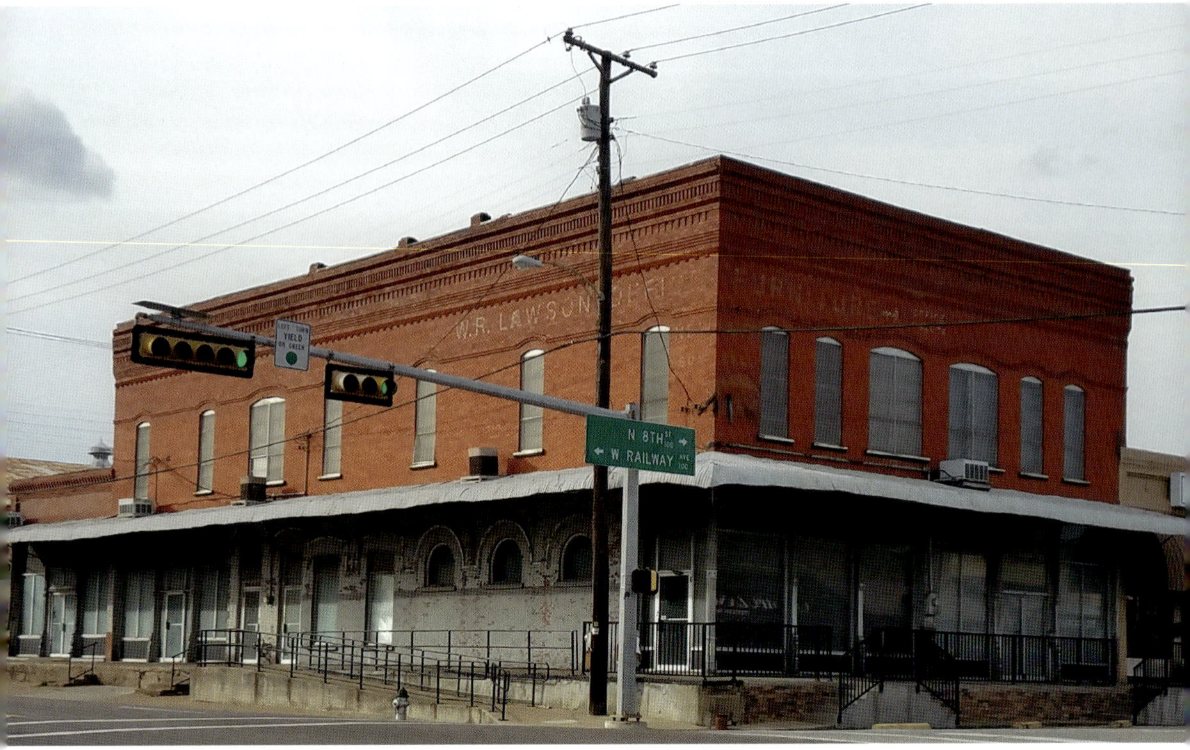

INDUSTRY BEGINS: The W. L. Hawkins building, per the 1910 Sanborn map (northwest corner of Ave G & 8th Street), housed the Twentieth Century Tire Protector Company which manufactured and sold a special tire patch invented by J. A. Posey and W. W. Major. The patch had a money-back guarantee. A patron who bought four tire covers and an extra described them as made of rawhide with steel buttons along the tread. The company was still in business in 1919 per the ad.

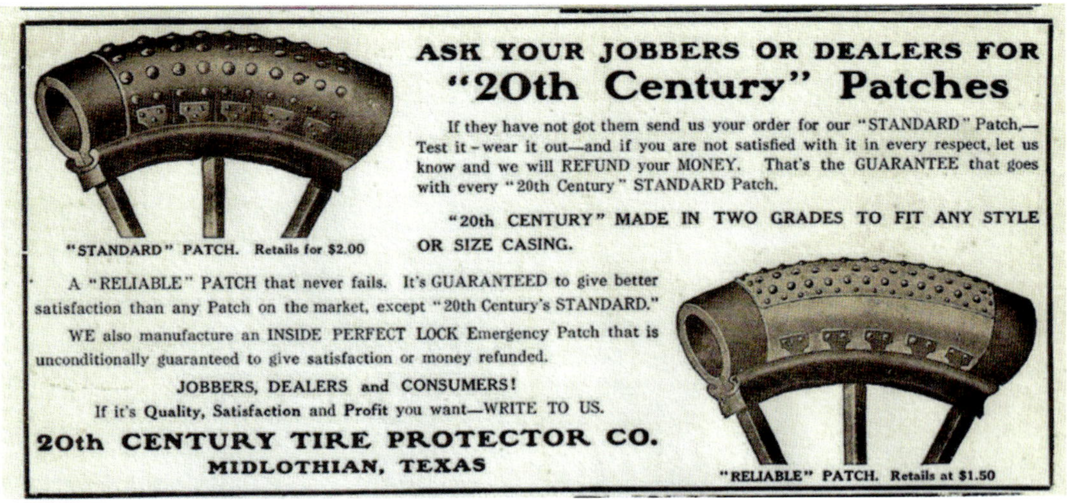

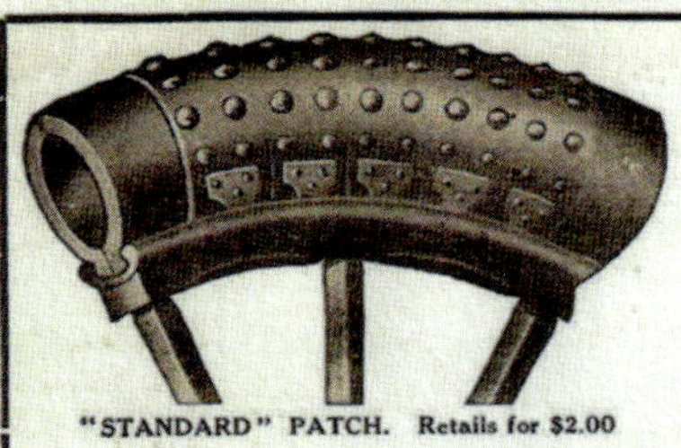

"STANDARD" PATCH. Retails for $2.00

ASK YOUR JOBBERS OR DEALERS FOR

"20th Century" Patches

If they have not got them send us your order for our "STANDARD" Patch,—Test it - wear it out—and if you are not satisfied with it in every respect, let us know and we will REFUND your MONEY. That's the GUARANTEE that goes with every "20th Century" STANDARD Patch.

"20th CENTURY" MADE IN TWO GRADES TO FIT ANY STYLE OR SIZE CASING.

A "RELIABLE" PATCH that never fails. It's GUARANTEED to give better satisfaction than any Patch on the market, except "20th Century's STANDARD."

WE also manufacture an INSIDE PERFECT LOCK Emergency Patch that is unconditionally guaranteed to give satisfaction or money refunded.

JOBBERS, DEALERS and CONSUMERS!

If it's Quality, Satisfaction and Profit you want—WRITE TO US.

20th CENTURY TIRE PROTECTOR CO.

MIDLOTHIAN, TEXAS

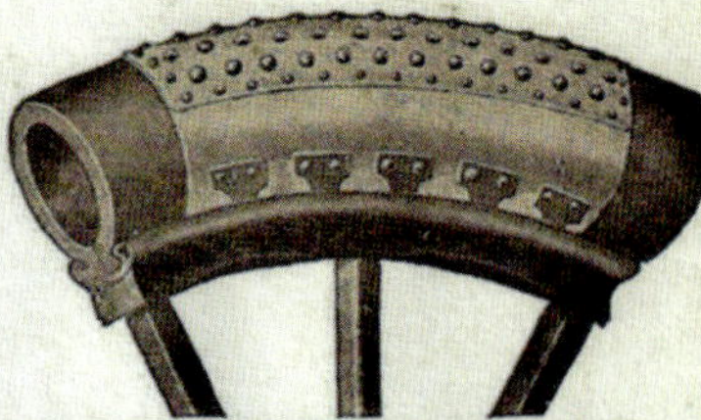

"RELIABLE" PATCH. Retails at $1.50

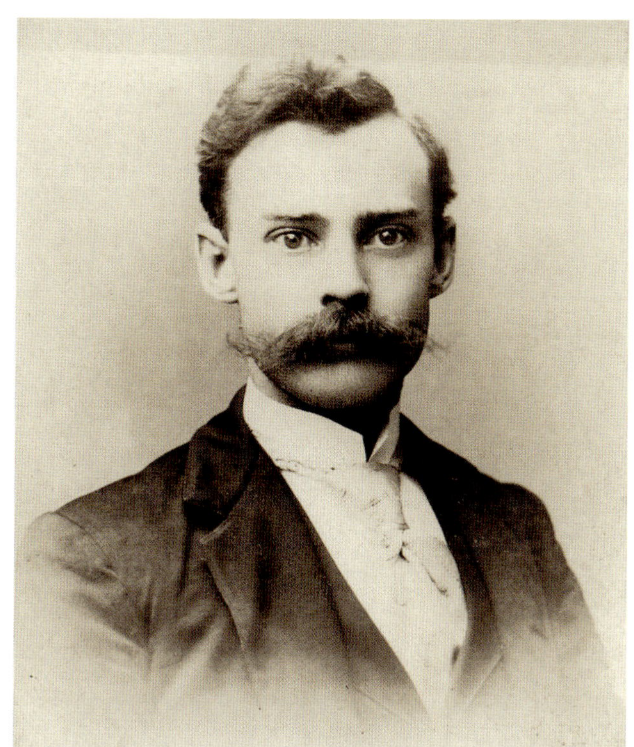

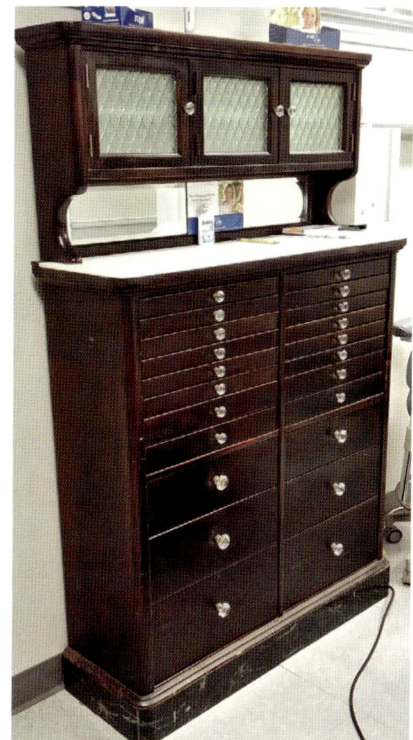

EARLY DENTISTS: Charles Jackson, dentist, housed his practice in an office of the Masonic Lodge building. Arriving in Midlothian about the time of Dr. Jackson's death (1930), Dr. H. J. Williams ("Doc") agreed with Widow Jackson to purchase her husband's practice, including his equipment and furniture. Doc was a new graduate of the dental college in Minnesota. Doc was a Presbyterian, Mason, served on the Midlothian School Board, and was a charter member of the Lions Club. The cabinet that Doc purchased from Mrs. Jackson was used in his sons' dental offices until the younger son retired in 2015.

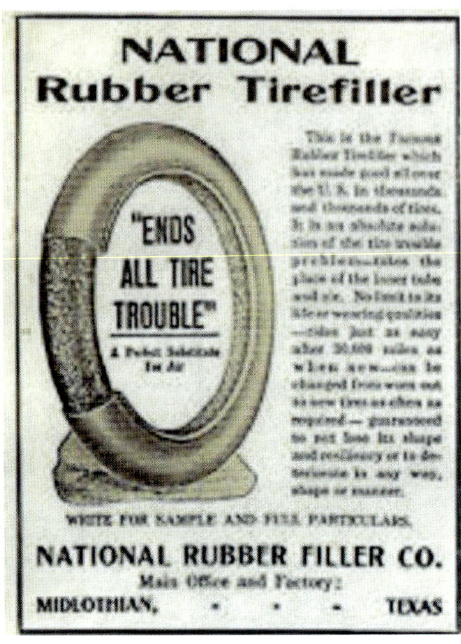

DEVELOPMENT OF INDUSTRY: Ed F. Aycock and W. W. Major organized the National Rubber Tirefiller Company in 1911. Its main office and factory were in Midlothian. Drivers were solicited to write for a sample and full particulars. This filler supposedly lasted for 30,000 miles in that it replaced the inner tube. So, tires became blow-out proof and puncture-proof. The building is now used as a dance studio.

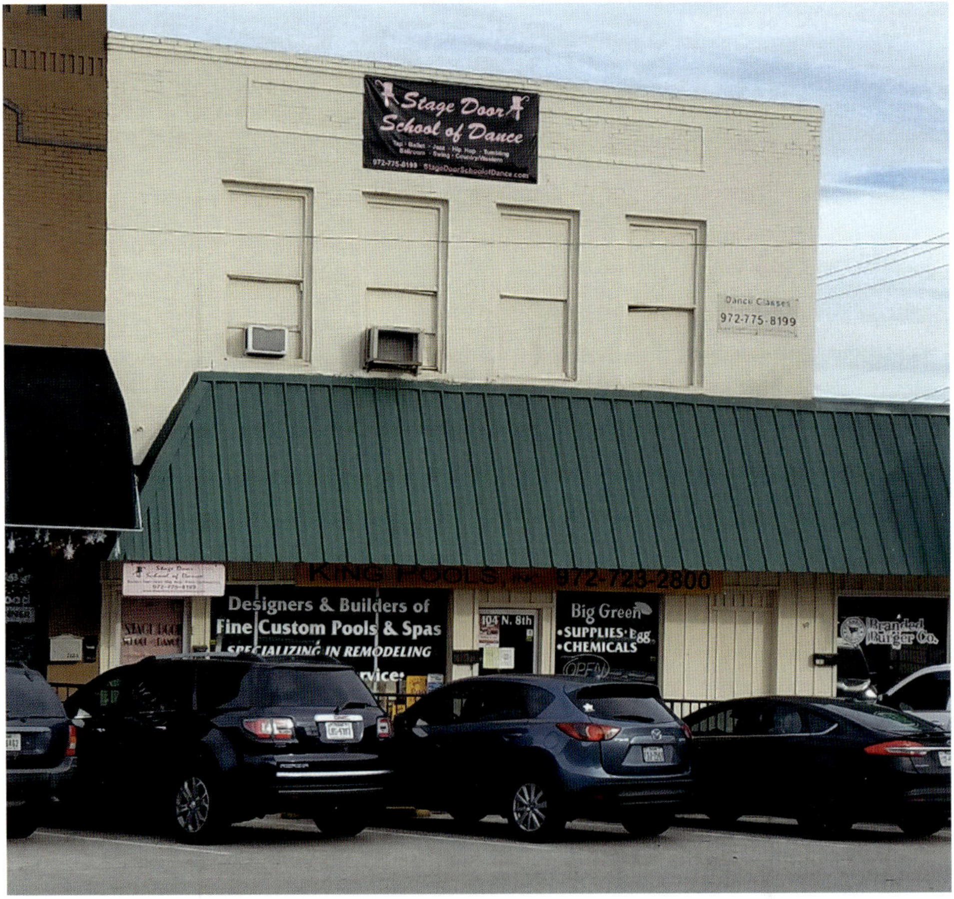

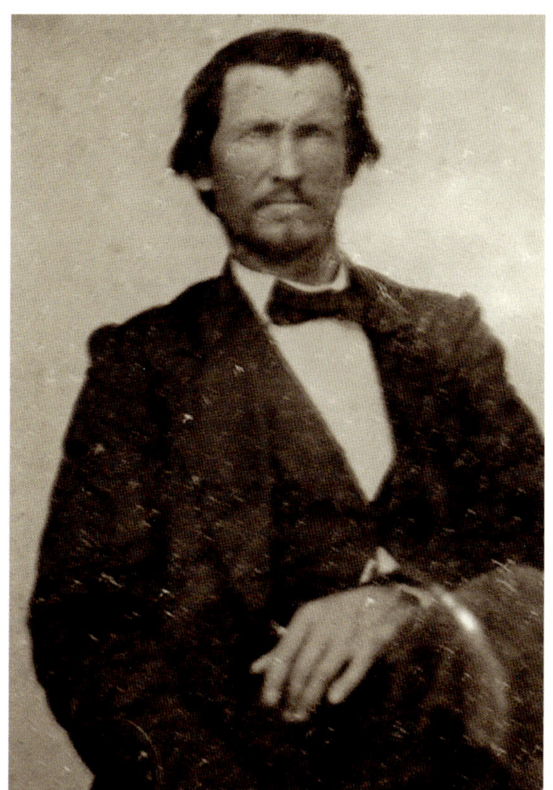

PHYSICIAN; DRUGSTORE: Dr. Martin Luther Haggard fought for the Confederacy in Co. "B," 25th Louisiana Cavalry. Coming to Midlothian after the war, he set up his practice and opened a drugstore. He lived in Midlothian until his death in 1897. In later years, 1940, Dr. Haggard's son, John Martin Haggard, ran the drugstore.

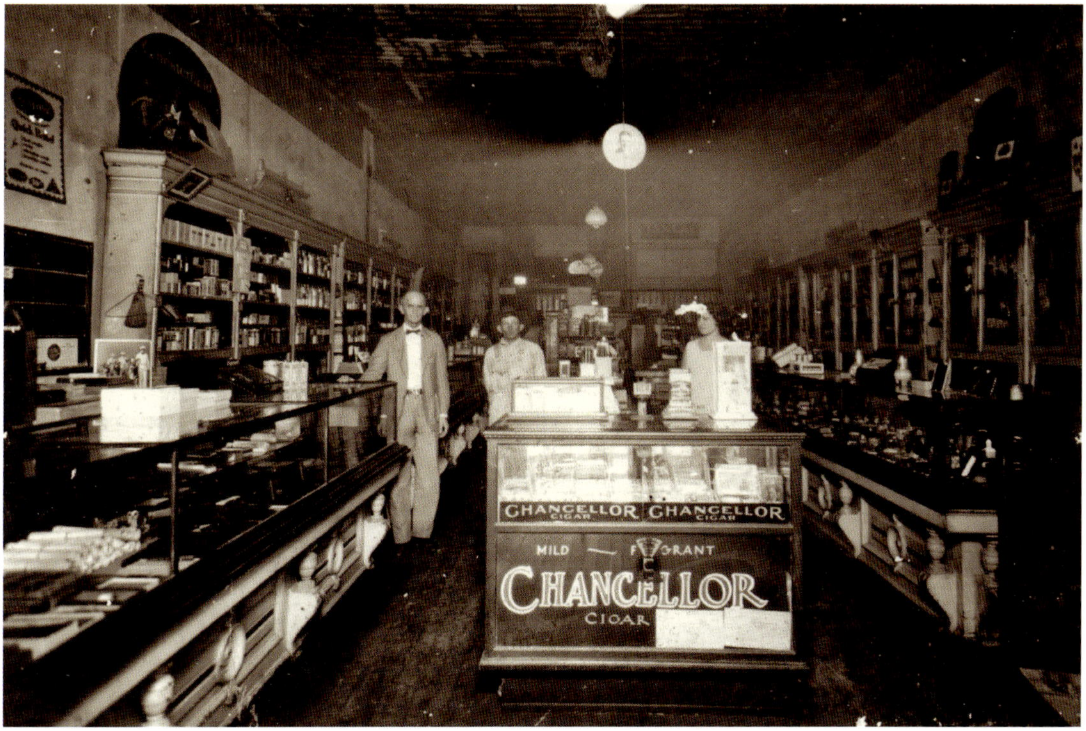

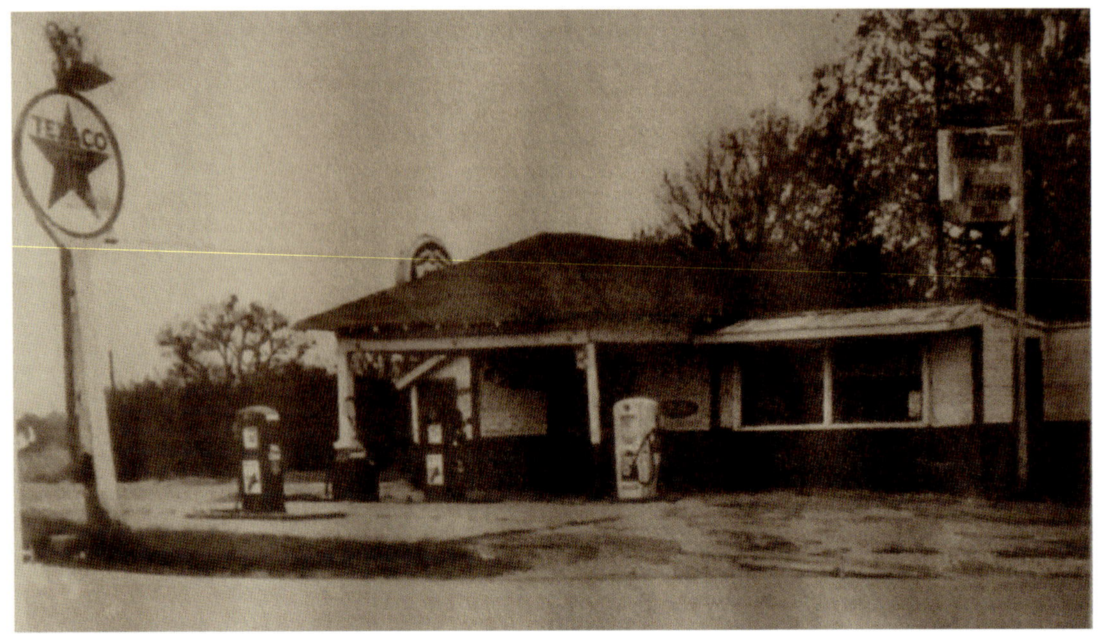

Transportation Needs: Briggs Texaco was long a fixture at the intersection of North 9th Street and East Avenue E, shown here in the 1950s. The building has been through many later owners, in 2018 serving as a tire repair facility.

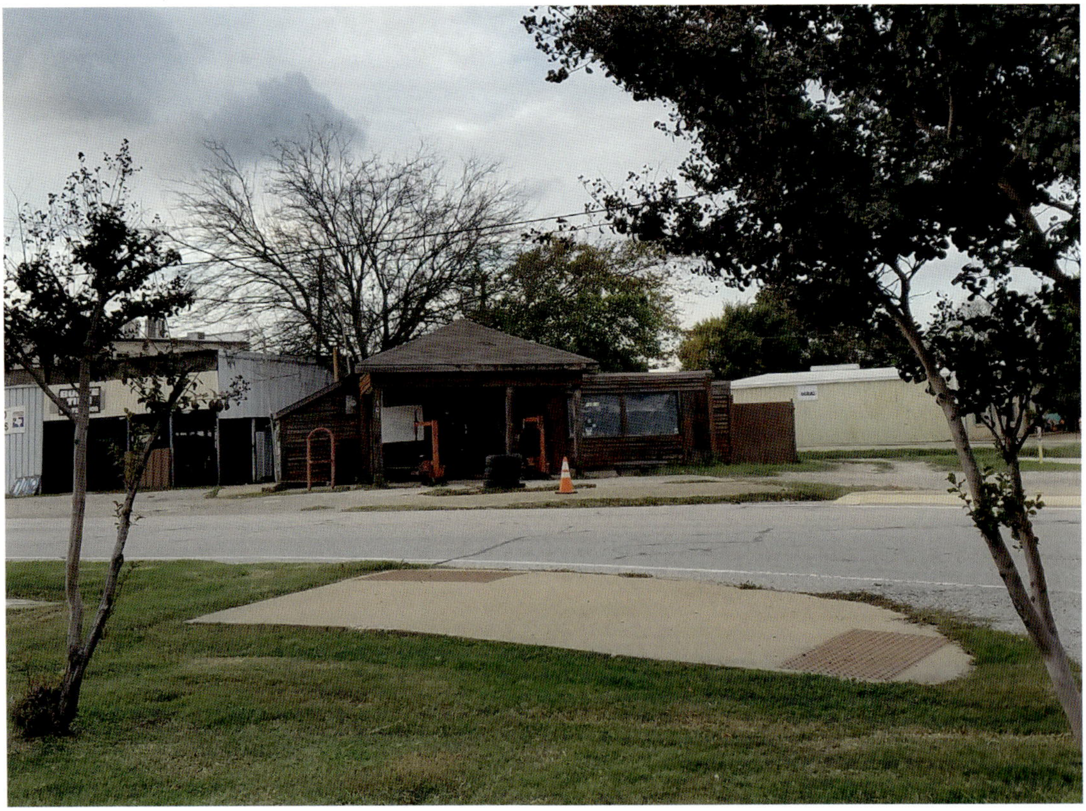

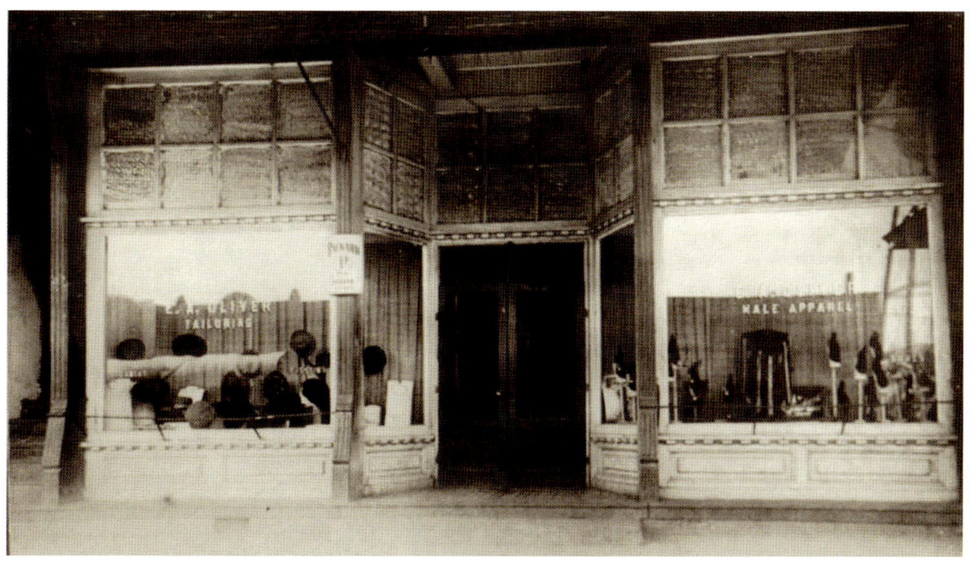

MEN'S CLOTHING: Ernest Albert Oliver ran a men's clothing store and advertised many items, for example, spring oxfords, lace-up shoes, button shoes, all leathers. He also listed underclothes, belts, ties, handkerchiefs, suspenders, garters, "Most any Thing for Man or Boy to Wear." His store windows advertised tailoring and male apparel. Ernest was Fire Chief in 1914. The shop is used as a restaurant in 2018.

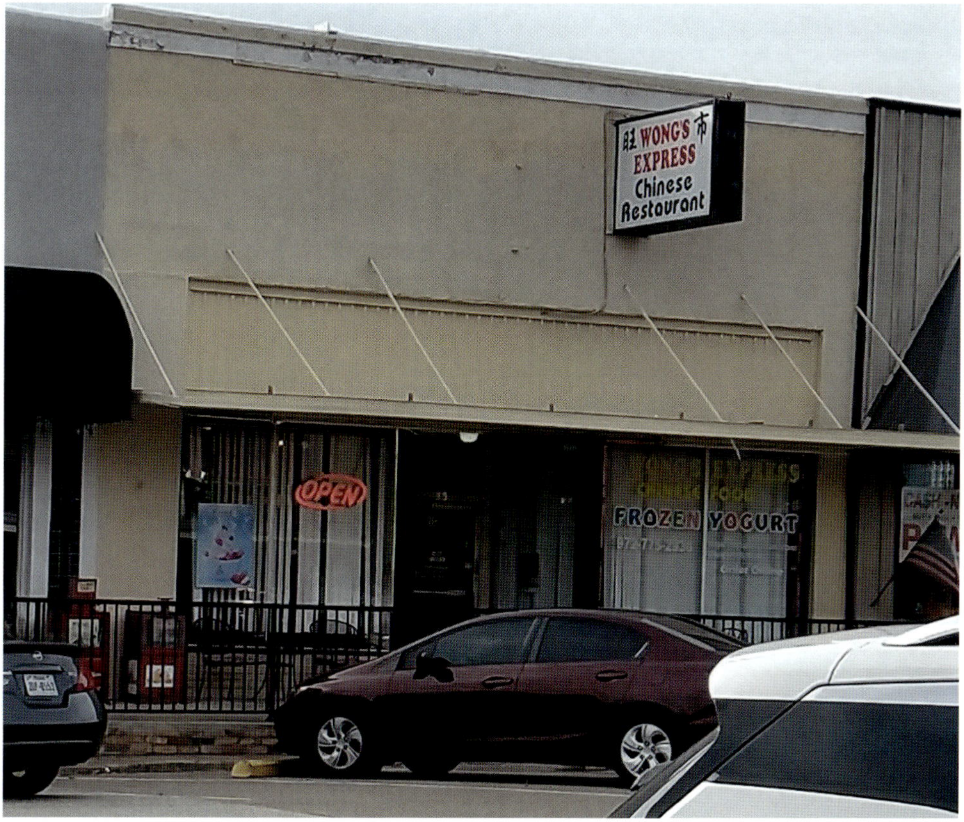

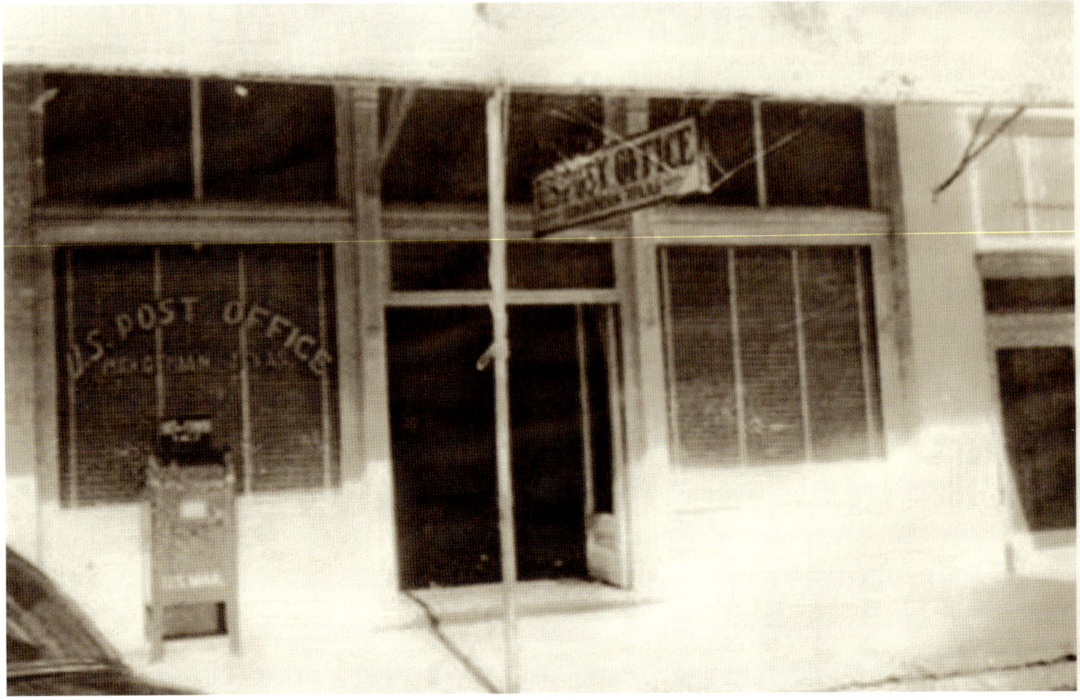

Post Offices: Before Midlothian was named, the mail arrived every Friday at Charles Barker's home. The rider came from Waxahachie, changed horses at Rev. Barker's, and went on to Wyatt and Cleburne. Next the Post Office was in a store in Lebanon, a village by the present cemetery. Midlothian, assigned a Post Office in 1883, occupied several locations before moving to the Woodmen of the World building on North 8th Street in 1917. In March 1961, land was bought from Clint Gouger's Garage, and the new building was dedicated on May 17, 1962.

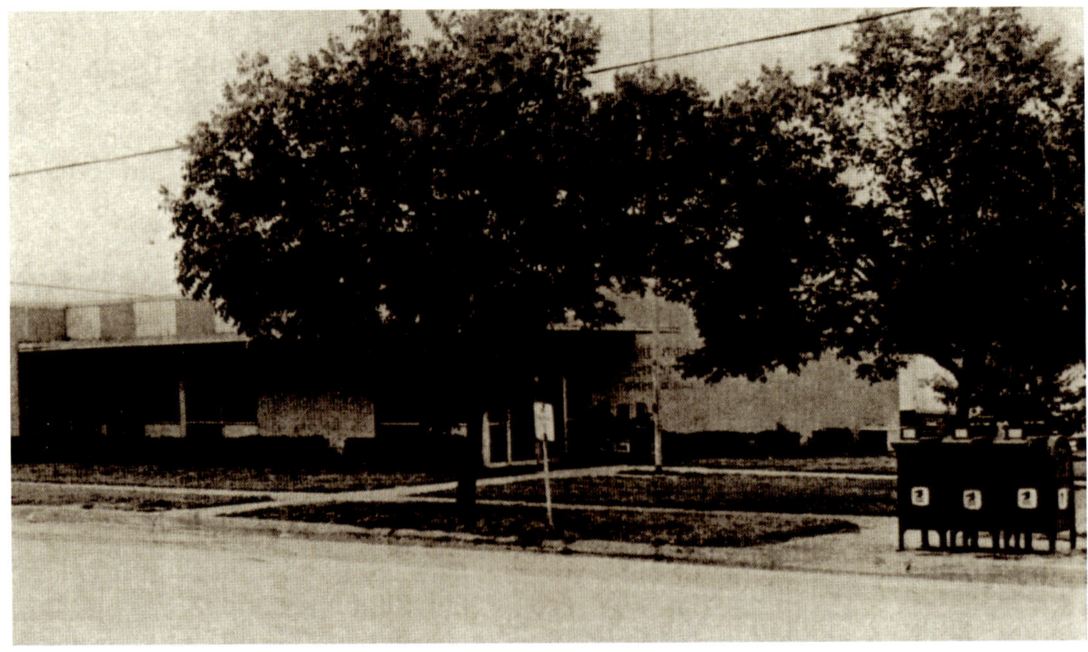

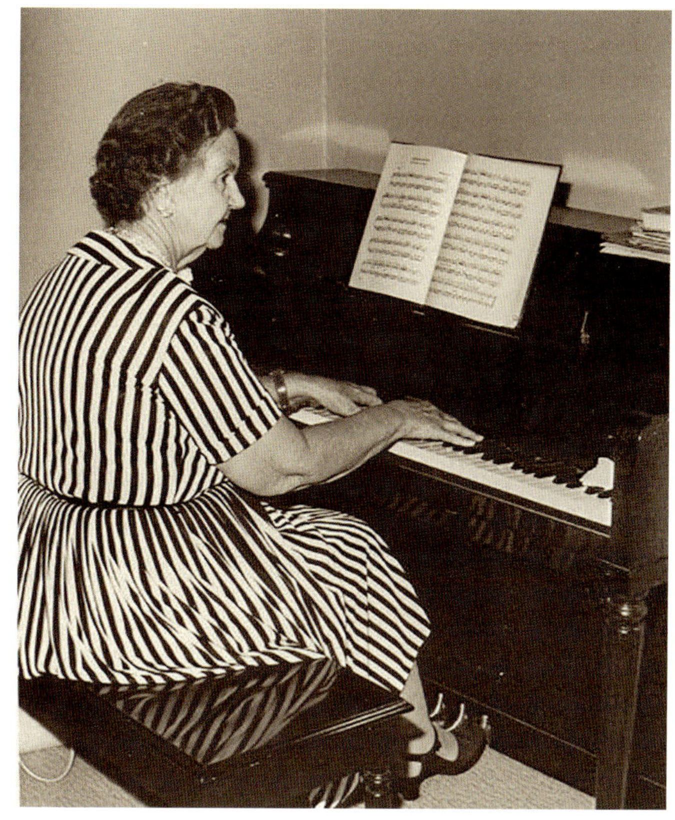

PHYSICIAN AND MUSICIAN: Dr. James Edgar Sewell, born 1870, Waxahachie, married Midlothian native, Edith Hawkins, born 1890. They built a lovely Craftsman-style home in 1915 where Edith gave piano lessons for about fifty years. She was organist at the Methodist Church and would give organ lessons to select students during the summers. Dr. Sewell is to the left of this photo in his drugstore. The other men are Moe Holland, J. M. Haggard, and Jeff Jennings. This was taken in 1932, shortly before Dr. Sewell died in 1933.

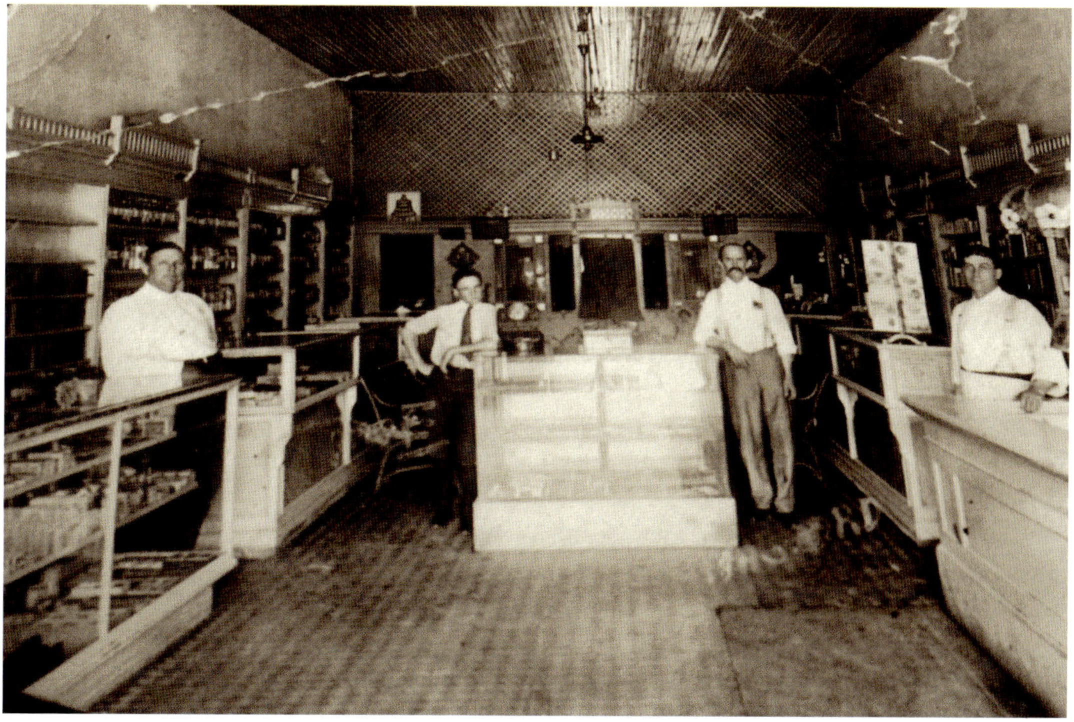

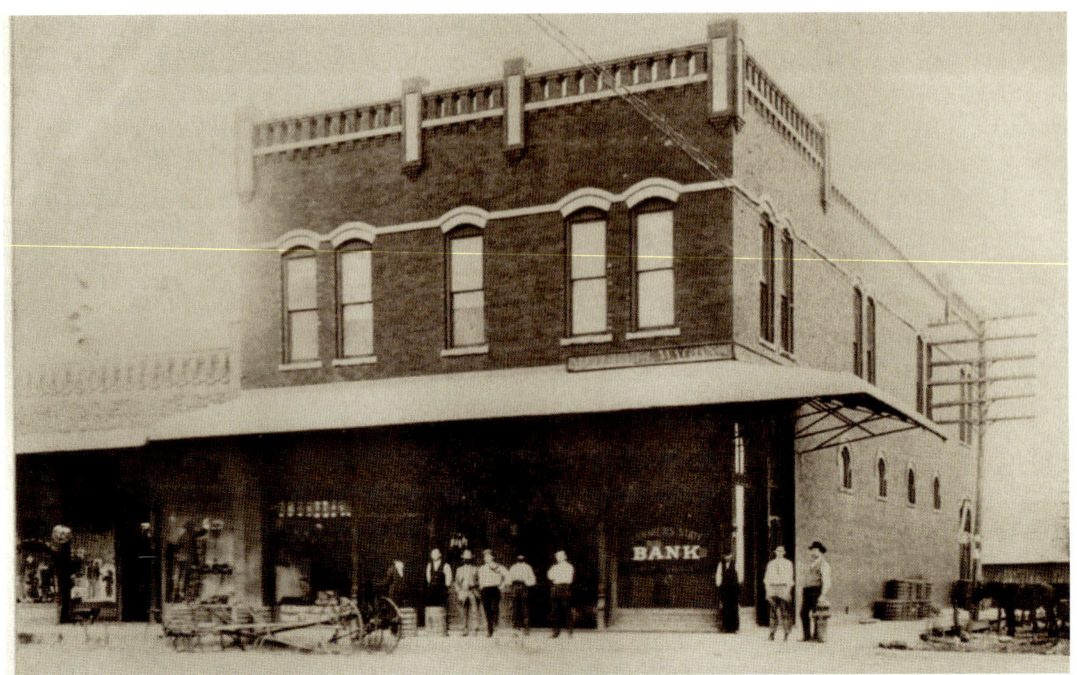

BANKS: G. C. Smith established a short-lived bank in 1895. William Hawkins established the First National Bank (FNB) in 1897. Although it is unknown when Citizens Bank began, FNB took it over in 1905. FNB bought the assets of Farmers National Bank in 1909. Farmers State Bank was founded in 1910 in the Martin-Hendricks building. It was consolidated with FNB in 1911, and the banks moved to Farmers' location under the FNB name. Farmers Guaranty State Bank was established in 1915 and consolidated with FNB in 1925. In 1937, FNB moved into the first brick business in town built by Sam Belew in 1892, below.

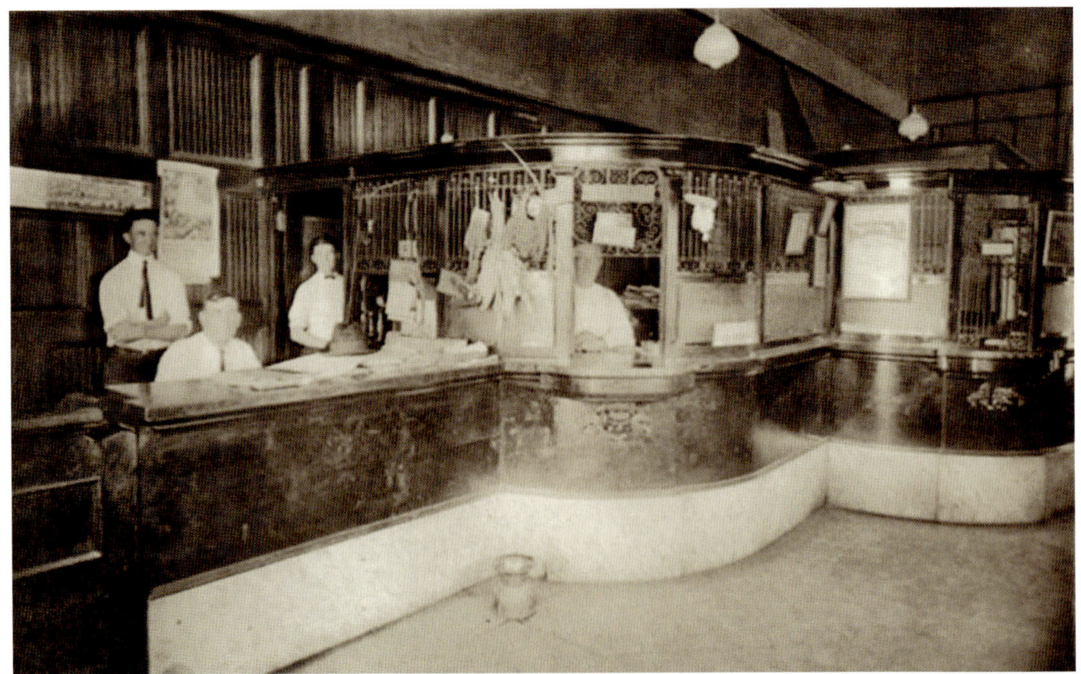

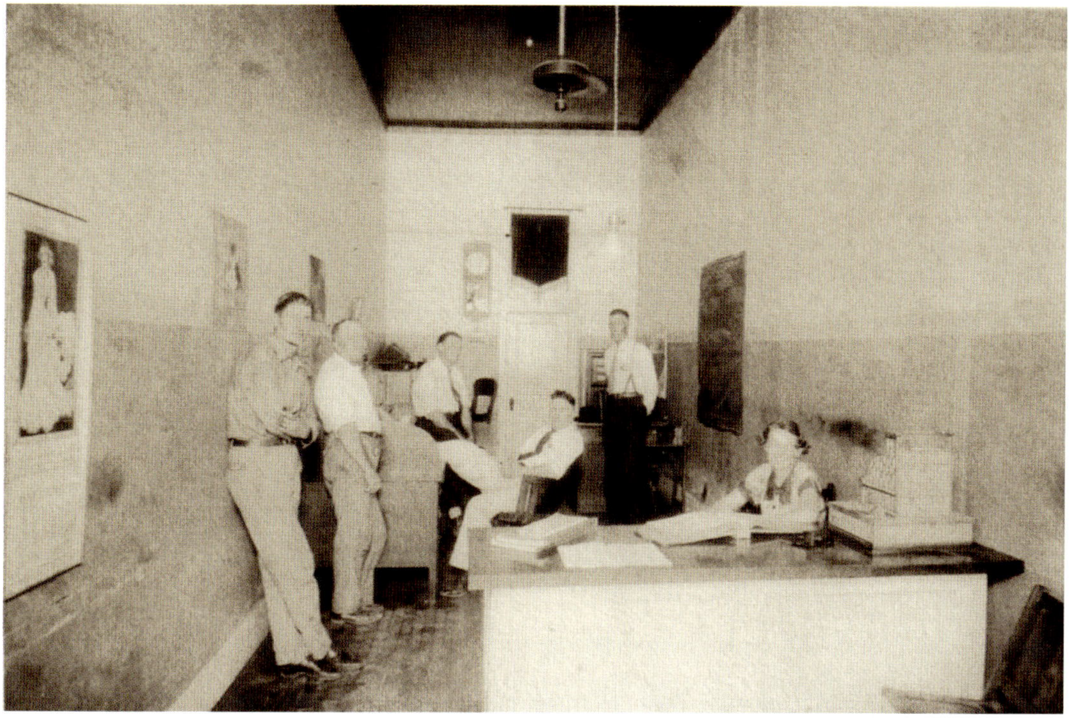

CITY HALL: In 1935, the City Hall occupied a very small store front on the main street. Shown are Charles Schultz, Bob Harris-Engineer for the Water Dept., Oscar Bennett-barber, Ernest Coward-employee of William Cameron Lumber Co., John Hays-Constable, and Alice Franks-City Secretary. By the mid-1940s, the office had been moved to a small room in the Fire Hall. Its entrance is at the far right of that building.

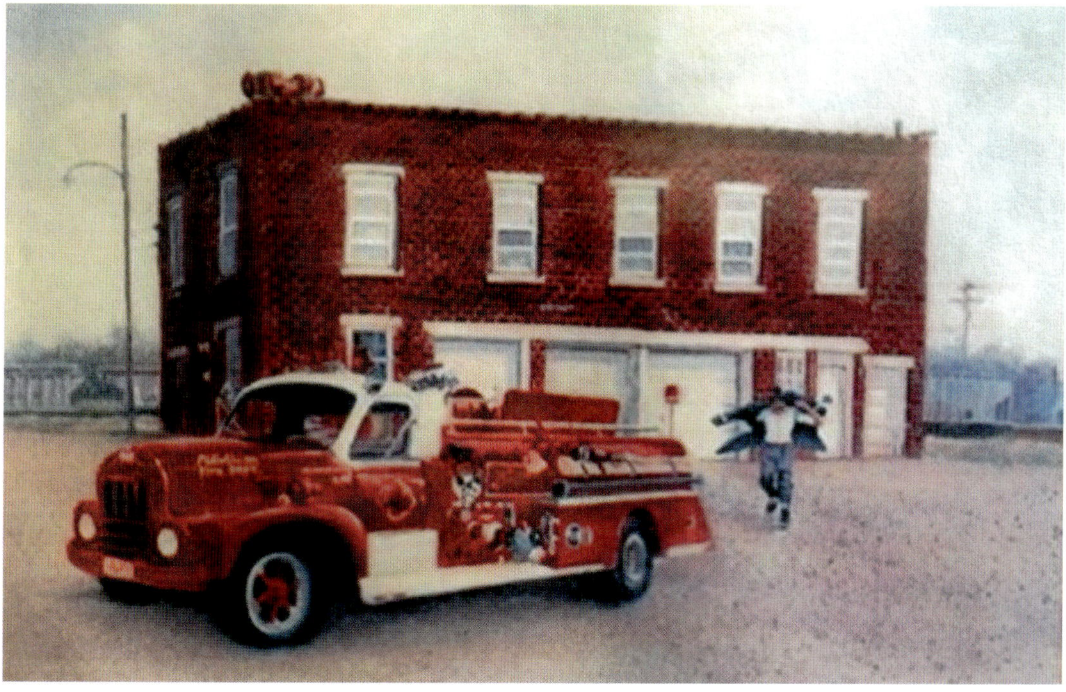

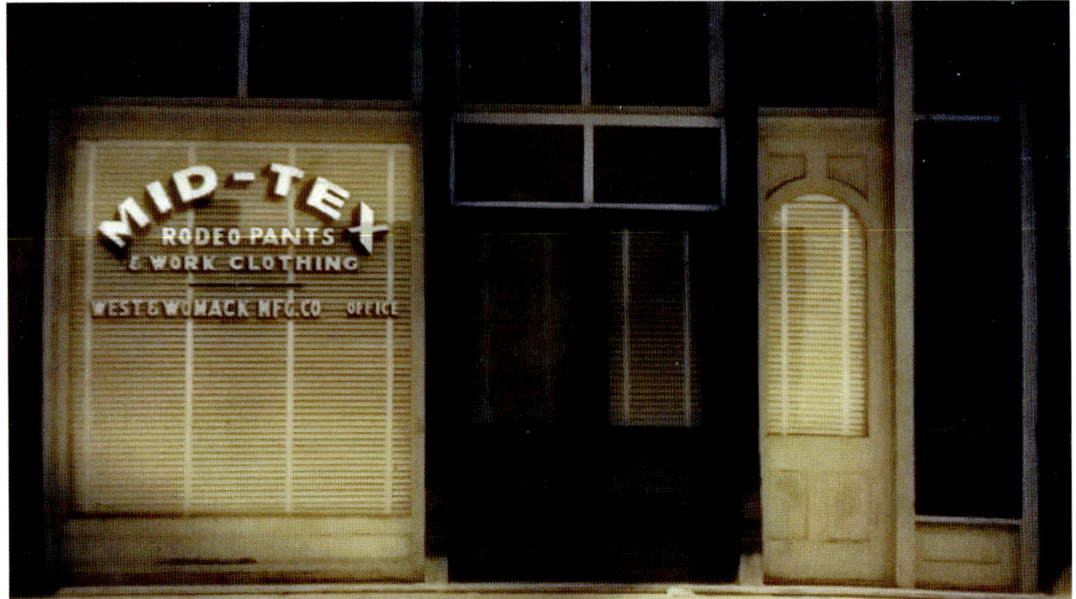

SEWING FACTORY: Mid-Tex occupied one of the store fronts of the two-story Martin-Hendricks Building, built between 1898 and 1901. Mid-Tex also used the second floor as a sewing room. The entire building was burned by an arsonist on September 30, 1960 while most of the Midlothian men were in Alvarado for a football game.

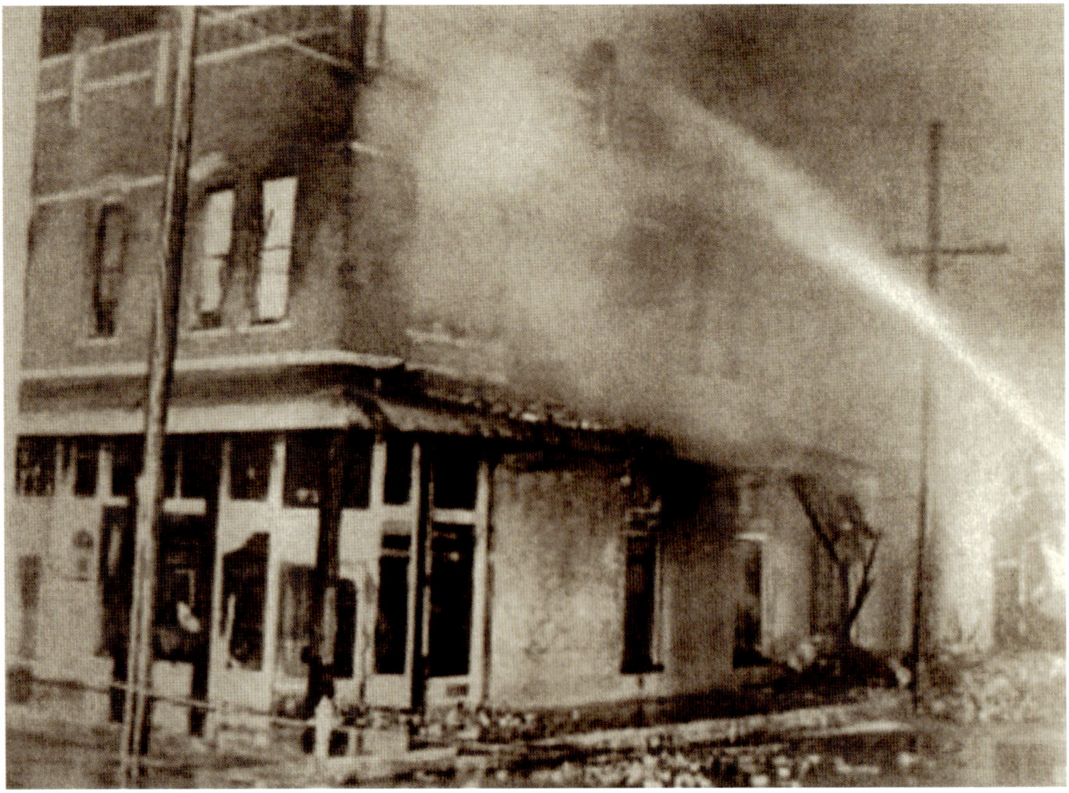

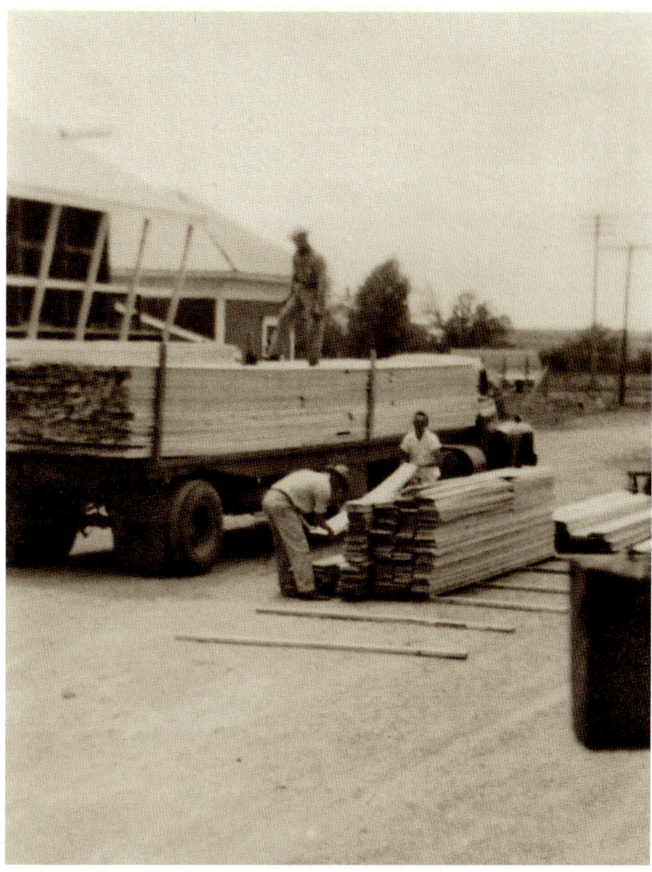

LUMBERYARDS: In 1882, Witherspoon and Chamberlain each ran a lumber yard in the area. E. R. Alexander ran a lumber yard along with several other businesses in 1889. Conway & Leeper ran a lumber yard in 1899, Farmers' Lumber Yard was open in 1904, and one in 1906 was named Citizens' Lumber Yard. Harris Fagg was transferred to Midlothian to manage the local William Cameron and Company in 1946, as shown in the yard. In the 1950s, the men in the office were Ray Ballard, Weldon Dillard, Manager Harris Fagg, Tommy Morgan and Philip Baxter.

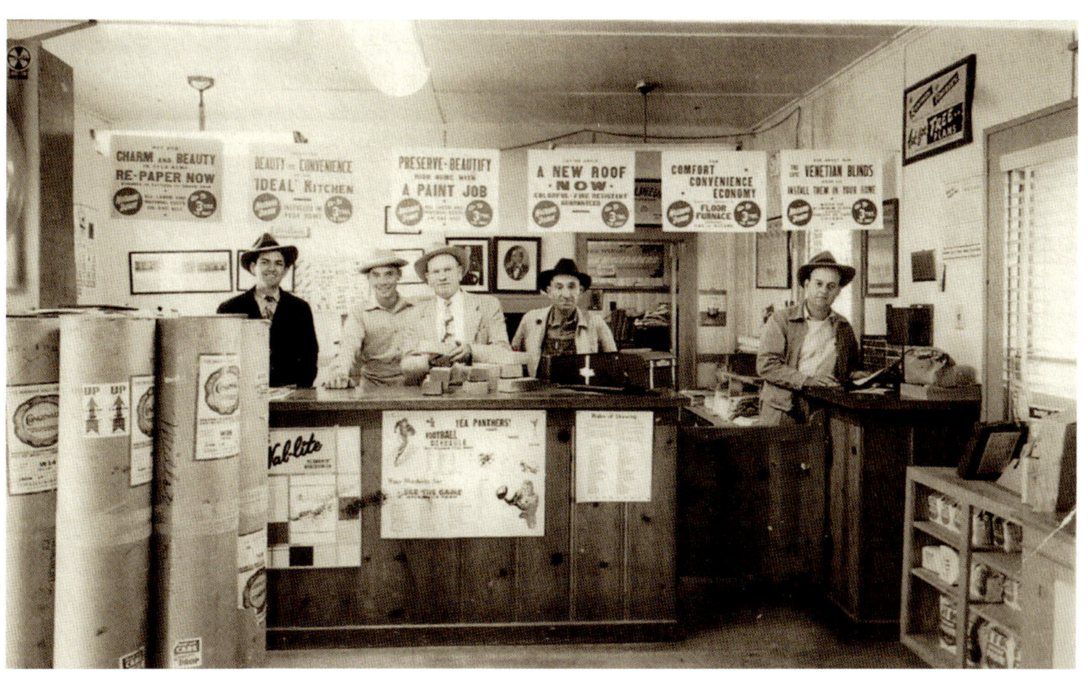

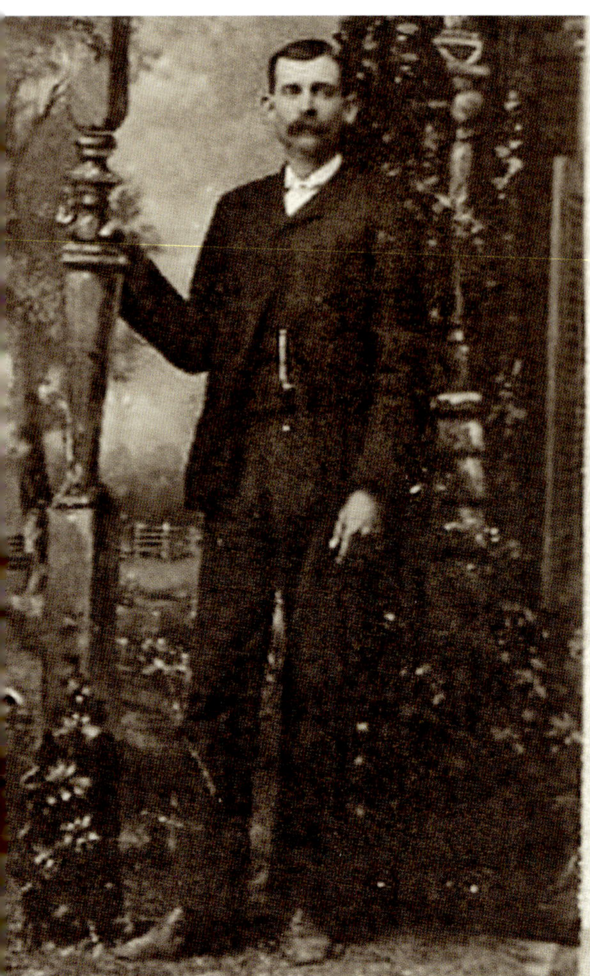

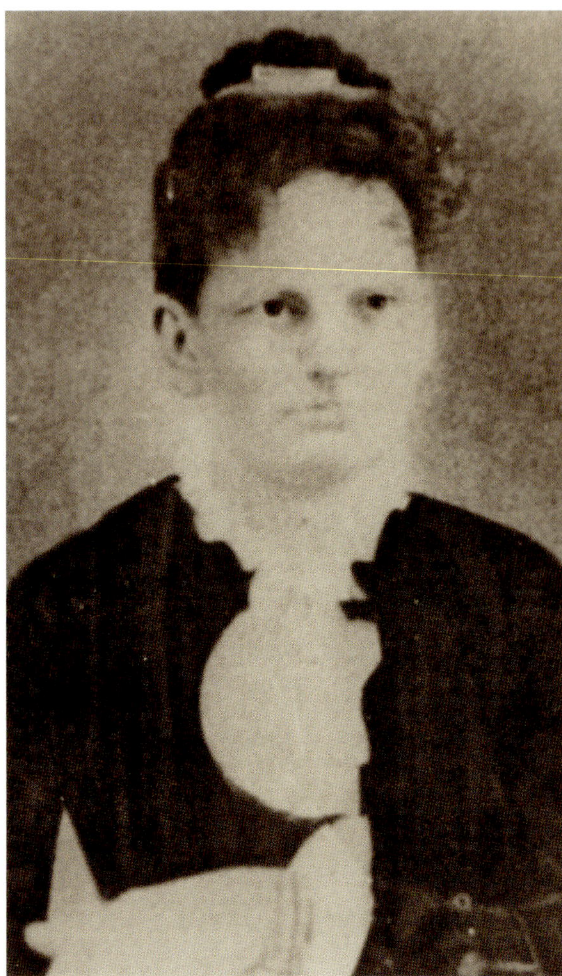

MERCHANT, INVENTOR: Ellanora Tucker, the daughter of Argyle and Marinda Tucker, married James Monroe Hopper in 1881. He was involved in a mercantile business, partnering with a Mr. Lawson. James built a new house for his family just before 1900. The home was remodeled and enlarged about 2009 to become an office.

Argyle William and Marinda Tucker first moved to Weatherford where Argyle, serving with the Texas Rangers, gained a great reputation as an Indian fighter. Argyle, brother Elihu, and father Laban were excellent machinists, gunsmiths, and silversmiths.

In 1861, they joined Tucker, Sherrad, and Company to manufacture arms for the Confederacy. Argyle and Laban created "The Tucker," a 44-caliber pistol with a 7½-inch barrel. When this business ended (April 1862), Argyle enlisted in Co. "C," 2nd Texas Infantry. After the war, Argyle moved to Midlothian to open a black smithy. He and Elihu opened the first photography studio in town and operated a mercantile store. Several of Argyle's inventions are recorded with the U.S. Patent Office, including this plan for a suspension bridge.

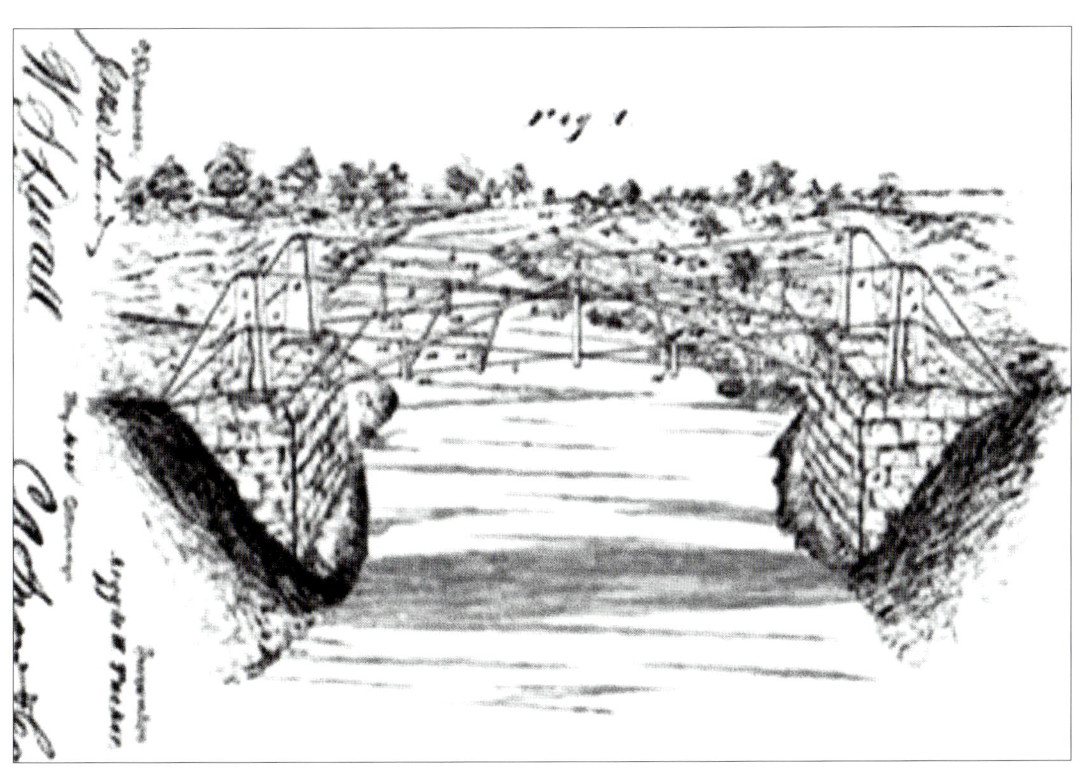

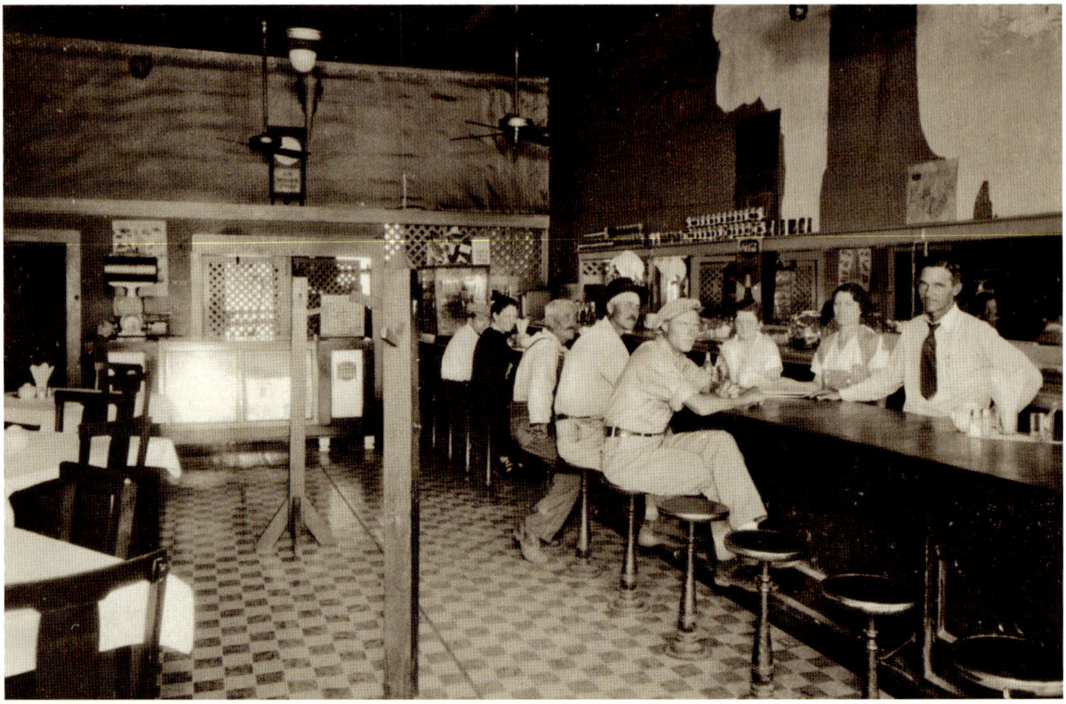

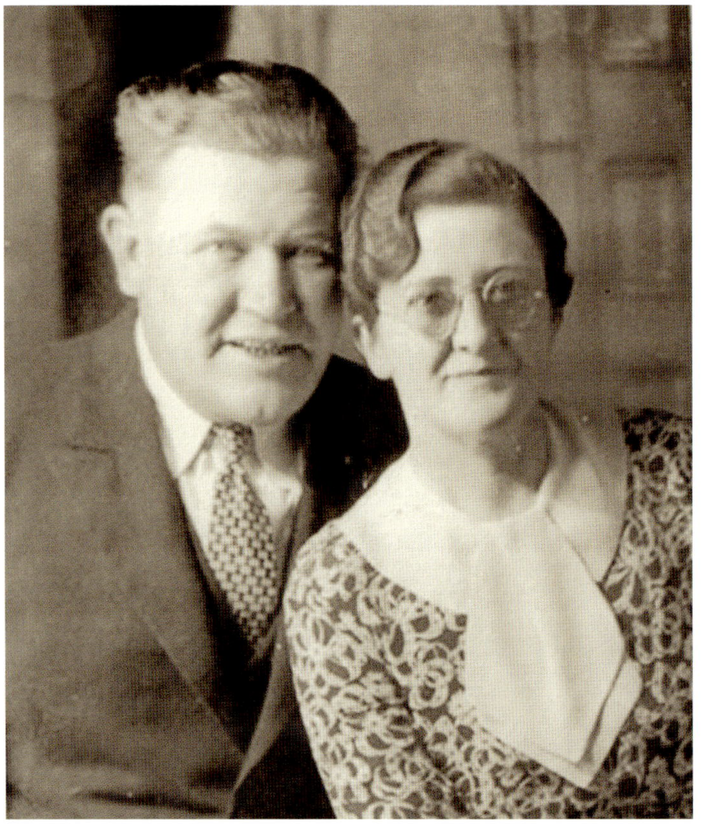

CAFÉ: The people in Briggs Café were (left to right) Bertha Hayes behind the counter, Ruby Briggs, and J. V. Briggs. In front, from left are Clint and Edna Eque, Jimmy Dorton, Sherwood Hendricks, and Frank Lawrence, in about 1934. Bertha Hayes had a wonderful reputation as a cook in Midlothian, and her pies were especially notable. She is pictured here in the 1950s with her husband Leslie "Pete" Hayes.

3

Society

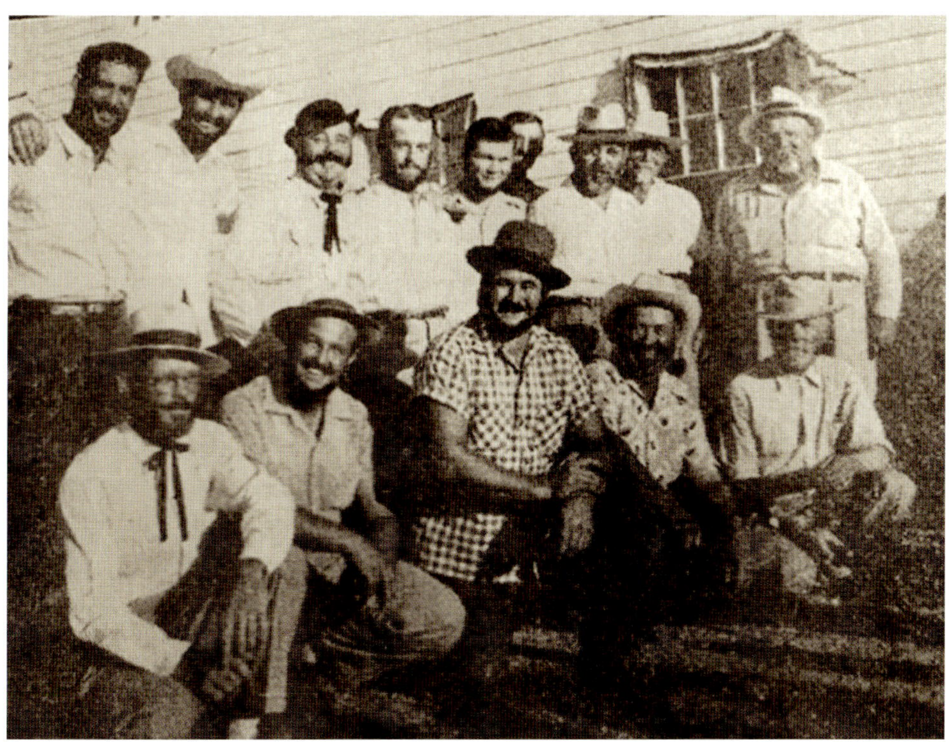

In 1956, men held a beard-growing contest. They are pictured at the old rodeo grounds: *From left to right, front row*: Milton Pegram, Odell Hayes, Buck Oatman, Reed, and Levy Ward. *From left to right, back row*: Pinkerton, H.C. Tucker, Robert Harrington, Hinton, Gilbert Hayes, Ray Crenshaw, Browning, Tom Davis, and M. T. Hawkins.

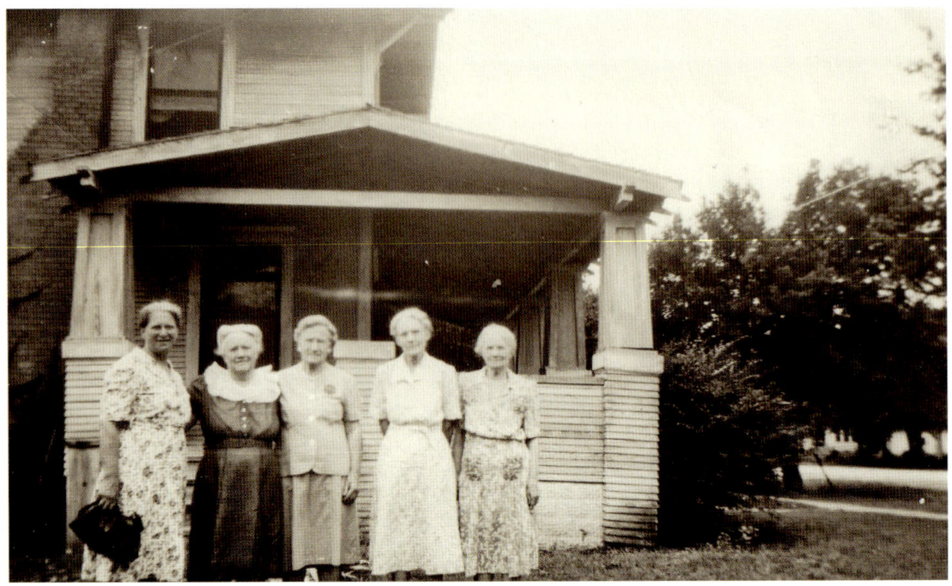

FRIENDS: These ladies visited in their friend Callie's home in the 1940s. *From left to right*: unknown, Ethel Page, two unknown, and Callie Lawson. Just east of her home (which appears again on the extreme left), neighborhood friends got together to play with their dogs in the mid-1950s. They are Penn Jones III, Mike Jones, Ray LaFrombois, and Moe Holland, Jr.

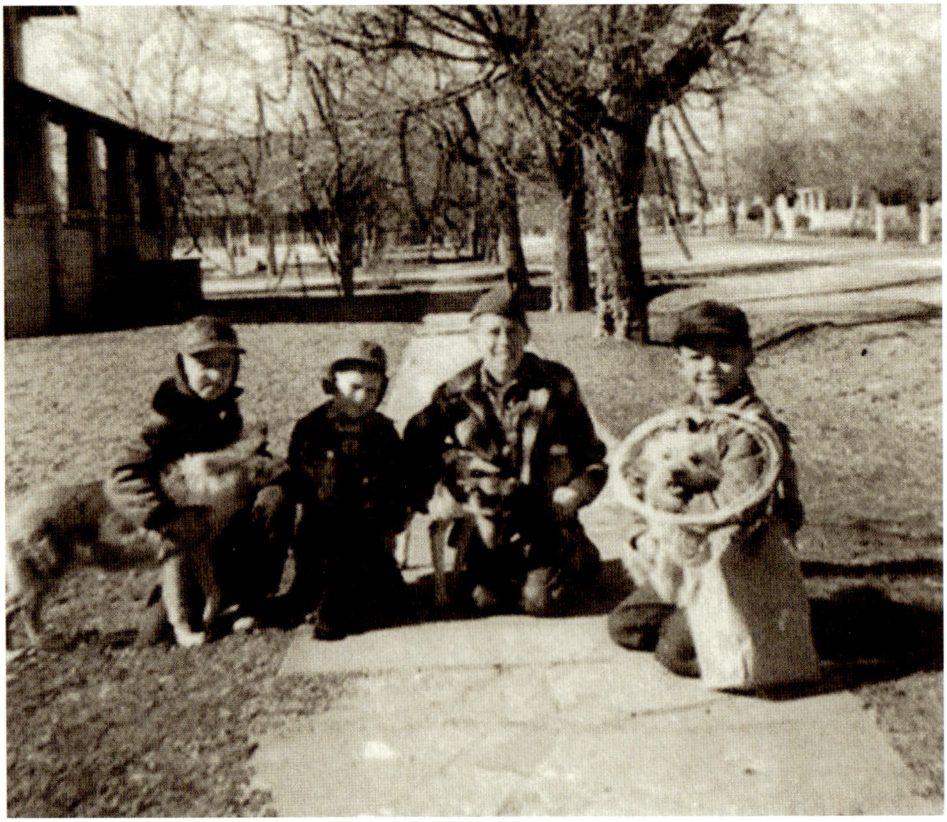

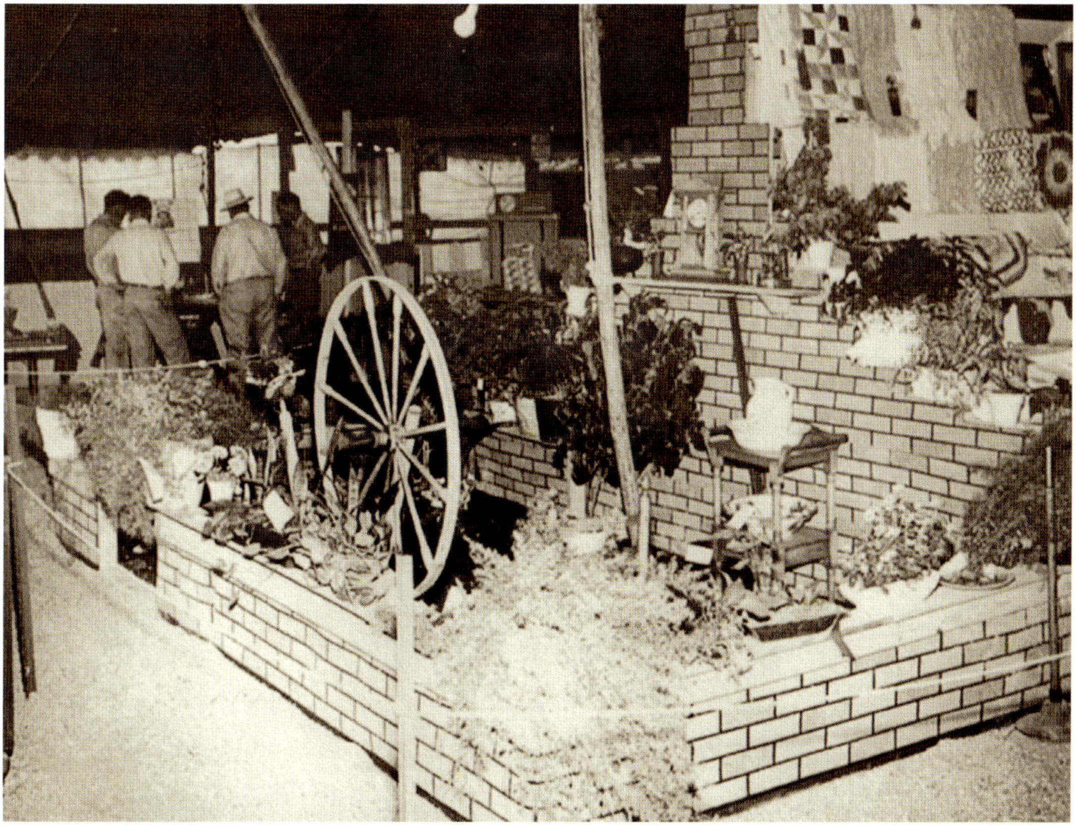

FAIRS: "Farm Exhibits" were held as far back as 1910. Also, many educational programs were presented in the Opera Hall (in WOW building). Early fairs were held in rented tents, and women showed their entries in the American Legion Hall. Local merchants awarded prizes and purchased the champion animals. A severe thunderstorm destroyed the tents during a fair in the early 1950s, so citizens decided to erect a building instead. The Civic Center Board began construction in 1955, with its completion in May 1957. Most of the work was done by volunteers, using donated materials.

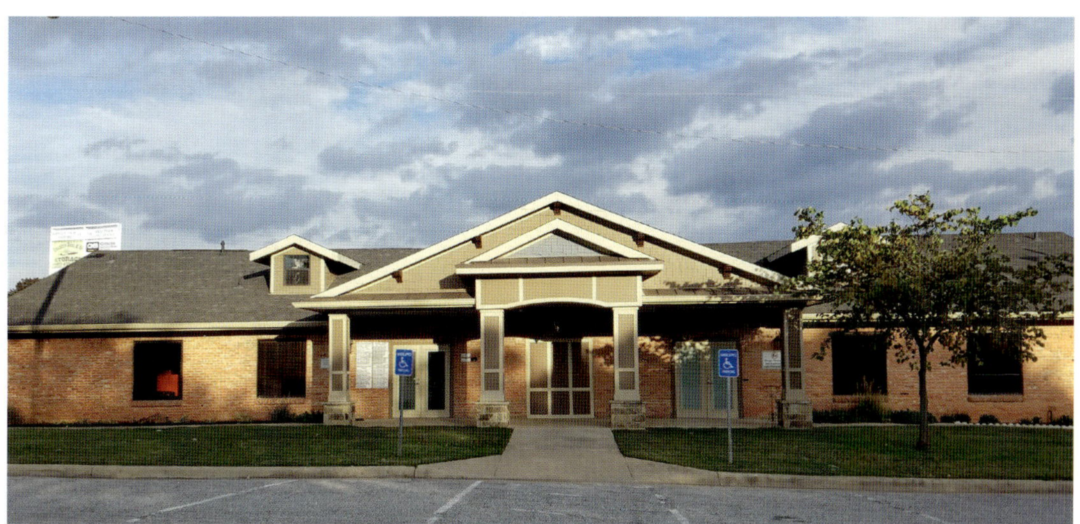

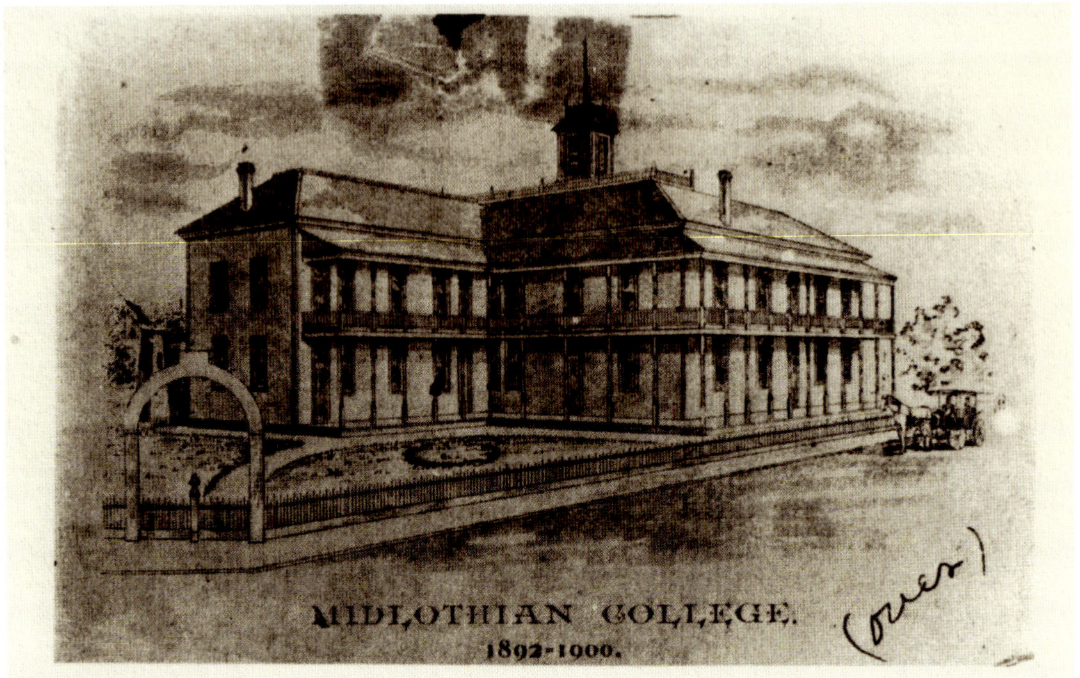

PRIVATE EDUCATION: William Works founded Polytechnic Institute in 1883. This private, coeducational school offered a wide variety of classes. After Mr. Works's death, Rev. Thomas G. Whitten operated the school, known as Whitten Institute. Then it was briefly named Midlothian College before being loaned to the public primary school for a short time. The building was dismantled in 1907. Former students continued to hold annual reunions, at least through 1948.

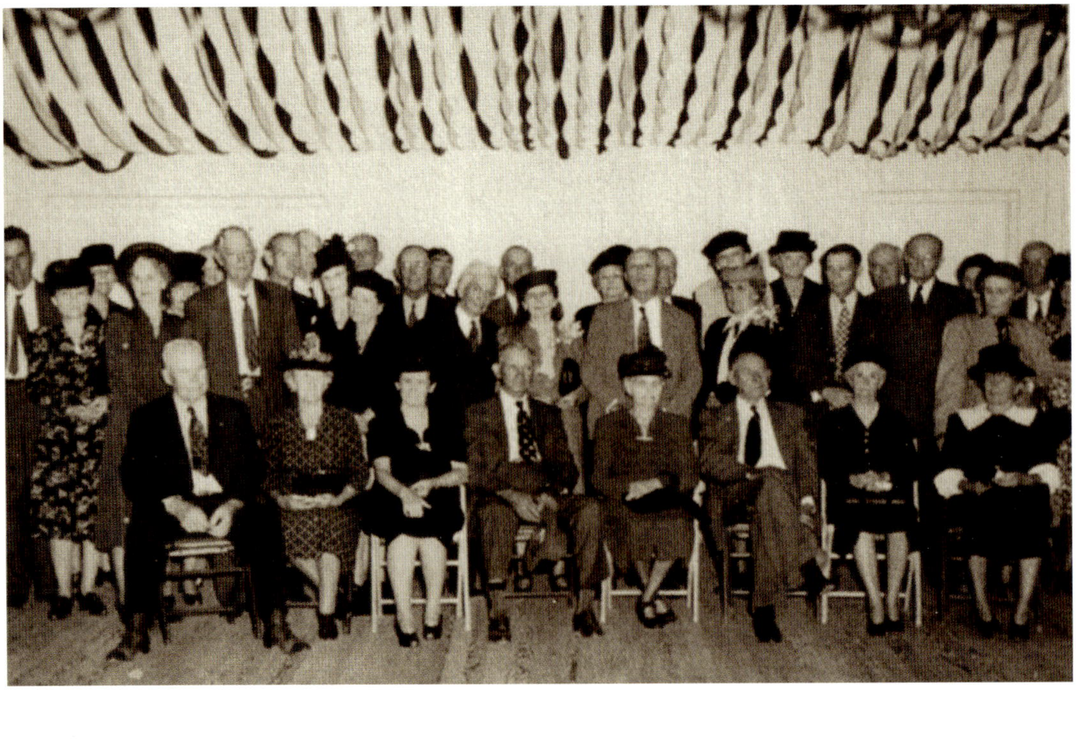

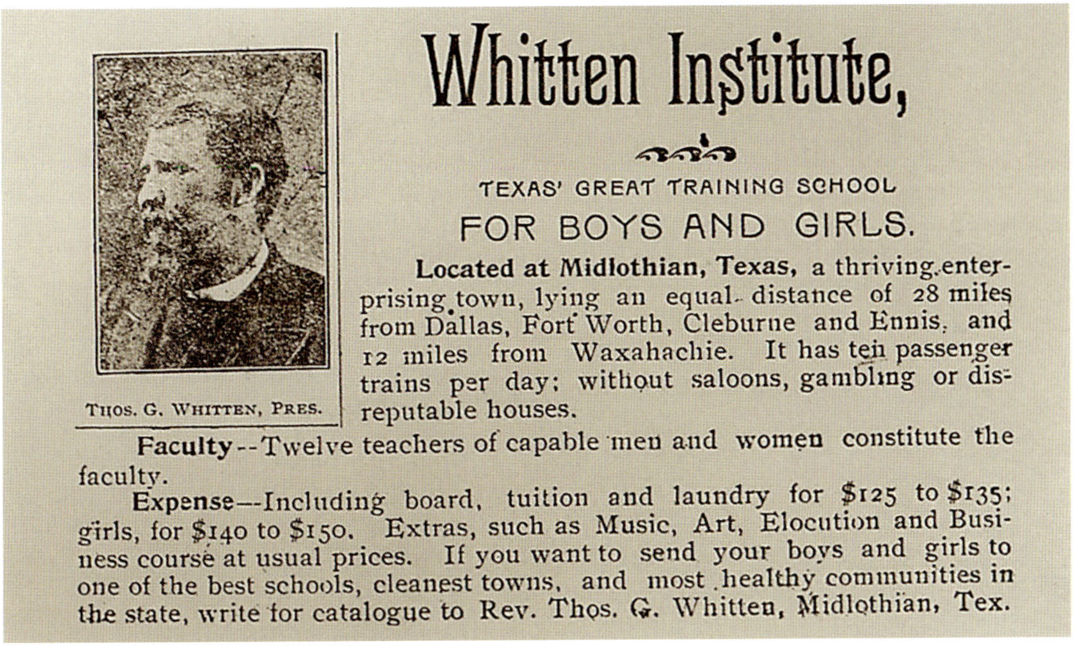

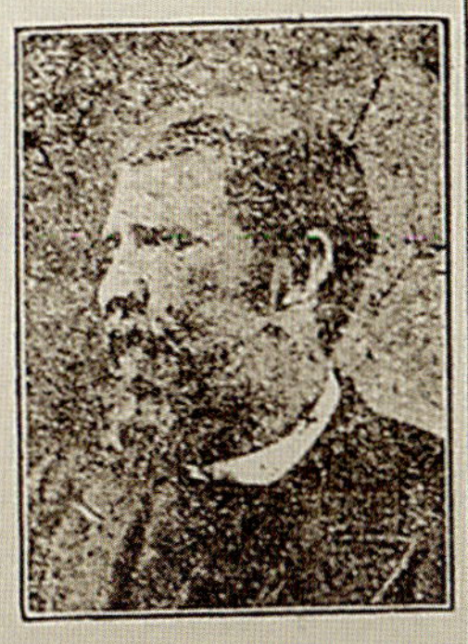

THOS. G. WHITTEN, PRES.

Whitten Institute,

TEXAS' GREAT TRAINING SCHOOL

FOR BOYS AND GIRLS.

Located at Midlothian, Texas, a thriving enterprising town, lying an equal distance of 28 miles from Dallas, Fort Worth, Cleburne and Ennis, and 12 miles from Waxahachie. It has ten passenger trains per day; without saloons, gambling or disreputable houses.

Faculty--Twelve teachers of capable men and women constitute the faculty.

Expense--Including board, tuition and laundry for $125 to $135; girls, for $140 to $150. Extras, such as Music, Art, Elocution and Business course at usual prices. If you want to send your boys and girls to one of the best schools, cleanest towns, and most healthy communities in the state, write for catalogue to Rev. Thos. G. Whitten, Midlothian, Tex.

FIRST CITY PARK: Stockholder J. C. Kimmel bought out the other stockholders, thus owning the entire city block. In 1915, his widow gave it to the city for use as a park. The bandstand was soon built, and children's playground equipment was installed, along with croquet and tennis courts. On the 100th anniversary of the donation, a celebration honored the Kimmel family. A grandson of the donor spoke, and many of the family came.

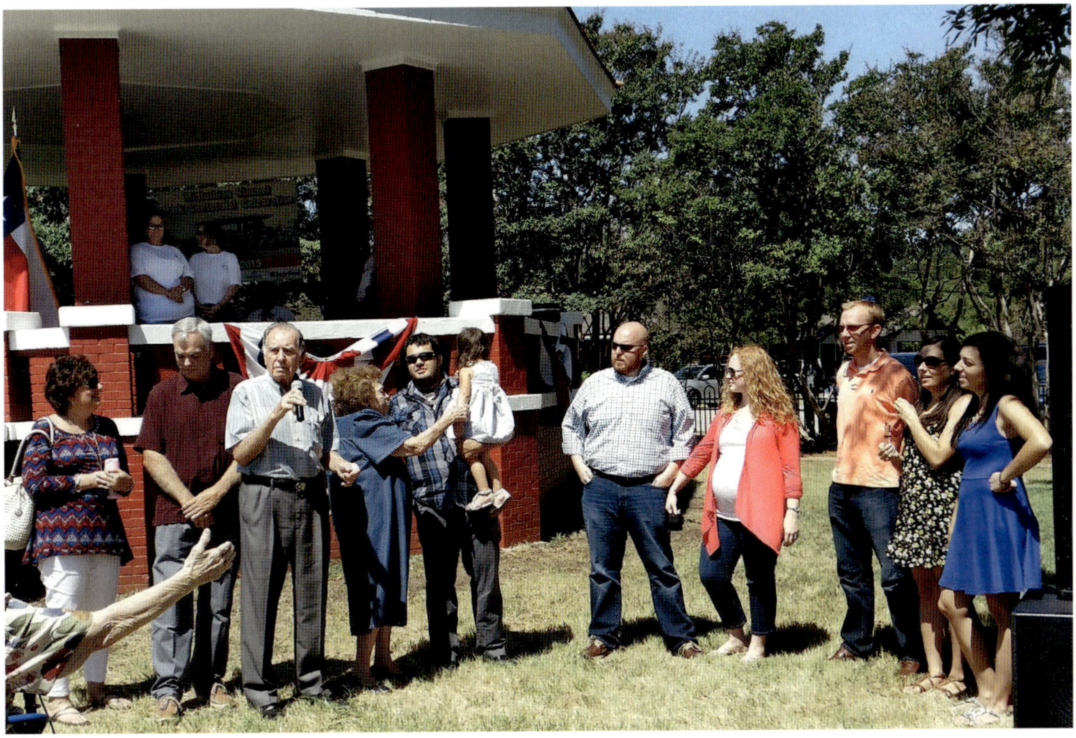

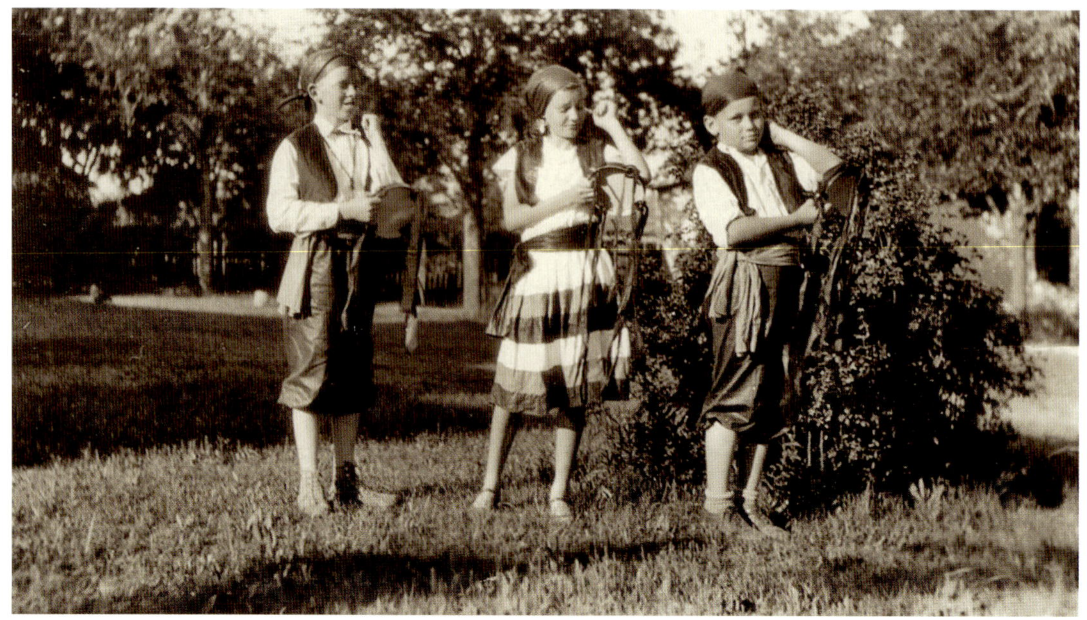

CHILDHOOD FRIENDS: These neighbors often played together, appearing as gypsies here, about 1930. They are Edward "Ubba" Harris, Charlene Morton, and Hubert "Buddy" Morton.

These girls enjoyed celebrating Beverly's sixth birthday at Kimmel Park, 1952. *From left to right*: Kathy McElroy, Lou Ann Wadley, Purnie Lefkosky, Beverly King, and Diane Morton.

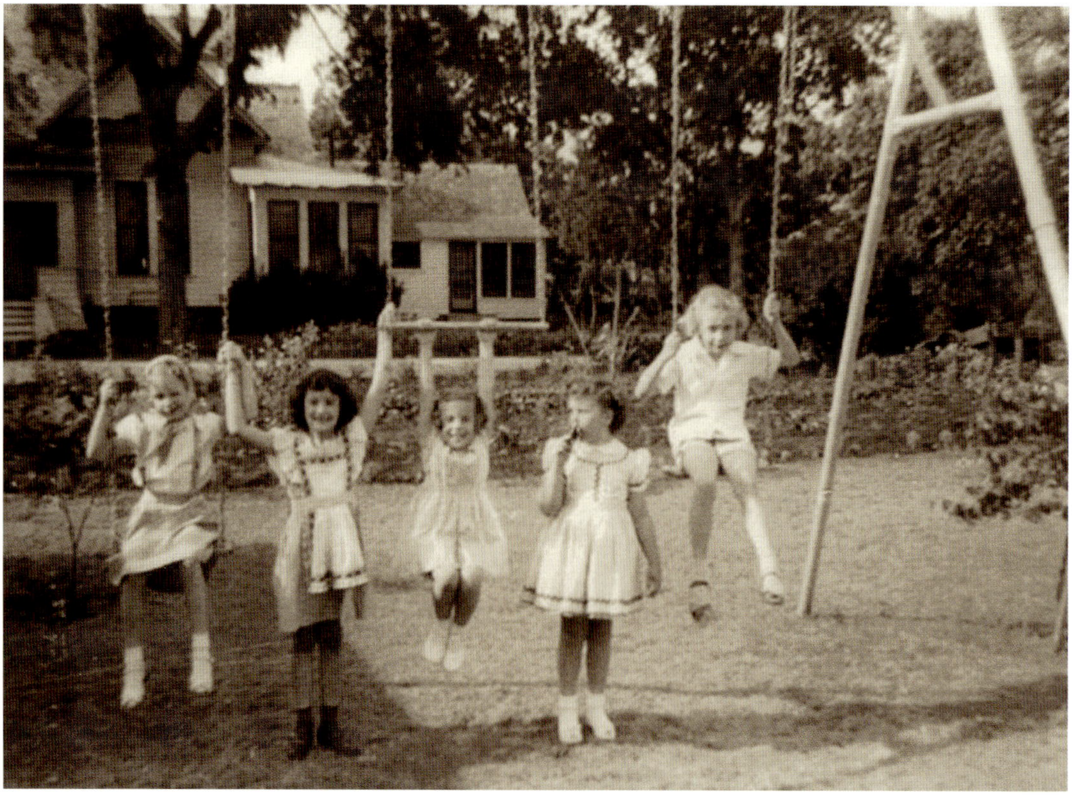

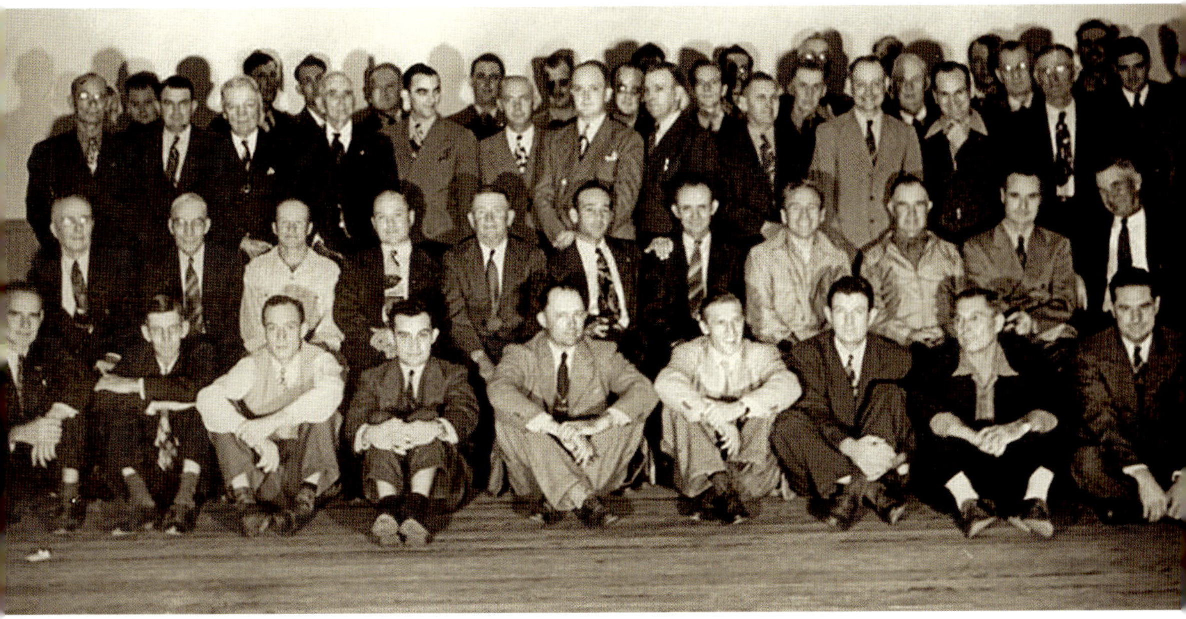

CHAMBER OF COMMERCE: Members of the Chamber of Commerce in 1946 were identified by surname only. Unfortunately, a few of the names are unreadable. *From left to right, front row*: Howard, Mason, Hilley, unknown, Aday, Cowan, Autrey, Ray, and McElroy. *From left to right, second row*: Hooper, Brundage, Moseley, Crow, Ward, Webb, Reed, Jones, Lupton, McElroy, and Mahanay. *From left to right, third row*: Byrd, Wadley, Hanson, Price, Turner, Mitchell, Page, Ralston, Eskridge, Goodwin, Kay, Morris, and Sewell. *From left to right, fourth row*: Spearman, McDonald, Griffin, Lewis, Forbes, Aycock, Page, Harris, True, unknown, Hendricks, Lee, Stell, Alderdice, and Few. Chamber of Commerce headquarters is on South 9th Street as of 2018.

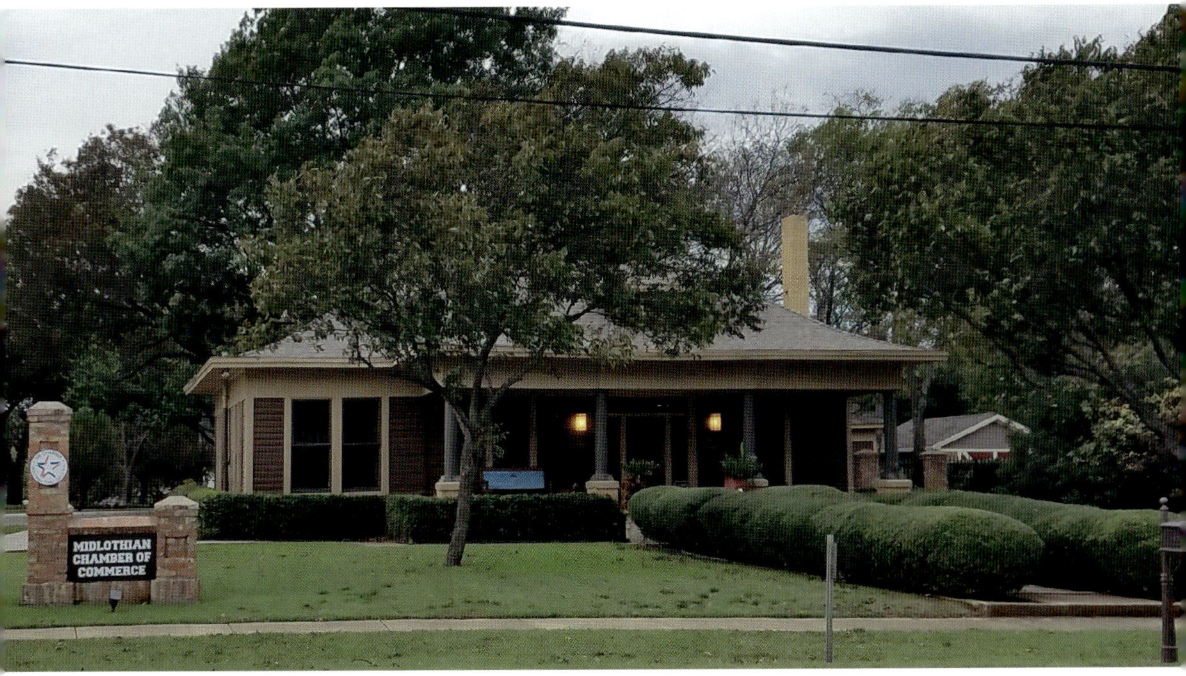

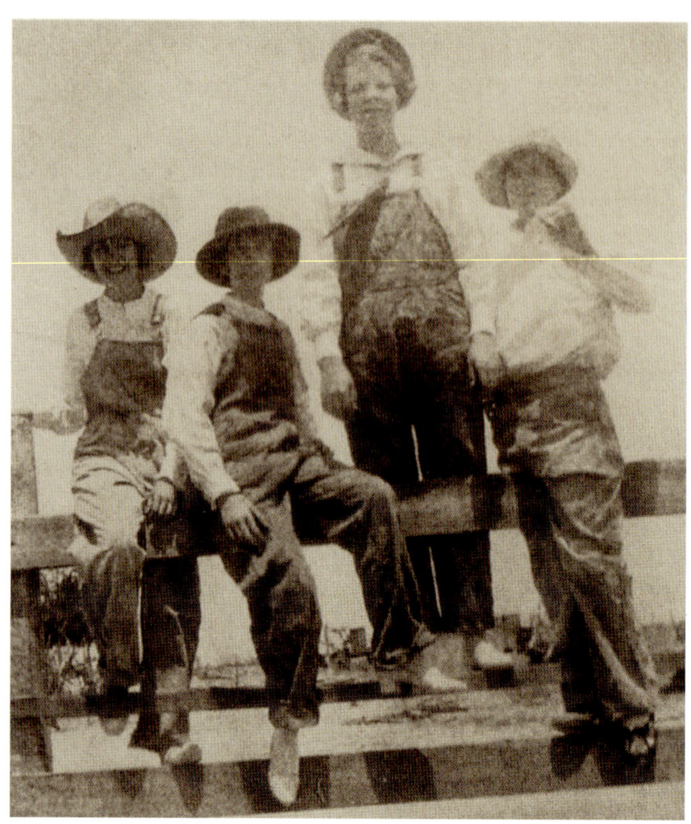

COSTUMES: In the mid-1920s, these girls enjoyed dressing up as boys, but it looks like some of them did not change their shoes. They were identified as Alpha, Bill, Oleta, and Phama. Across town, another group of girls decided to do likewise. *From left to right, in the lower picture*: Grace Eldridge, Nell Hopper, Zelma Eldridge, and Bertha Hopper.

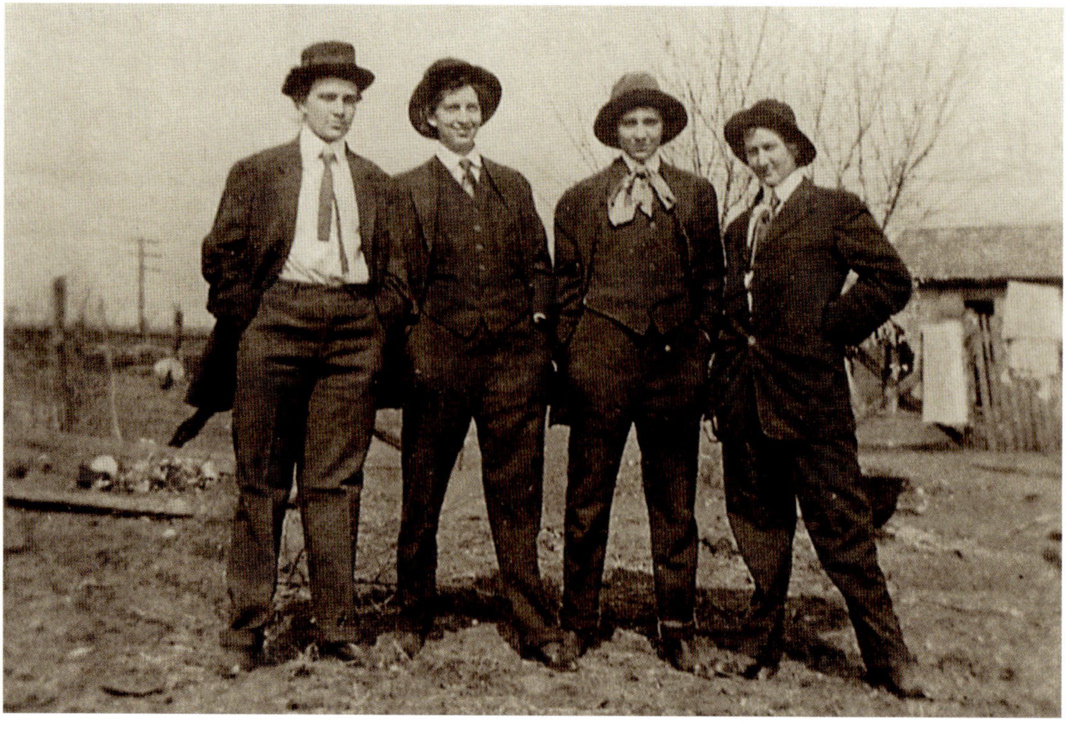

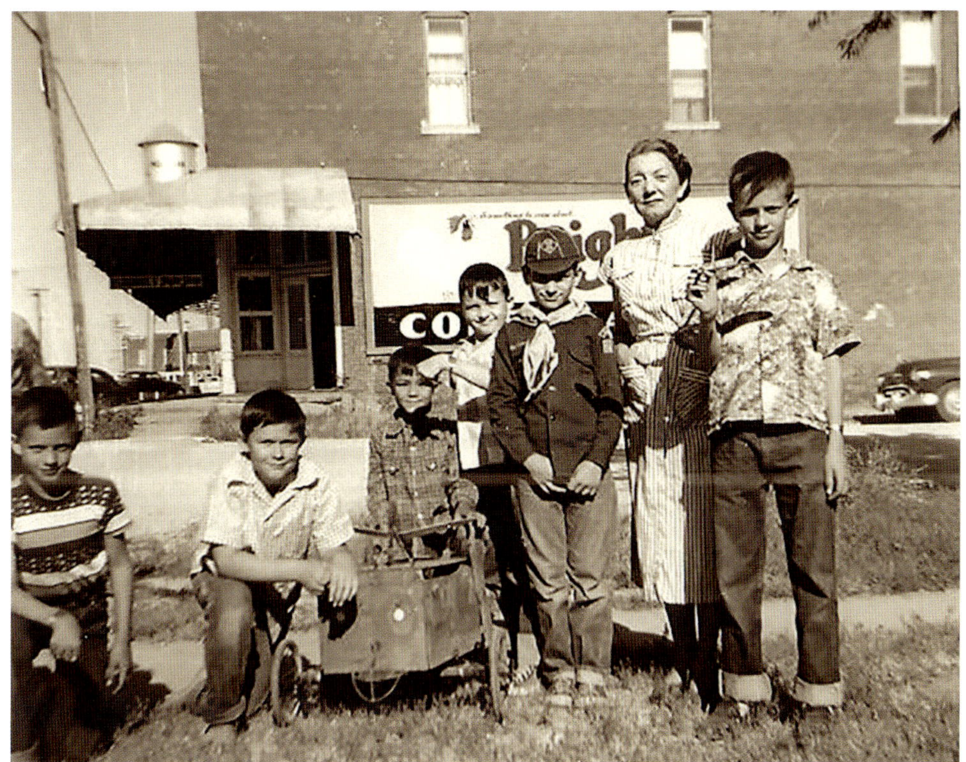

BOY SCOUTS: These Boy Scouts gathered in the Moe Holland, Sr., yard about 1953. They are Fred Howard, Danny Spearman, Moe Holland, Jr., Hal Edwards, Stanley Springer, Mrs. Moe Holland, Sr., and Ted Howard. The home and yard are now a warehouse, but one can still look east on West Avenue F toward the now-restored Fire Hall. However, the water tower has been dismantled.

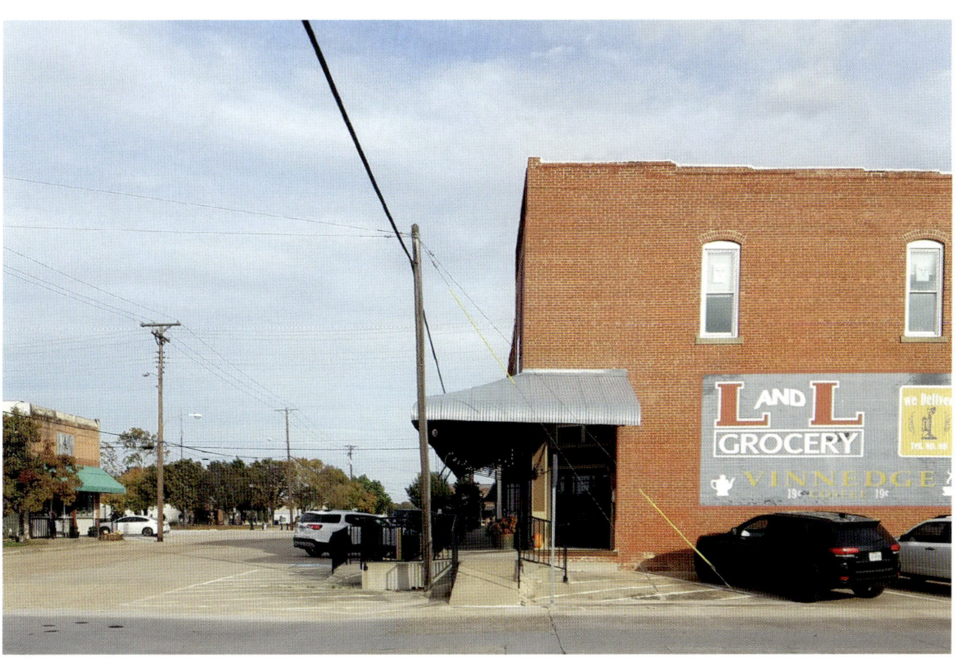

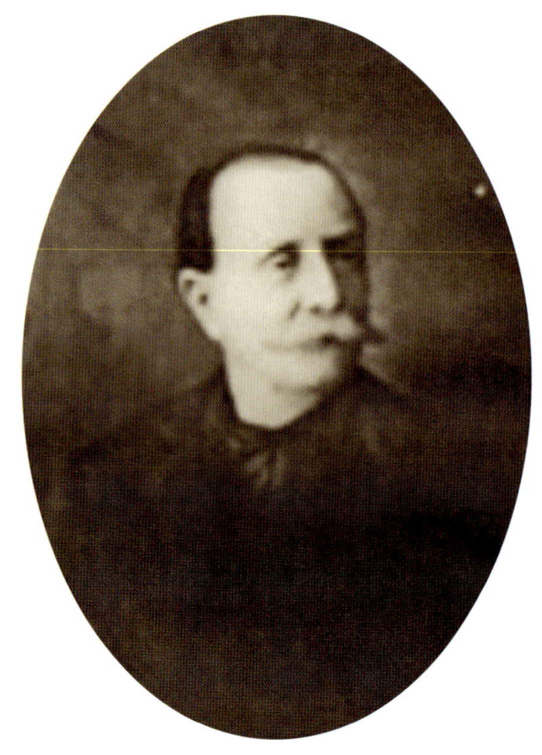

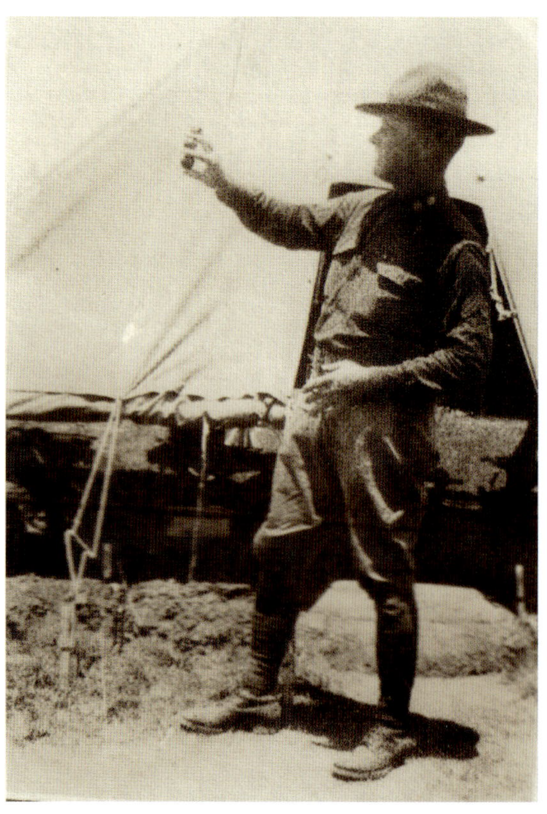

WORLD WAR I: George Washington Goodwin, born in 1841, Mississippi, came to Texas with his family about 1855. He fought for the Confederacy in Co. "H," 1st Texas Cavalry. He first married Sarah M. Lowe who bore two sons. Secondly, he married Mrs. Martha Ellen Guiles by whom he had six children. George was a member of the Church of Christ and of the Farmers Union. His grandson, Isaac Burton Goodwin, was sent overseas during World War I. "Burt" liked to entertain his fellow soldiers with some magic tricks.

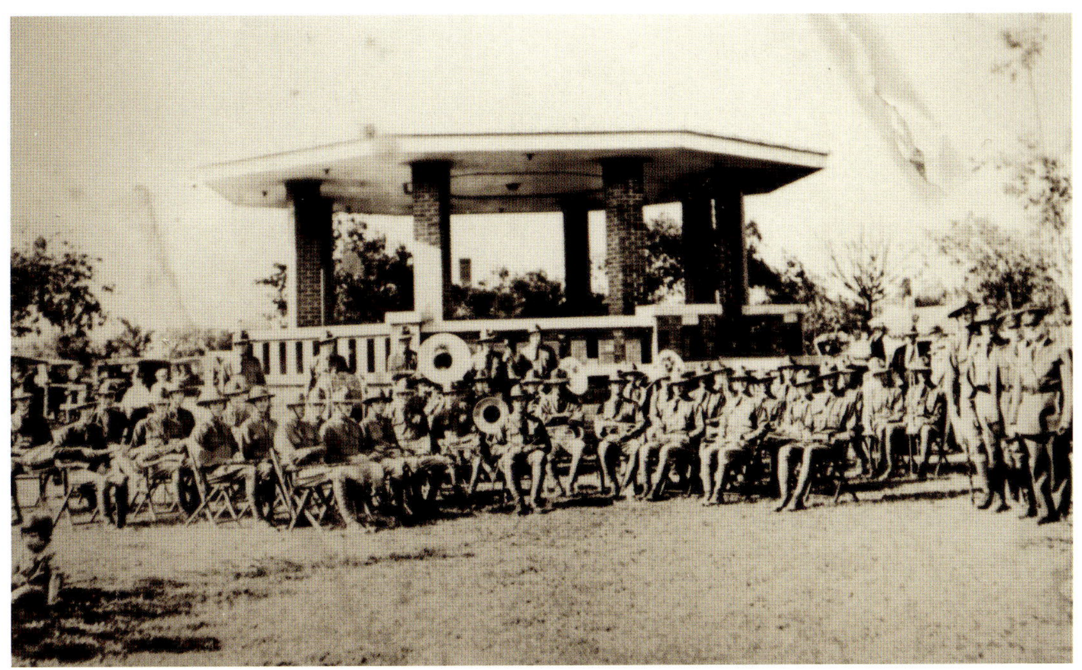

144TH INFANTRY BAND: The 144th Infantry Band was a large part of Midlothian social life from 1919 until World War II. In the 1920s, the band played a concert at the Bandstand in Kimmel Park almost every Sunday afternoon. Girlfriends and families would take picnic lunches and blankets to the park to enjoy the music. As a part of the U.S. National Guard, the band had drill every summer at the National Guard camp in Palacios, Texas. They are in Glen Rose, TX, in the lower photo.

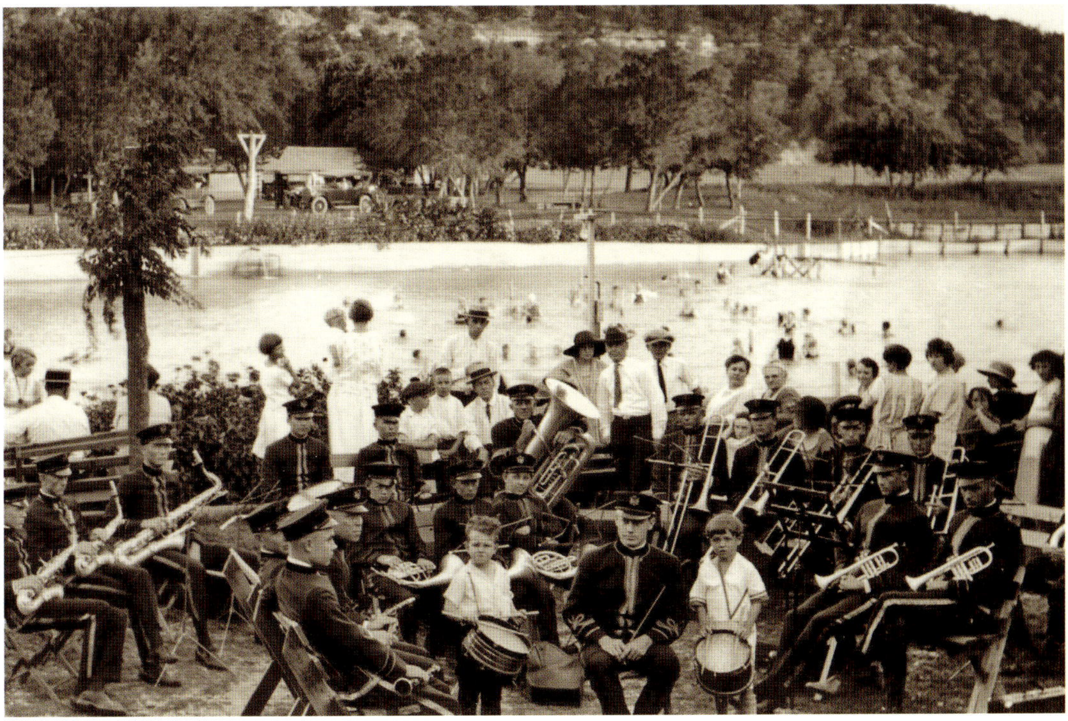

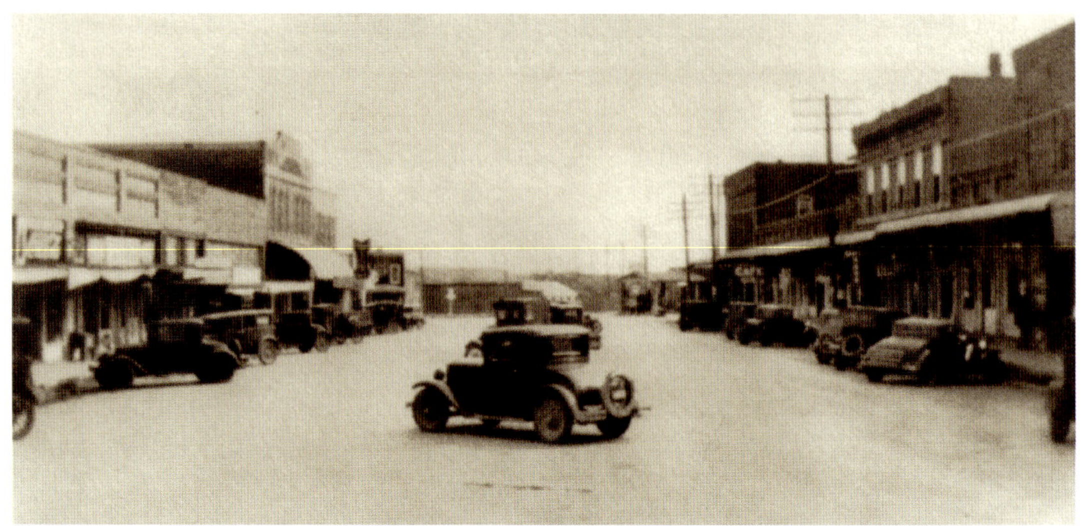

THE MAIN STREET: Back in 1925, people parked many different ways on the main street. The brick buildings on each side have been completed, and the lumber yard is seen at the back end of the left side. After World War II ended, the citizens held a public barbecue every July 4. The street was blocked off for uninterrupted eating and dancing, as shown in 1950.

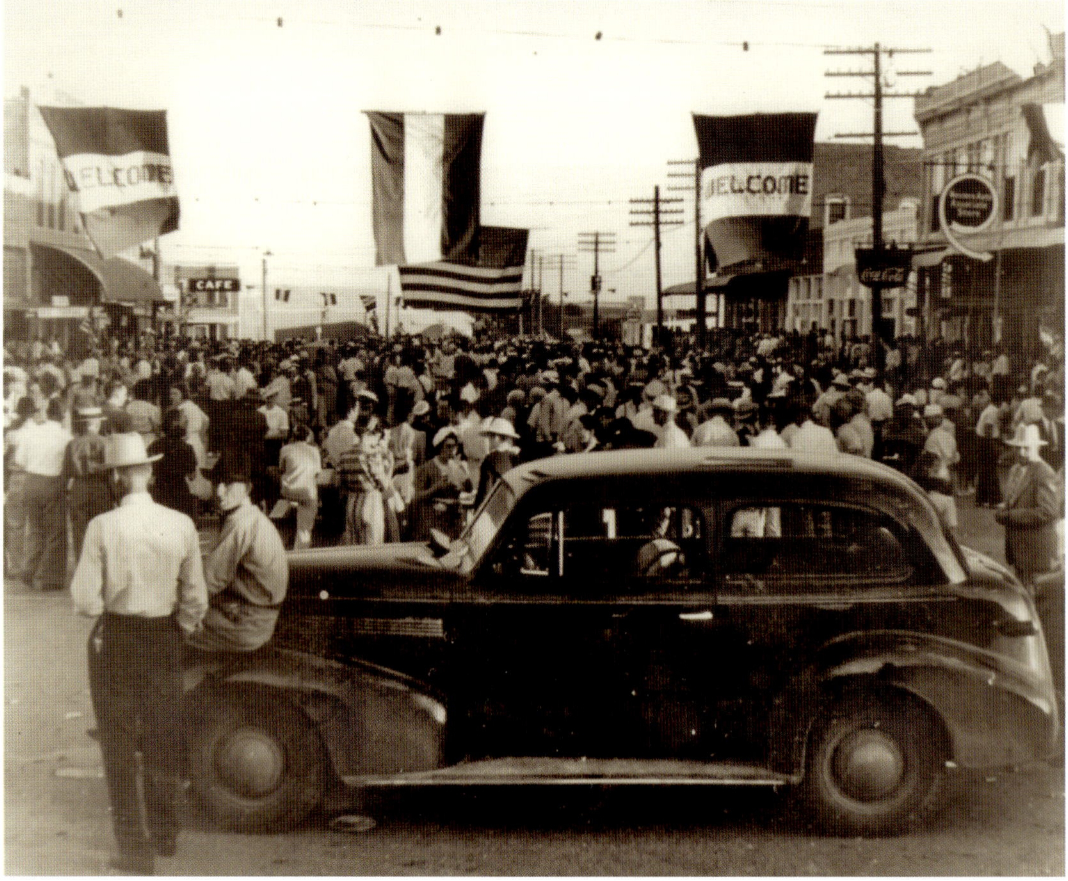

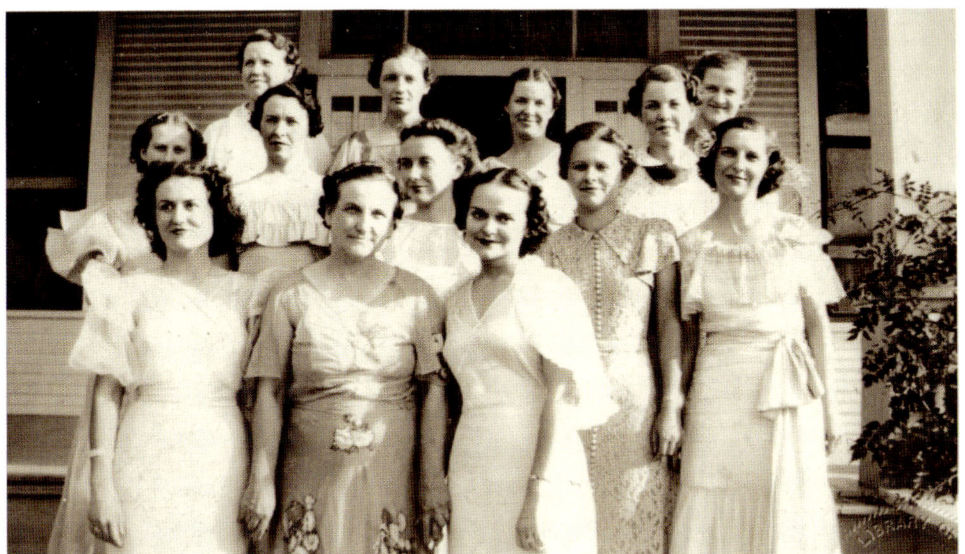

LADIES' MEETING: In 1930, Midlothian ladies held a meeting at Mattie Warren's home. *From left to right, back row*: Phama Duke Few Kay, Mary Wadley, Alice Lloyd, Oneta Sewell, and Olivia Bynum. *From left to right, middle row*: Frances Beddow, Unidentified, Hazel Warren, Christine Reese, and unidentified. *From left to right, front row*: Catherine Martel, Mattie Warren, and Clarine Warren.

Son of Mattie and husband of Hazel, Major Miller P. Warren, Jr., was killed January 9, 1945 while a POW of the Japanese. He graduated U.S. Military Academy, Class of 1933. After being in the Bataan Death March, he died on a hell ship, *Enoura Maru*. General Jonathan Wainright presented his Silver Star to son, Jon Miller Warren.

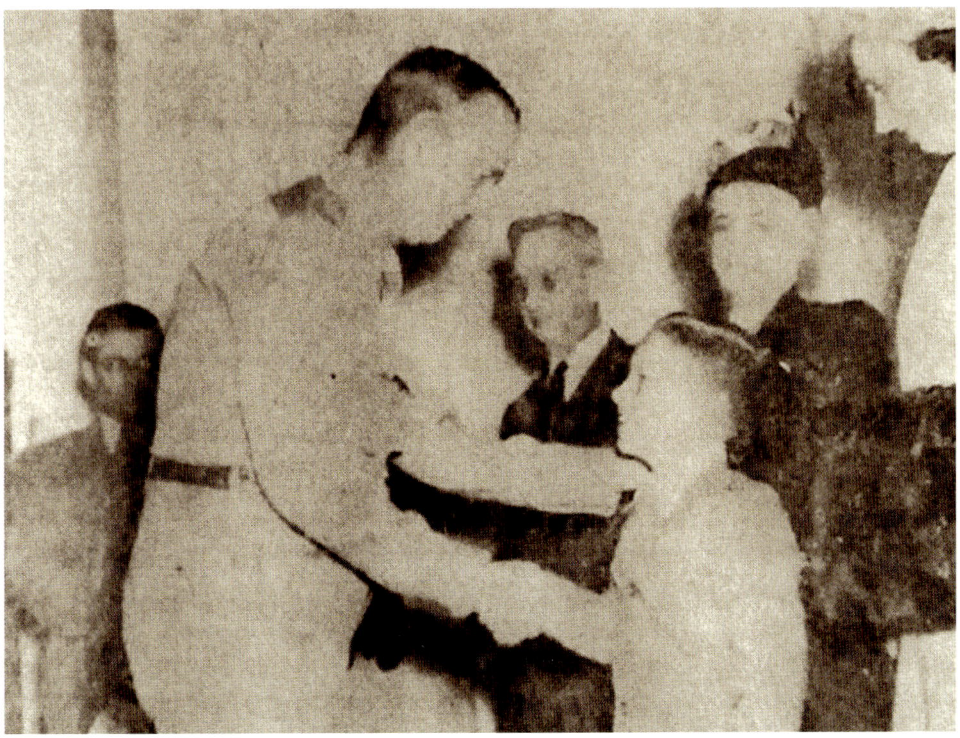

ıort Name: R. H. Cornelius
ıll Name: Cornelius, R. H. (Rufus Henry), 1872-1933
rth Year: 1872
eath Year: 1933

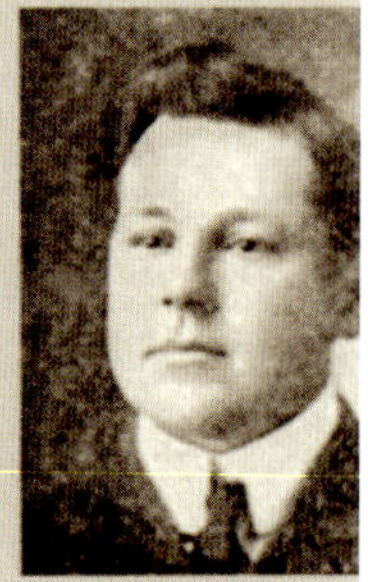

www.hymntime.com/tch

H. Cornelius, known as Rufus Cornelius by his friends, was born in Blount Co., AL., January 24, 1872. He was ucated in the public schools of Oneonta, the county seat. He began teaching in the public schools at an early e and at one time was associate Principle of the Oneonta High School. It was while teaching in the high hool that he became interested in church music and began to study with some of the best teachers of the ne. His first major teacher was the late A J showalter in one of his normals at Eden, AL. He continued his ıdy with this wellknown teacher until he had finished the courses a second time. He soon felt that the study of rmony was his first love in his study and soon became one of the best harmon teachers of his time.

ıar the close of the century, he moved to Texas and settled in Midlothian, Ellis Co., where he established a ıblishing house and published many fine gospel song books that sold by the thousands. However, before coming to Texas, he was associ th The Showalter-Patton Co. who published his first compositions. Soon after coming to Texas, he devoted much time to teaching singin hools (Cornelius Normal Musical Institute) and soon became one of the best known teachers of that great state, often having many more lls for schools than he could have time for. In many cases his schools were dated years ahead. he had possessed a beautiful tenor voice ıs of a very pleasant personality. This caused his to be loved by all who knew him. About 1914 he was called to Southwestern Baptist ıminary as head of the music department. After several years here in the Baptist School in Ft Worth, Texas, he felt he was more needed ıck in the field of teaching and songbook publishing. Soon after coming to Texas, he married Maycon Temperance Burleson, who was a fi ıger and musician and wrote many songs.During the first 32 years of the 20th Century, this couple of musicians blessed the State of Tex th their singing and teaching. Of all the fine song written by Mr. Cornelius, "Oh, I want to See Him" will carry his memory for years to co ıe Cornelius' were members of the Baptist Church and were devoted Christians.

. Cornelius passed away in 1932. Mrs. Cornelius lived only about two years, passing away in 1934. In the passing of these fine gospel ıger and teachers, church music suffered a great loss. By C C Stafford

GOSPEL MUSIC: Rufus Henry Cornelius, born in AL in 1872, was greatly interested in church music and studied it in depth until he found that the study of harmony was his favorite. He came to Midlothian about 1900 where he established a publishing house and began to teach singing schools. His 1912 songbook, as well as others, was well received. He soon married Maycon Temperance Burleson, a fine singer in her own right. Together they wrote many songs and were asked to conduct more singing schools than they could schedule.

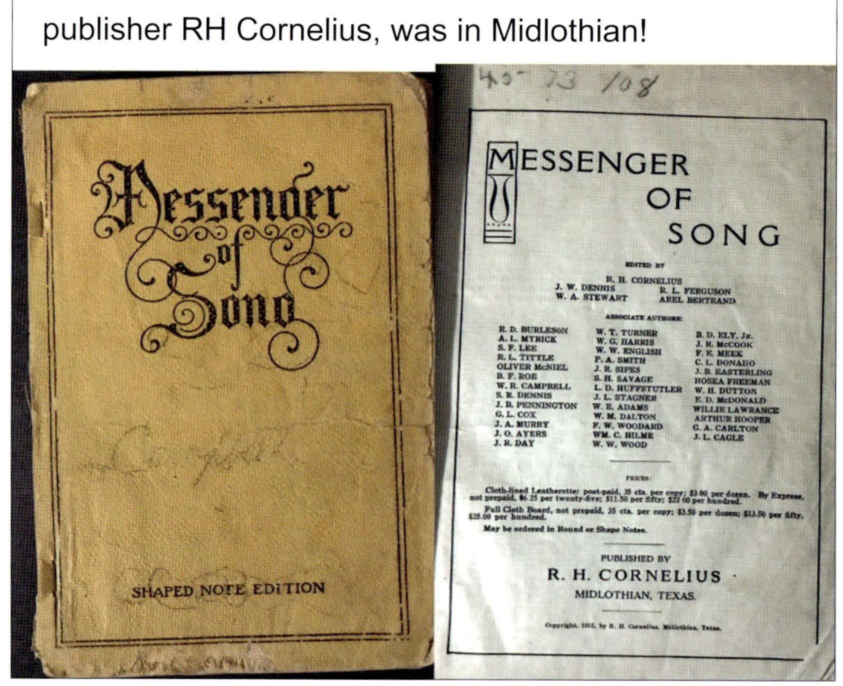

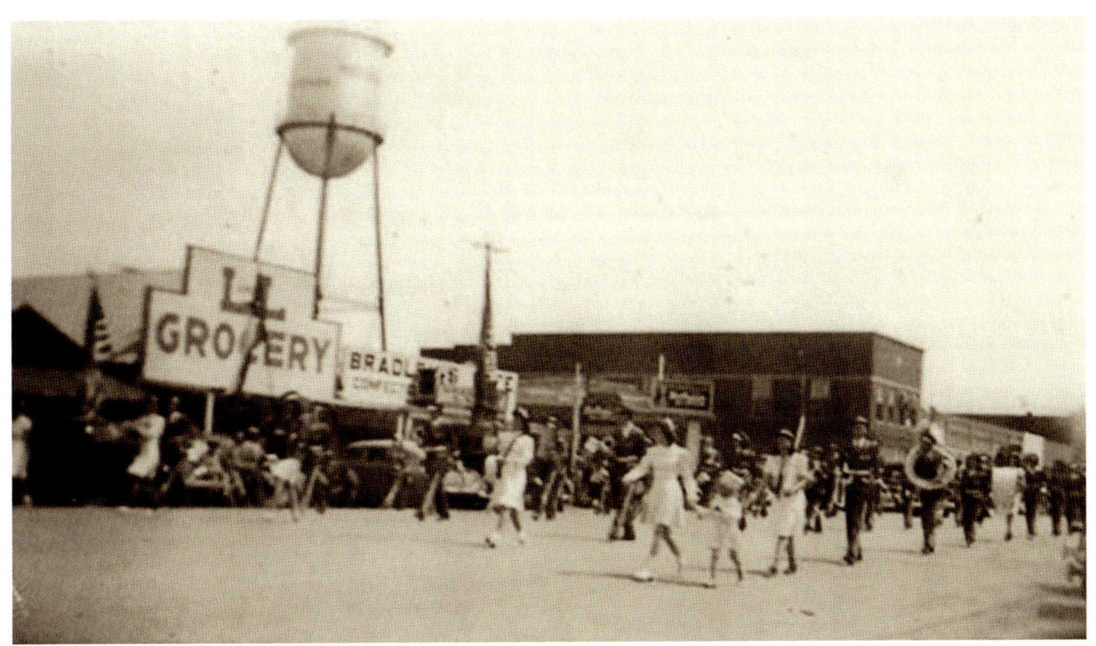

PUBLIC SCHOOL BAND: About 1940, the MHS Band paraded north in the 200 block of North 8th Street, followed by floats. Note the old water tower, which razing is still deplored locally. Beneath it, on the east side of the street, appear L&L Grocery, Bradley's Café, and other small businesses. After the parade ended, people walked west across the street beside the two-story Martin-Hendricks building, which would be torched twenty years later, the Good Luck Café, and a filling station on the end of the block where Fire Station No. 1 was later built.

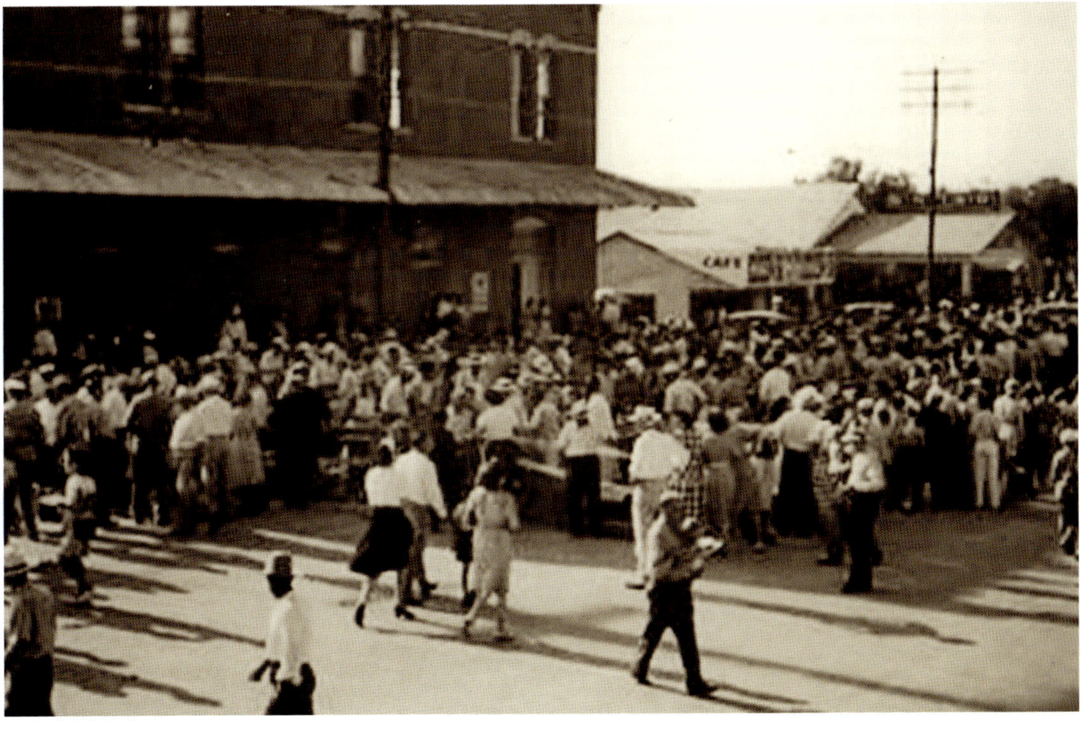

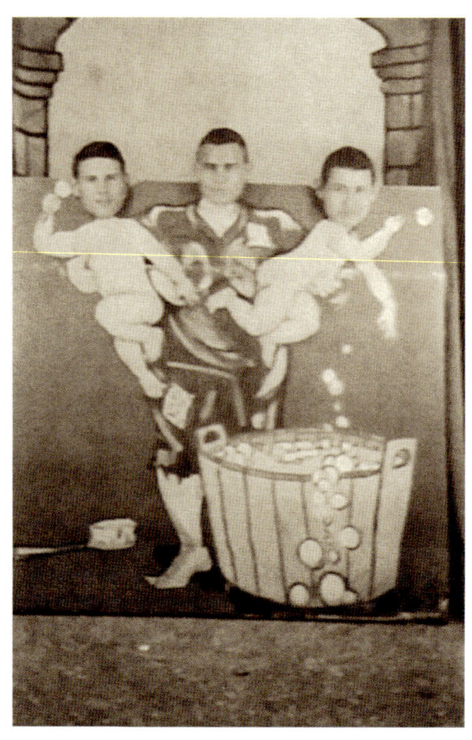

Long-time Friends: These three friends were seniors at Midlothian High School when they visited the Texas State Fair in Dallas and had this funny photo taken in 1965. At a class reunion in 2018, Ellis Christie, on the left, was deceased. But Jerry Miller, center, and Dwaine Rayburn, right, were still glad to pose together.

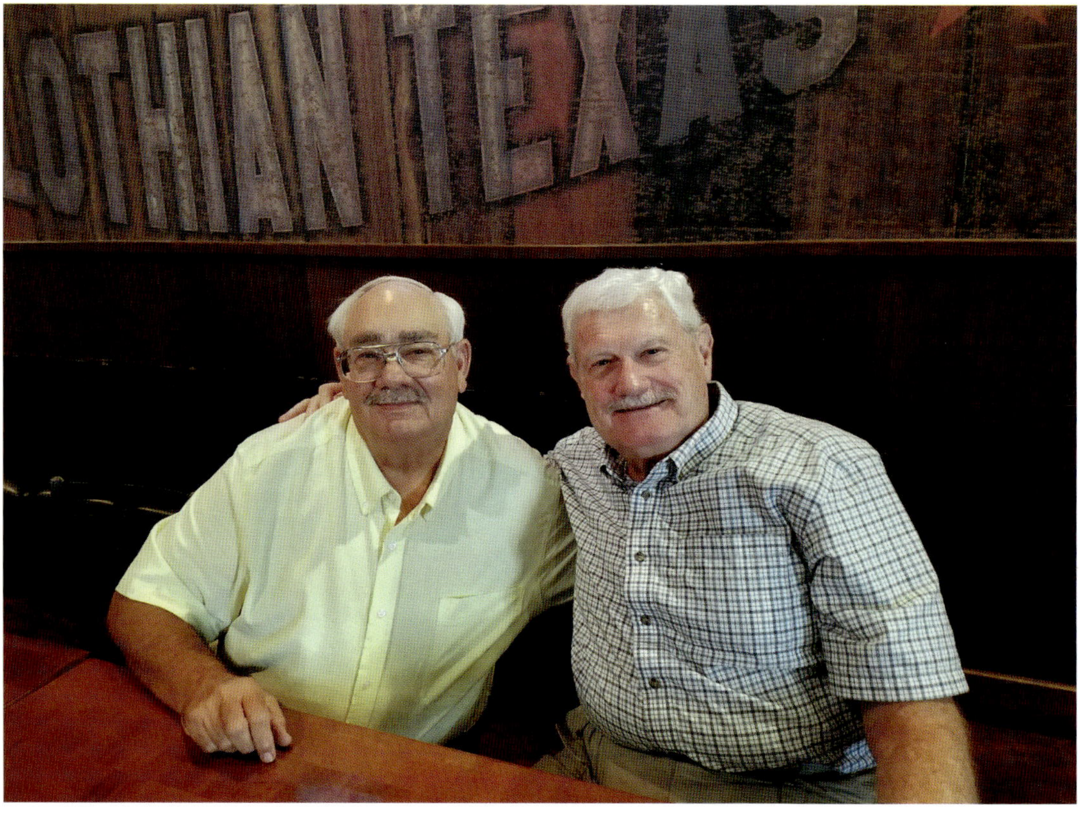

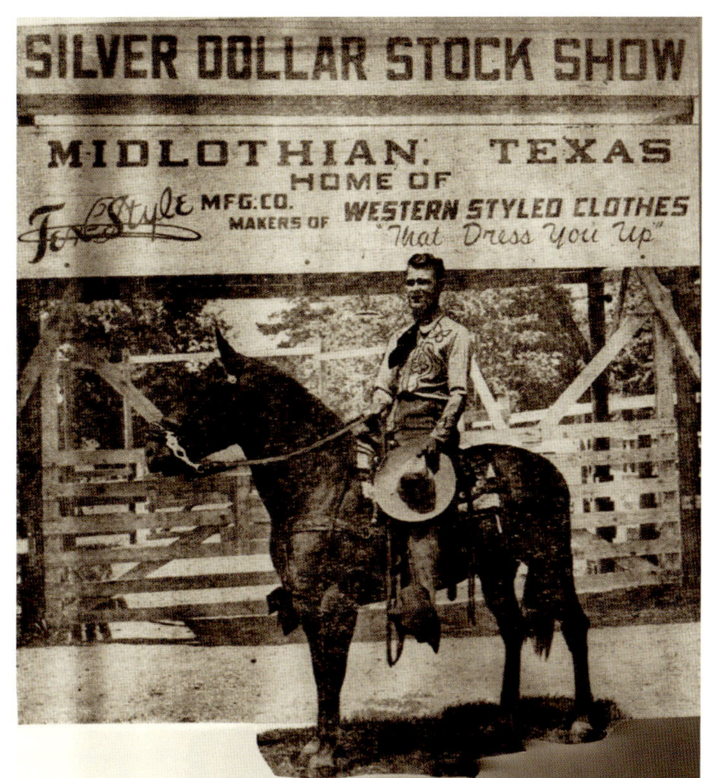

RODEOS: Rodeos were scheduled in conjunction with local fairs, and businessmen offered prizes. The Chamber of Commerce bought several acres and built an arena, grandstands, and auction barn. They also owned the herd used in the rodeos. A special series of rodeos was called the Silver Dollar Rodeos, with silver dollars awarded as prizes. For a while, Henry F. White and his wife, Mollie O'Daniel, daughter of the Governor, lived in Midlothian and took a big hand in promoting these rodeos, as in this ad in the 1947 *Midlothian Mirror*. The land has been cleared and is used for soccer fields in 2018.

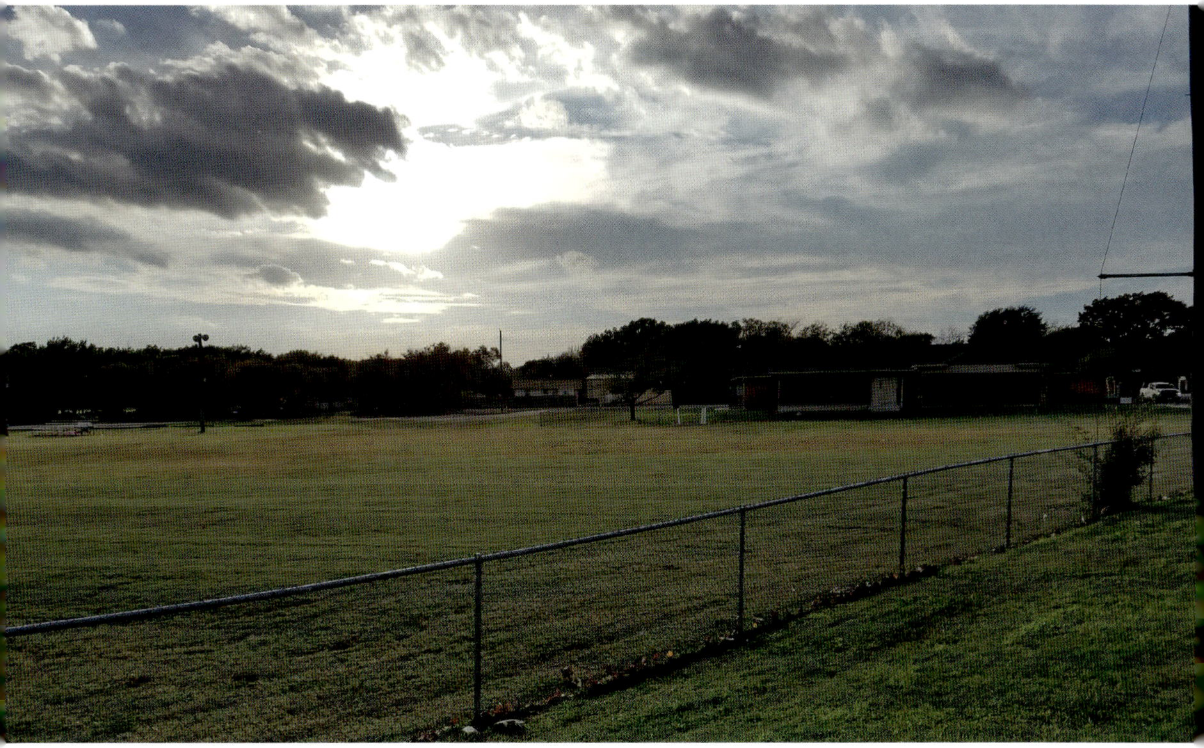

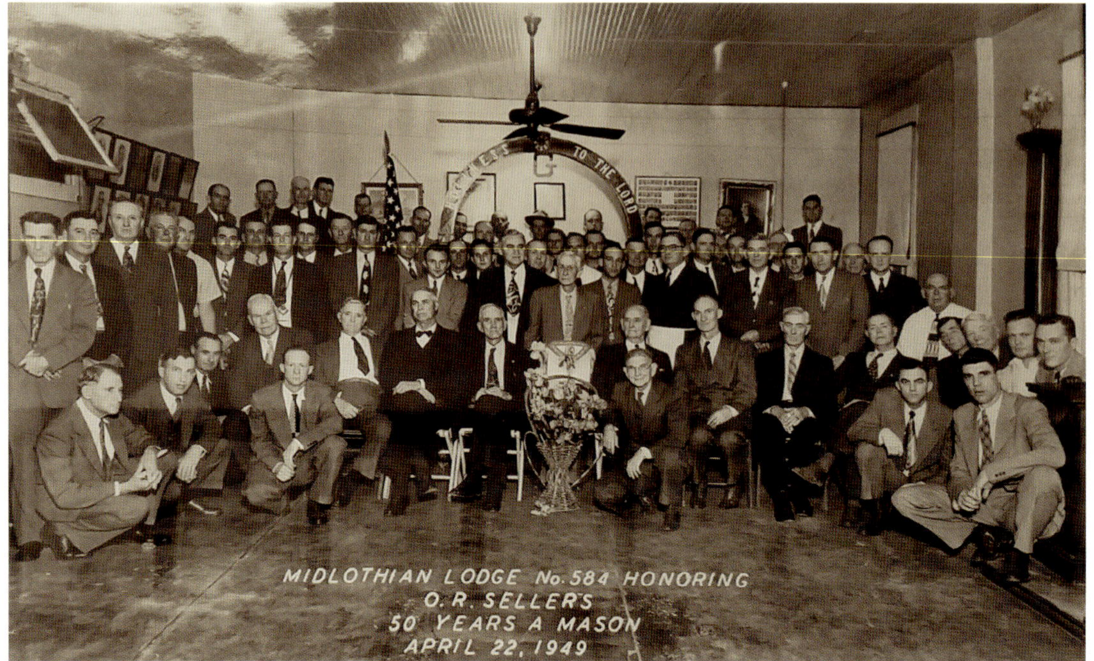

MASONIC LODGE: The Midlothian Masonic Lodge No. 584 held a Called Meeting on April 22, 1949, to recognize Brother O. R. Sellers for fifty years of membership. He served as Worshipful Master in 1915. Brother Sellers is standing immediately behind the flower arrangement with his son Earl at his right. Seated on the viewer's left of the flowers are W. H. Price (nearest flowers), P. S. Hendricks, Unidentified, J. P. "Jake" Sewell. To one's right of the flowers are T. J. Dorsett (nearest flowers) and L. F. Hughes, all Past Masters. The Master then was Milton Pegram, wearing the hat in the back center of the platform. The Lodge is shown in 2018.

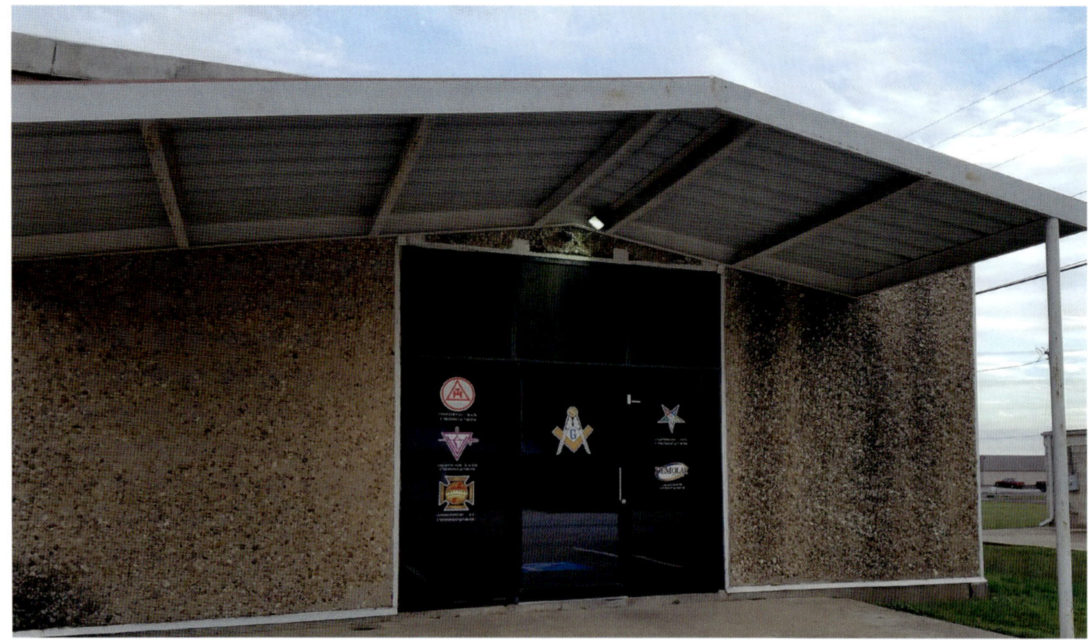

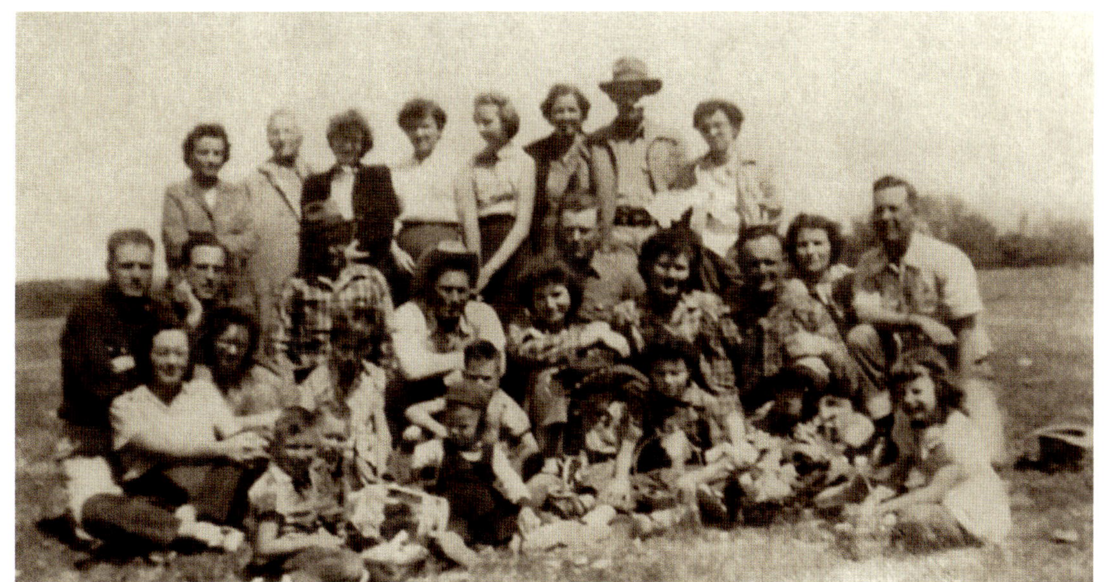

EASTER PICNIC: Mountain Peak residents shared a community picnic, Easter 1950, held on the Curtis Ray farm. *From left to right, back row*: Mr. & Mrs. Hollabaugh, Vera Ray (hostess), Yvonne Wooten, Carolyn McAlpin, Myrtle McAlpin, Bill Woods, and Linnie Woods. *From left to right, middle row*: Eldon Morgan, Carl Martin, Bill McAlpin, Curtis Ray (host), Mildred Smith, Bobby Smith, Margaret McClendon, M. M. "Sard" McClendon, Tennie, and Clen Hollabaugh. *From left to right, front row*: Loree Morgan, Wilda Martin, Buddy Martin, Dickey Ray, William Hollabaugh, Carol Hollabaugh, Ricky McClendon, and Susan Martin. Little boys in front are Gary McClendon, Wayne Ray, and Ronnie Morgan. In 2018, housing additions are being built around Mountain Peak, but there is no "town center."

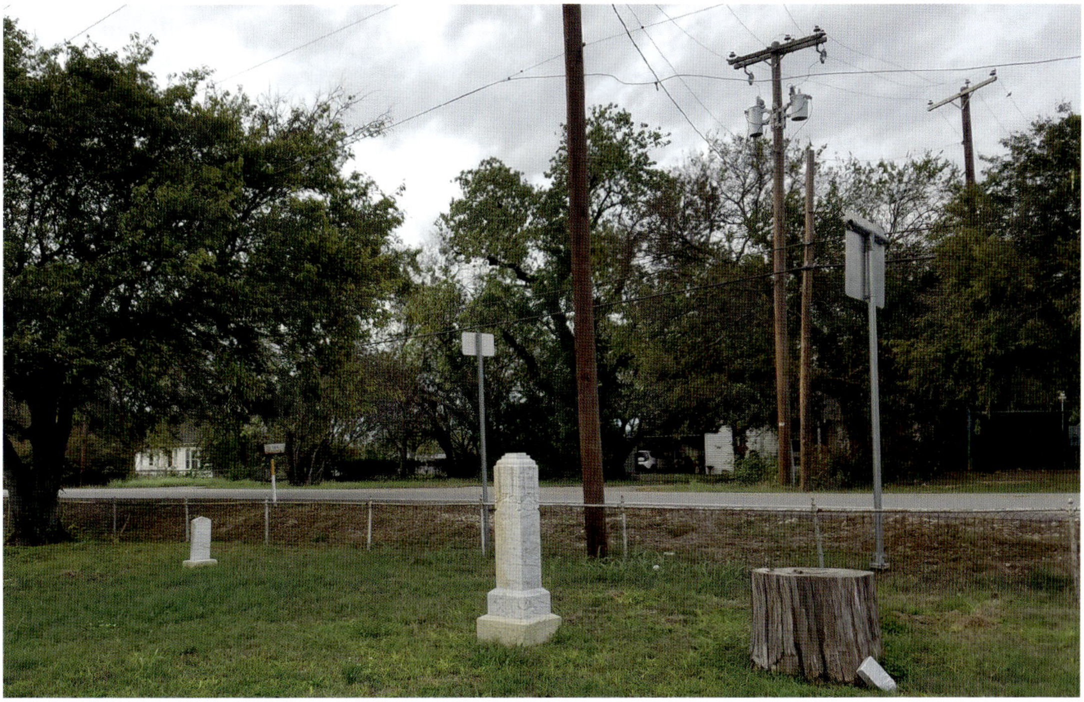

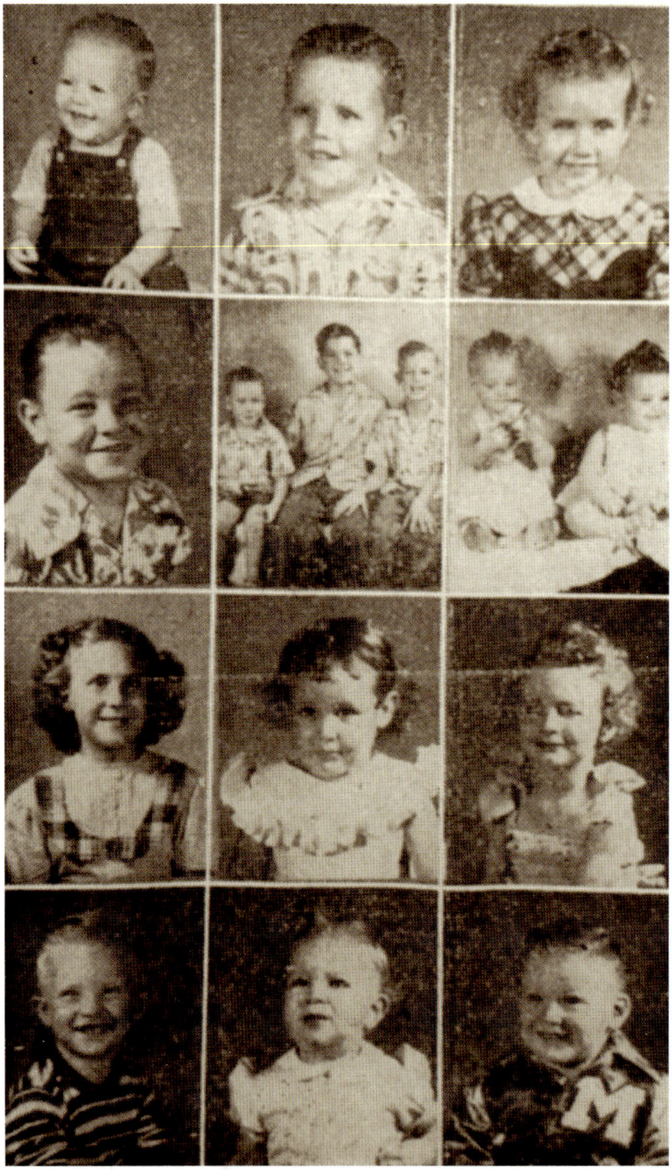

CHILD BEAUTY CONTEST: In 1950, Hallmark Studios of Dallas held a "picture contest" of Midlothian children. The studio chose the winners and awarded prizes. Some of the entrants are seen here. *From left to right, top row*: Mack Seeton, Bryan Hayes, and Jennell Ralston. *From left to right, second row*: Jack Duvall, Jr., James, Joe and Ray Barksdale, and Lonna and Donna Hayes. *From left to right, third row*: Betty Seeton, Carolyn Hayes, and Kathy McElroy. *From left to right, bottom row*: Ronnie McMichael, Jeanne Ralston, and Jerry Massey. The four winners were First Prize—Markland Hayes, Second Prize—Patricia Ann Barnett, Fourth Prize—Patricia Duvall, Third Prize—Jennie Lou Hyslop.

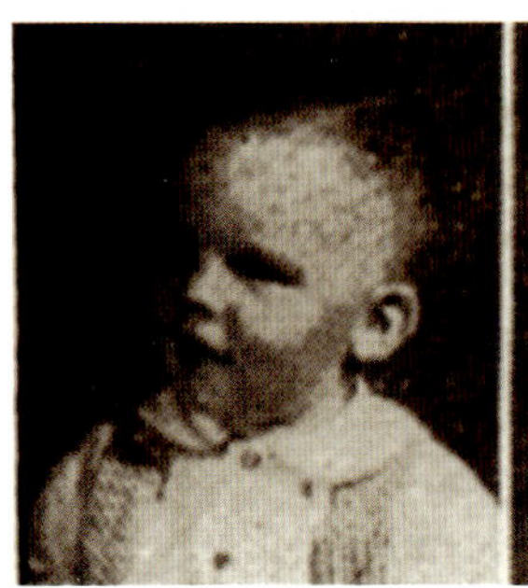

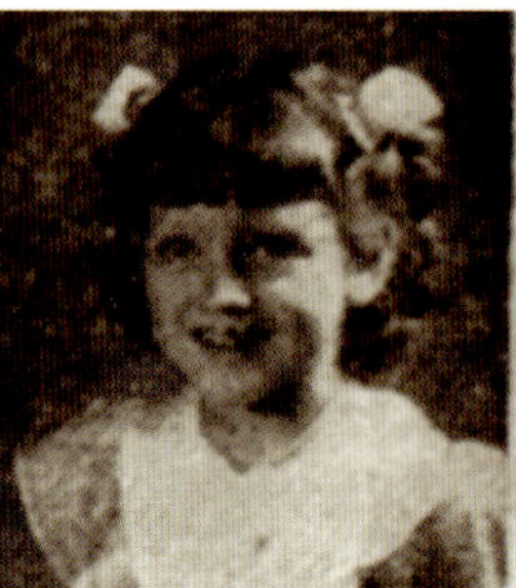

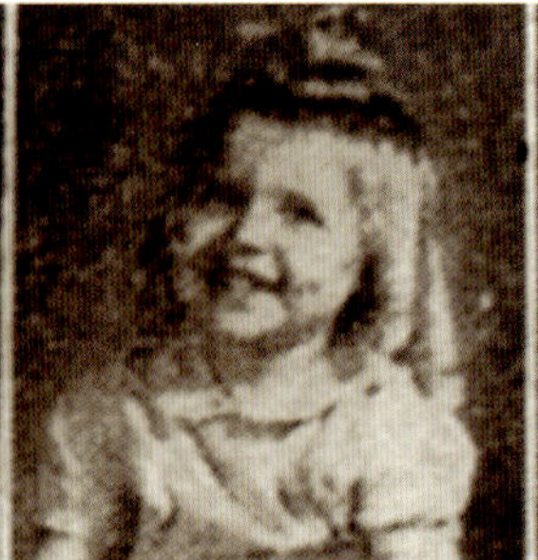

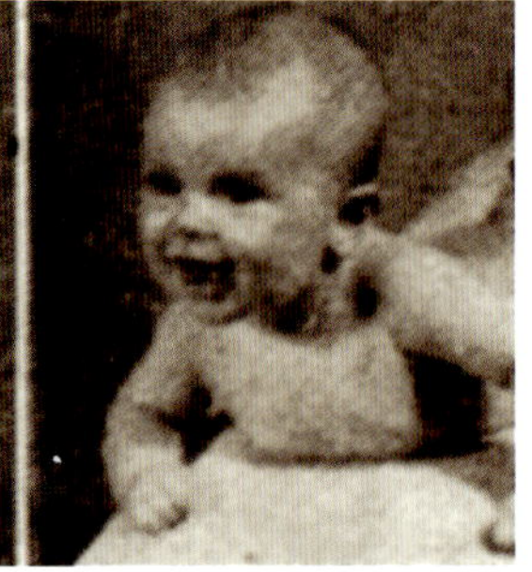

4

Churches

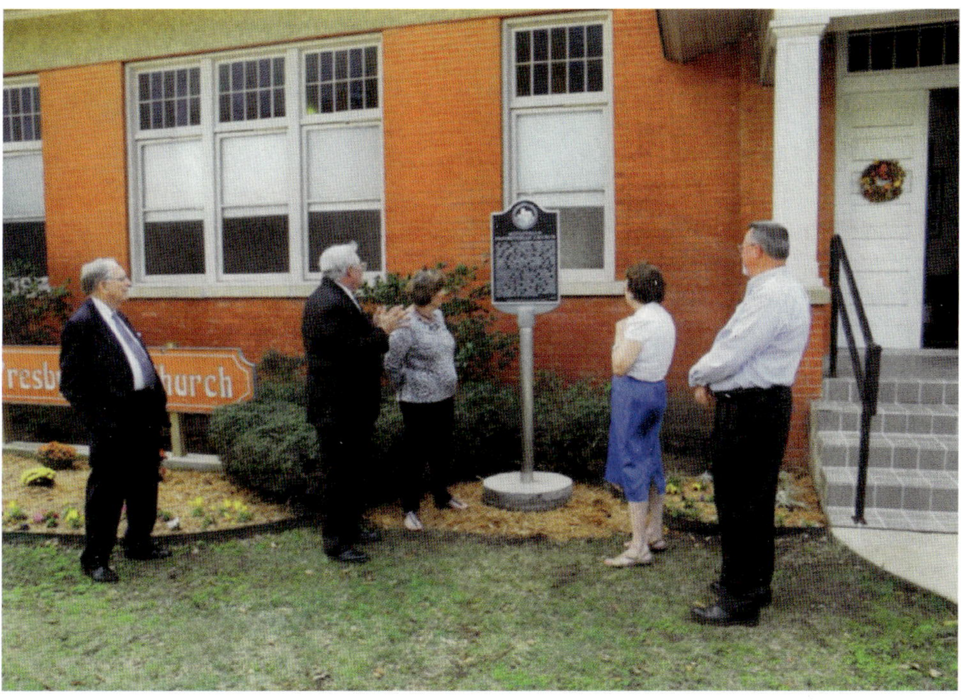

This Presbyterian edifice was built in 1913 on the lot deeded to the Cumberland Presbyterian Church in 1884 by the GC&SF. The "Old Style Presbyterians" joined with this congregation in 1911 to become the First Presbyterian Church and jointly construct this building. The congregation obtained a Texas Historical Marker in 2010.

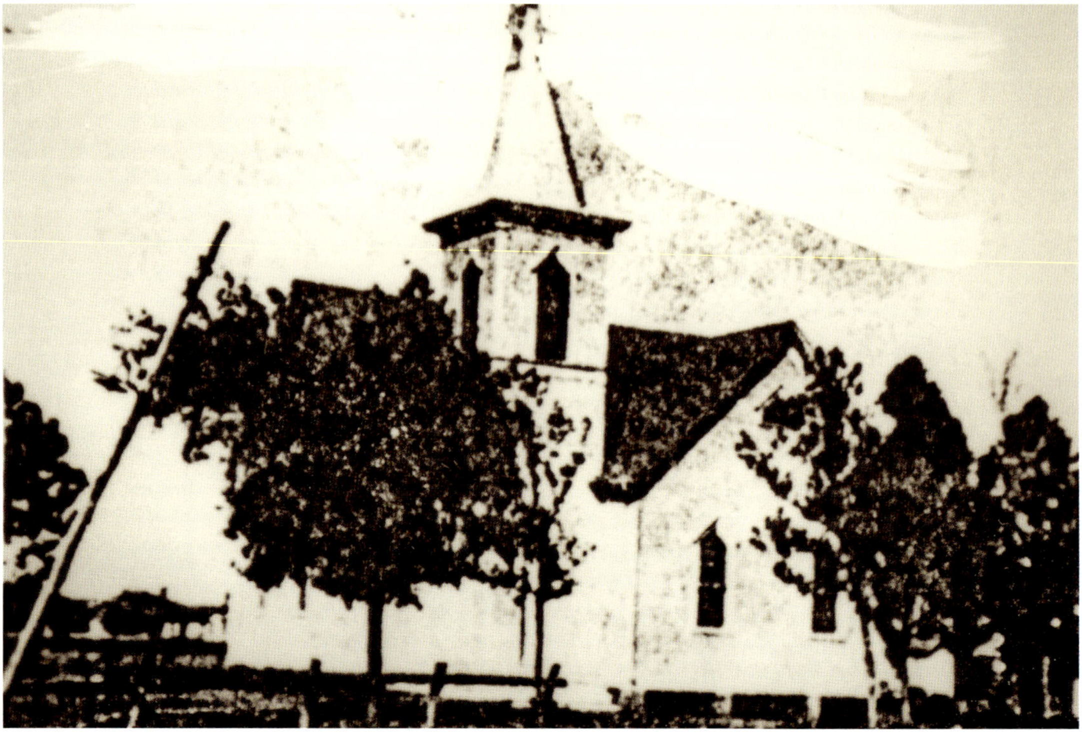

CHURCH OF CHRIST: The first Church of Christ built in Midlothian began hosting worship on January 18, 1903, with thirteen members present. It was remodeled in 1952. By 1968, it was too small for the congregation, and they purchased acreage for a new building.

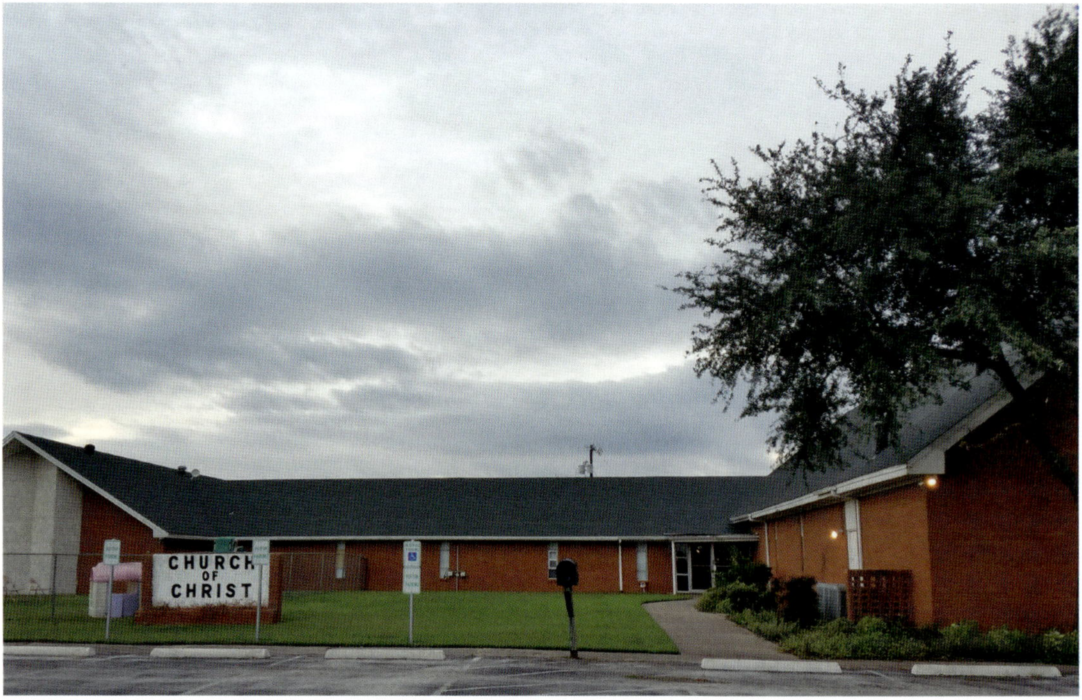

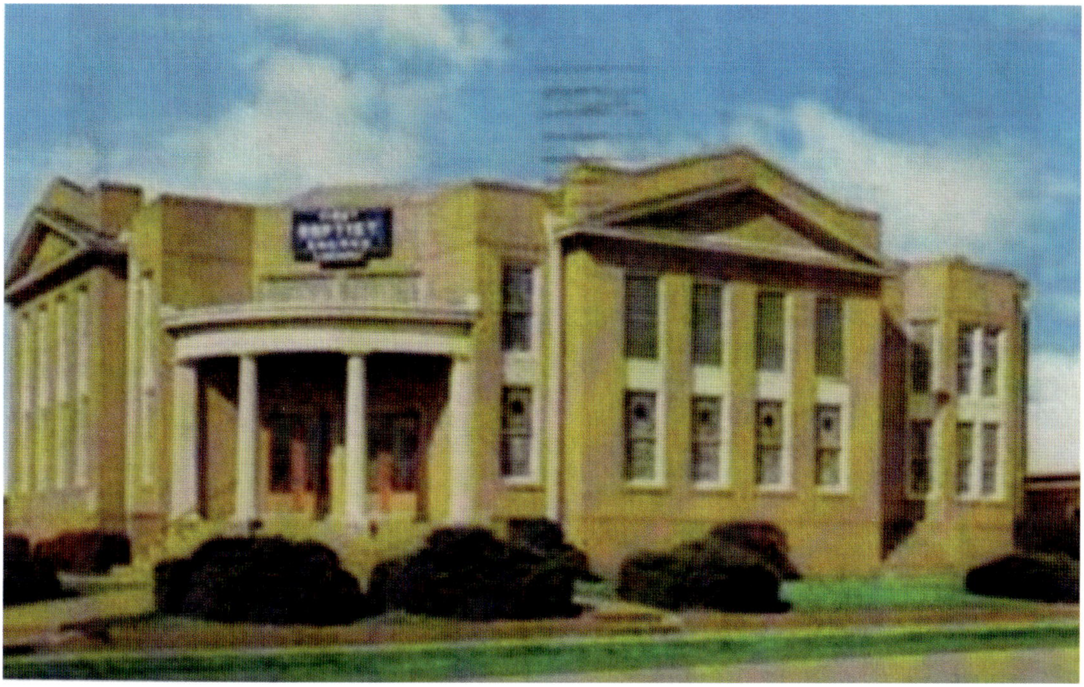

BAPTISTS: Founded in 1886, the First Baptist Church erected its first building in 1895. Twenty-five years later, they built the larger, pseudo-Greek style, which is occupied, as of 2018, by Grace Baptist Church.

The Ladies' Sunday School Class held a dinner in 1958. *From left to right, standing at rear*: Willie Moore, Burt Goodwin, John Milton, unidentified, John Spivey, Charlie Crenshaw, unidentified, Barnett Jenkins, and Hugh Inman. *From left to right, seated in chairs*: Leat Yeager, Sally Jenkins, Betty Joy Jenkins, Dorothy Middleton, five unidentified, Lubelle Redman, Mae Crenshaw. On the floor are Joycy Milton, Laura Jenkins, Addie Spivey, and Minnie Goodwin.

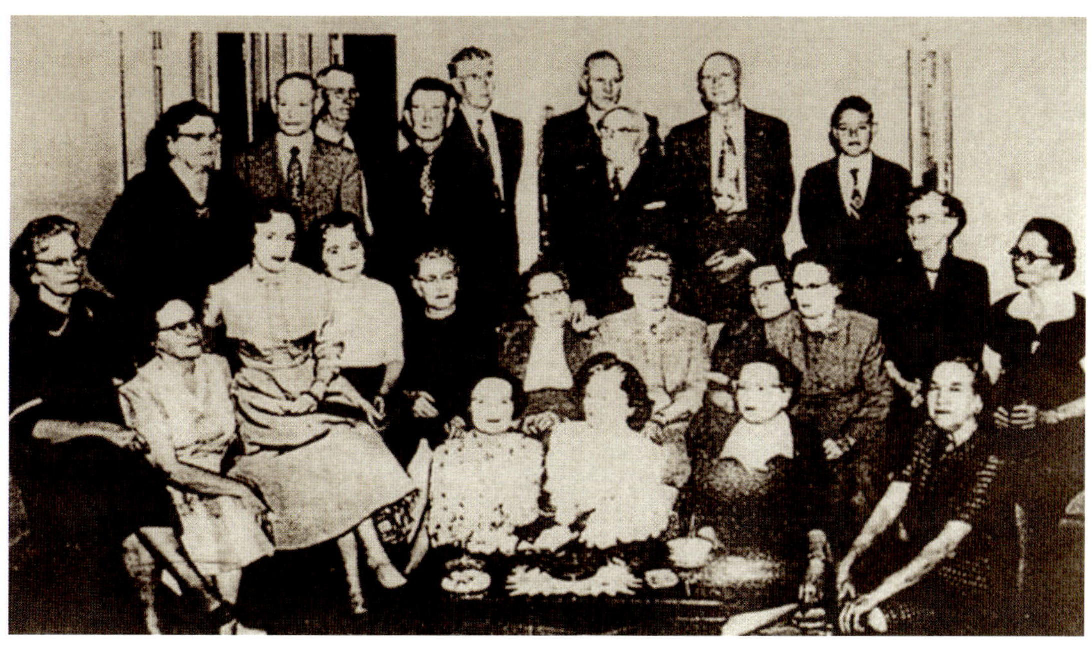

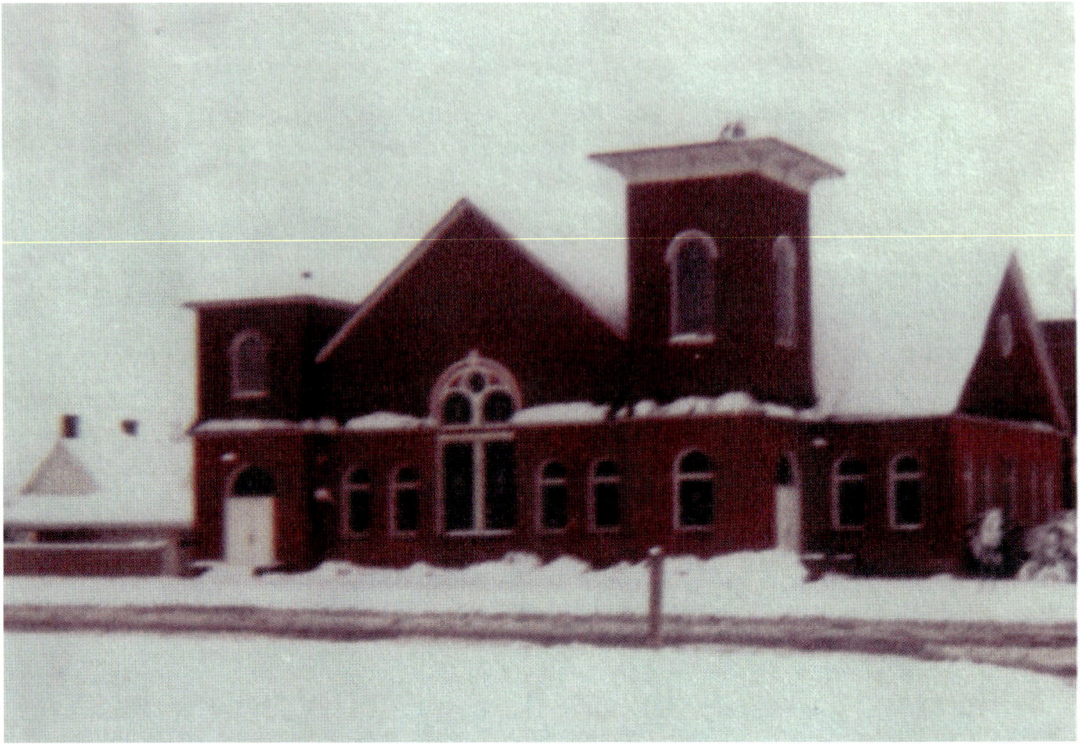

METHODISTS: The Methodist Church began at Lebanon where it met in a floorless log cabin. When Midlothian began, a wooden building went up there in 1884. The red brick church dated from 1901. The congregation moved into the brown brick church in 1969.

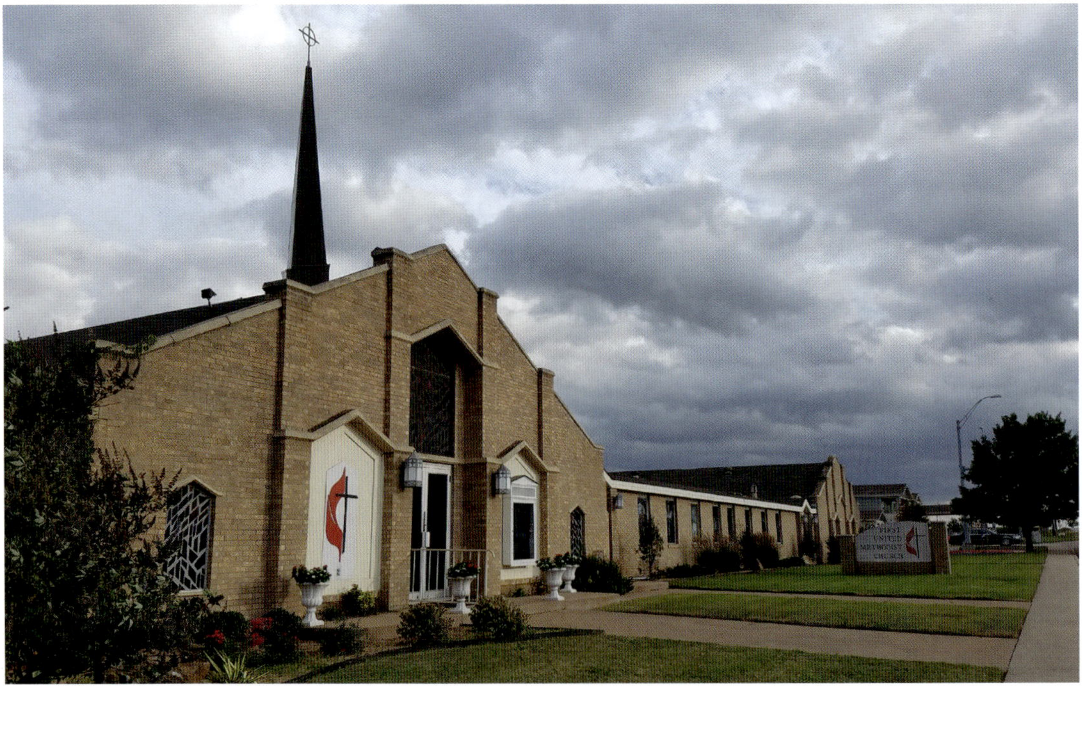

5

SCHOOLS

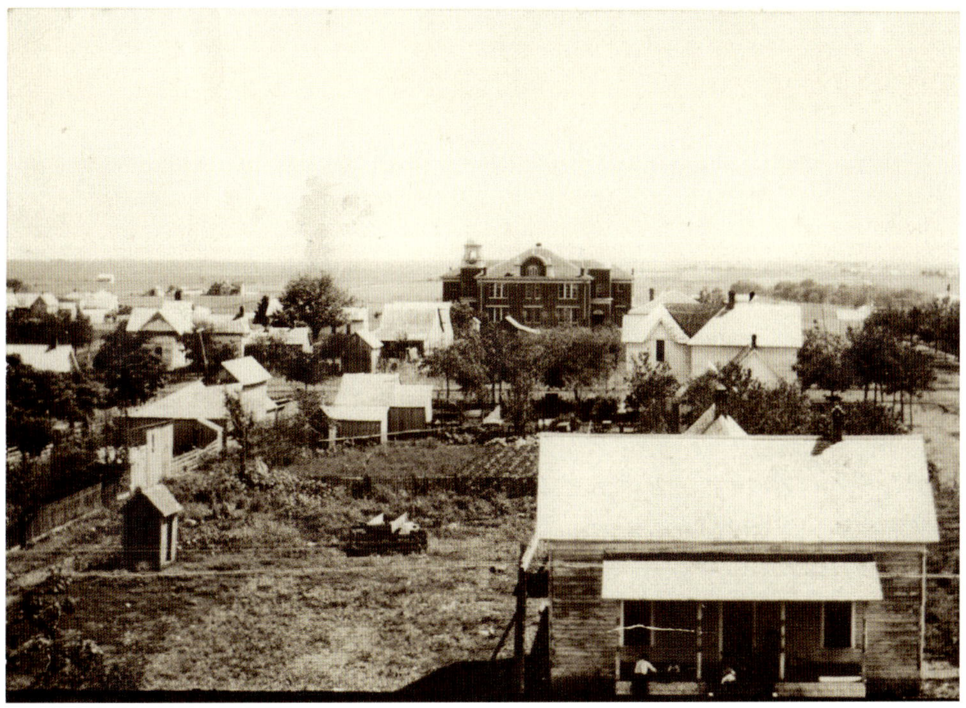

This is an unusual view of Midlothian High School, built in 1907. The photo would have been made before 1915 when another two-story school building was constructed to the left of this one. Also, city sidewalks were put in this part of town in 1915. The Sewell family owned the house in the front. It was greatly enlarged in 1916 when Mr. Sewell bought an entire wing of the building across the street at Midlothian College. The two-story house behind Sewell's is that of Constable John R. Hays.

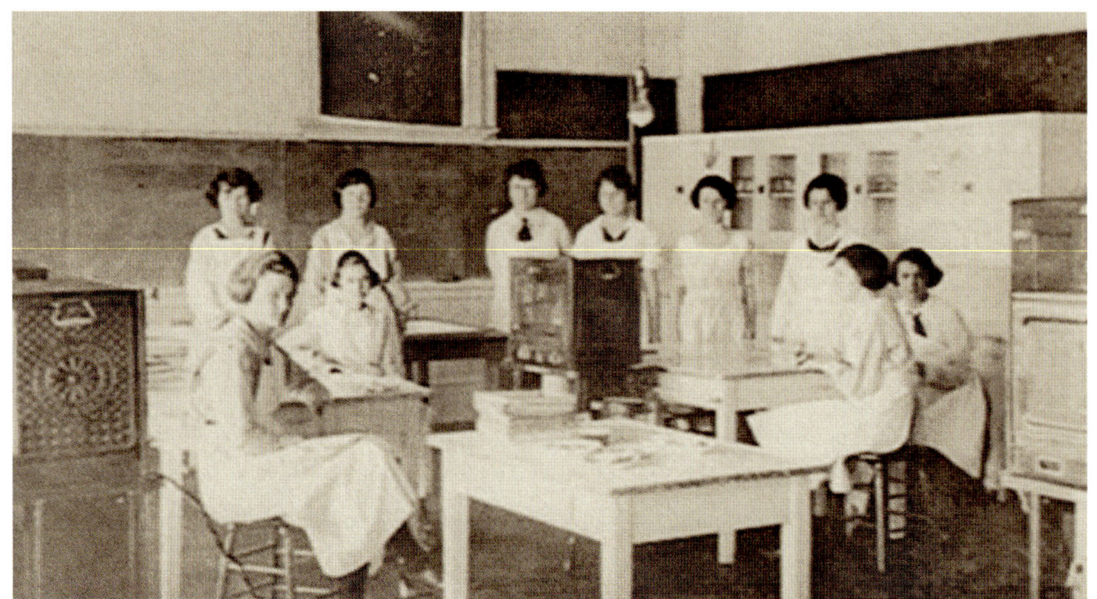

CLASSES: The MHS Home Economics Class was photographed during the 1921–1922 school year. The only girl identified was Frances Gross, fourth from the right. Some of the girls' handwork also appears.

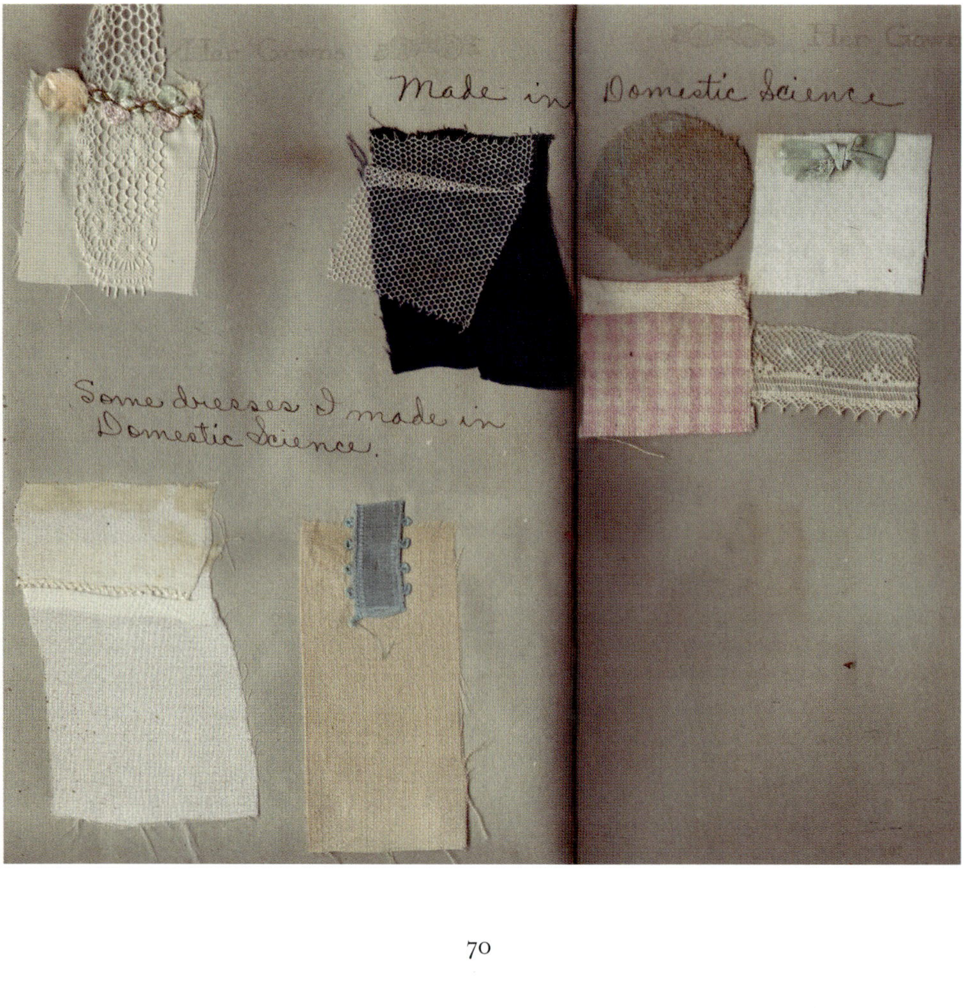

Made in Domestic Science

Some dresses I made in Domestic Science.

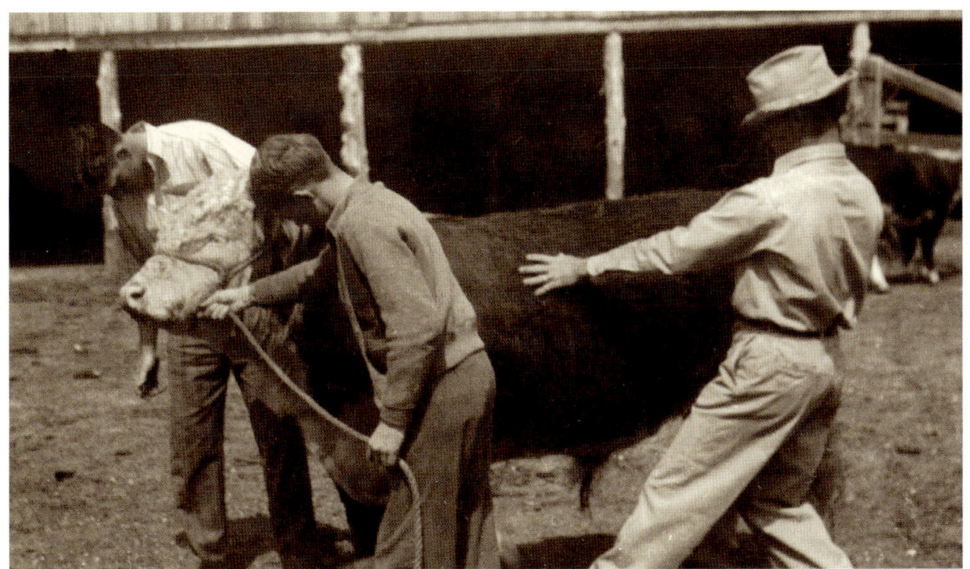

VOCATIONAL AGRICULTURE: James T. Kay, Jr., was the agriculture teacher at Midlothian High School, 1939–1941. Each student had one or more animals for his own "Project." The teacher was expected to visit the home farm of each student to evaluate the animals each semester. Former student Parks Tucker, Jr., appeared in the October 1962 *Midlothian Mirror*. His prize Texas Hampshire boar would be competing against Iowa Hampshires at the Texas State Fair. Because of the movie *State Fair*, filmed in both Texas and Iowa, Texas fair officials had challenged Iowa to send Hampshire boars for the "Blue Boy" competition, named for the mock competition held in the movie.

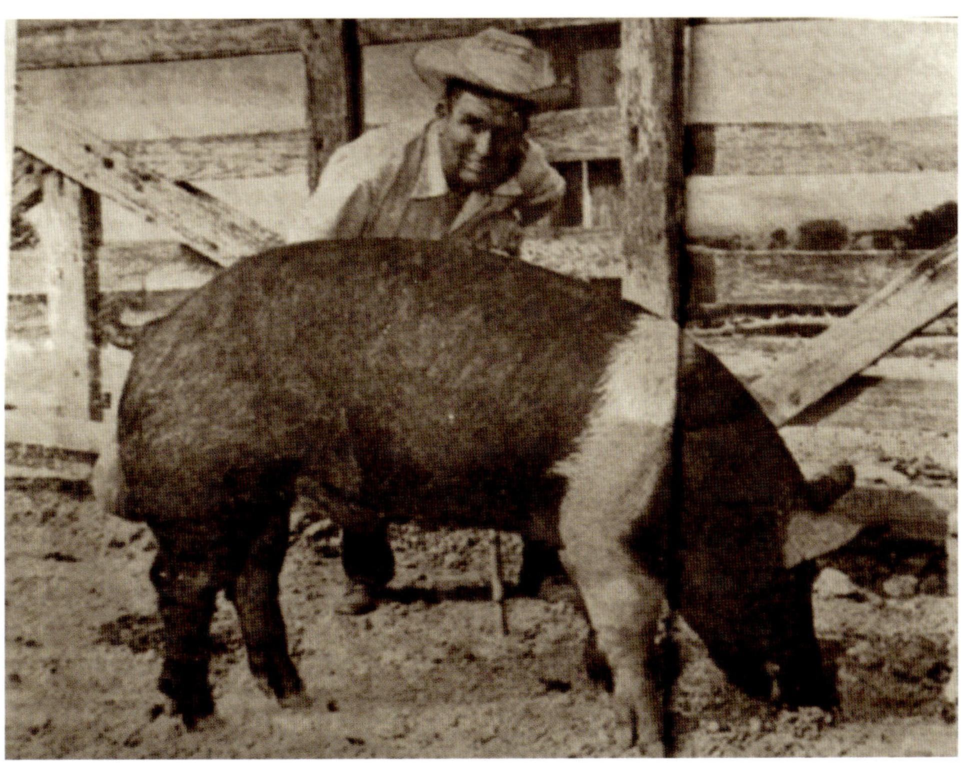

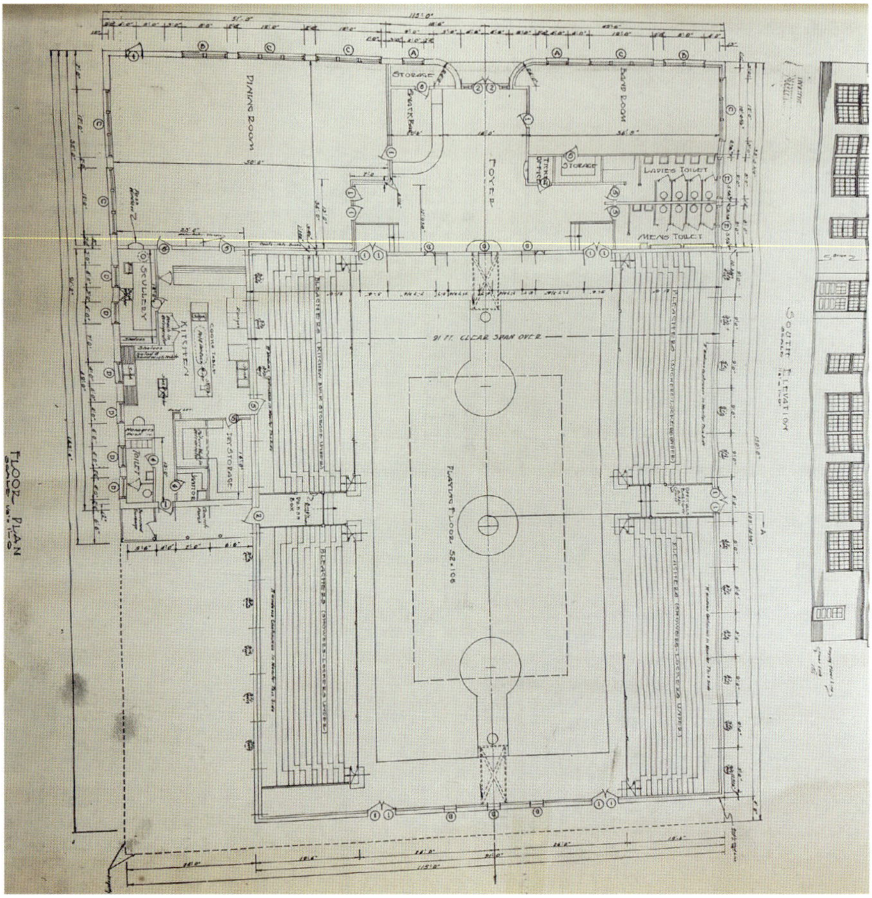

FINALLY, A GYM: Although there had been schools in this area since the days of Lebanon, through the creation of Midlothian Independent School District (MISD) in 1903, there had never been a gym in town. The School Board decided to remedy that situation in 1949 when they had blueprints drawn up. The plans included a band room, snack bar, ticket office, kitchen, dining room, and scullery. During construction, one can clearly see the use of Lamella design in the ceiling.

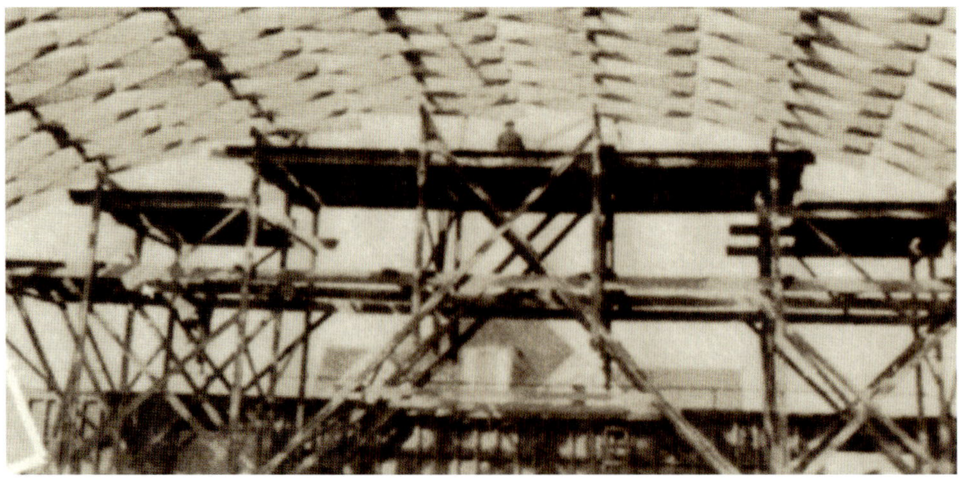

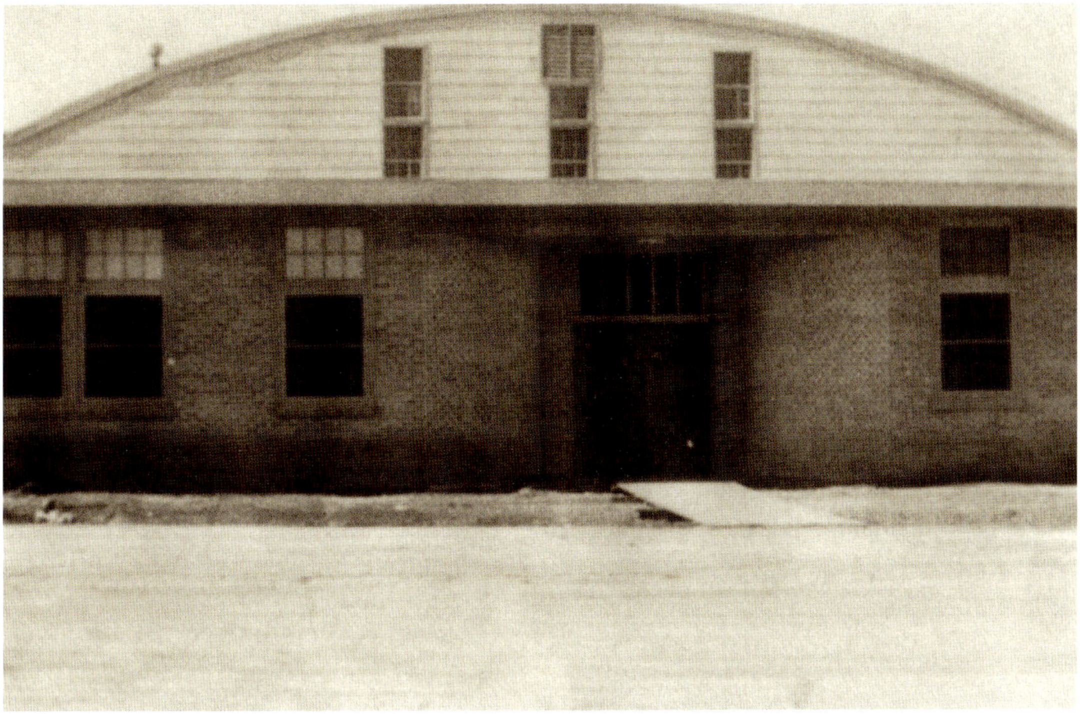

Using the New Gym: When the gym was finished in 1950, the students enjoyed it from the beginning. One of the boys relished a basketball game in 1955.

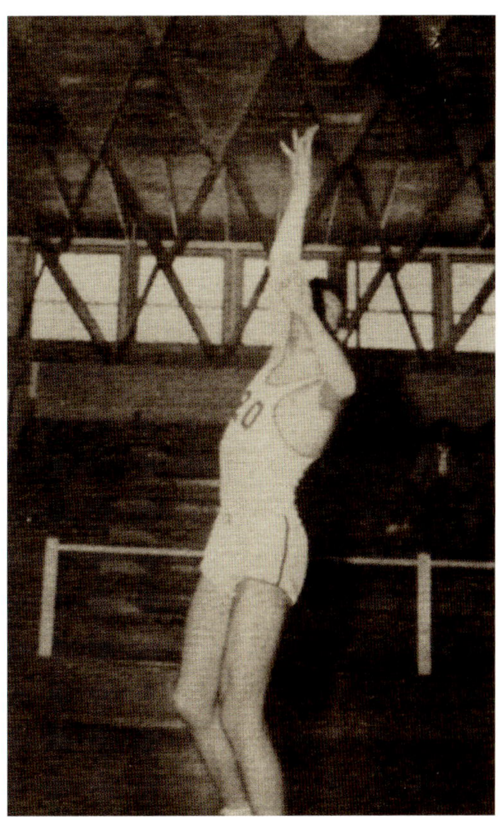

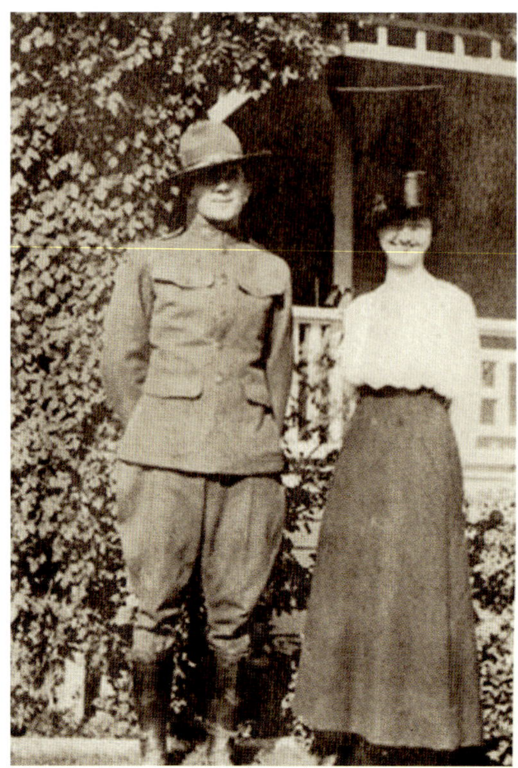

WEDDING DAY: In 1918, Robert Jeff Davis Harris "Bob" and his wife, Hattie May Smith, posed on their wedding day in front of the boarding house where they had met. He was on his way to World War I, leaving the City of Midlothian without its engineer to supervise the Ice, Light & Water Works. Hattie was a teacher for MISD. The house where they boarded soon became a private home and has been enlarged twice, as of 2018.

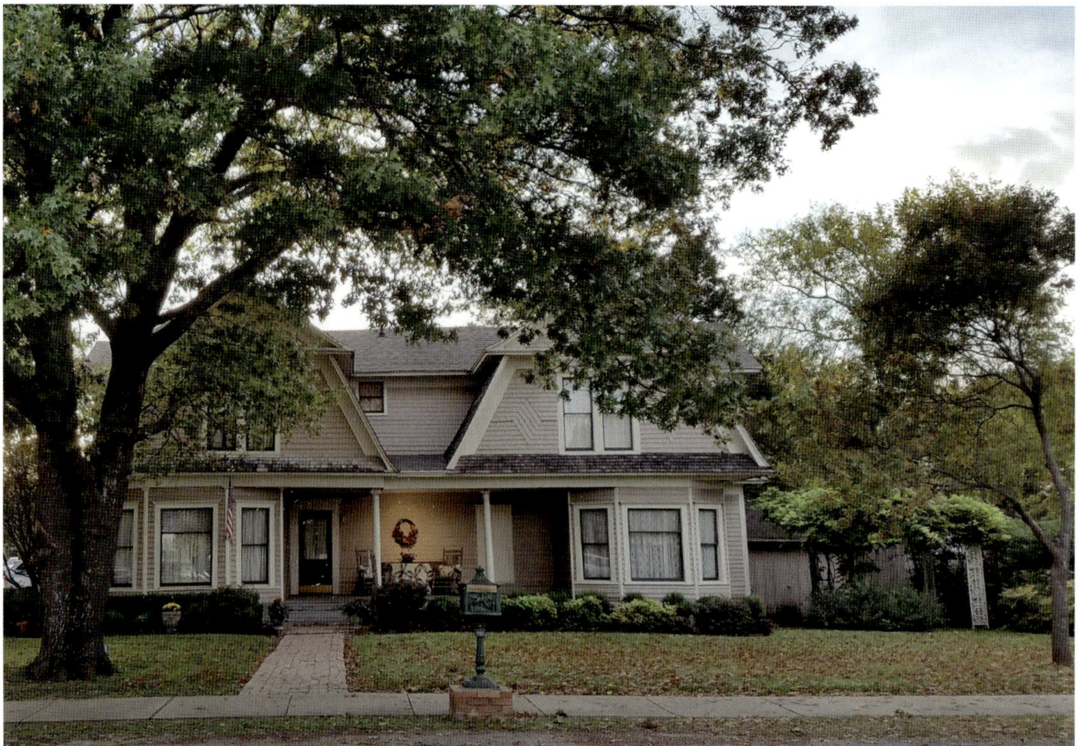

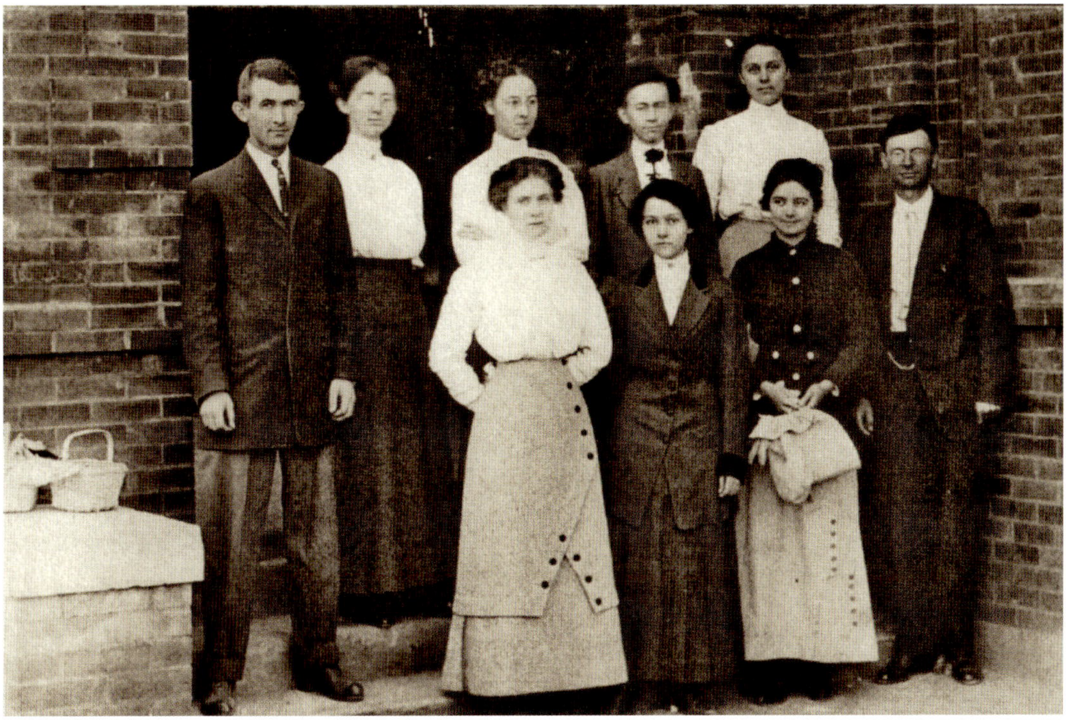

MIDLOTHIAN TEACHERS: The above photo of MISD teachers is dated 1911–1914. *From left to right, front row*: Annie Laura Bivins, Exie Campbell, Sybil Woolay, and M. H. Morris—Superintendent. *From left to right, back row*: Frank Poindexter, Hattie May Smith, Zephyr Hart, Clyde Duncan, and unidentified. There were eventually some changes in the teaching staff. *From left to right, front row*: B. F. Crews, Mana Winn, Superintendent M. H. Morris, Victoria Newton, and Frank Poindexter. Standing are Hattie May Smith, Annie Brown, Charles D. Duncan, and Annie Laura Bivens.

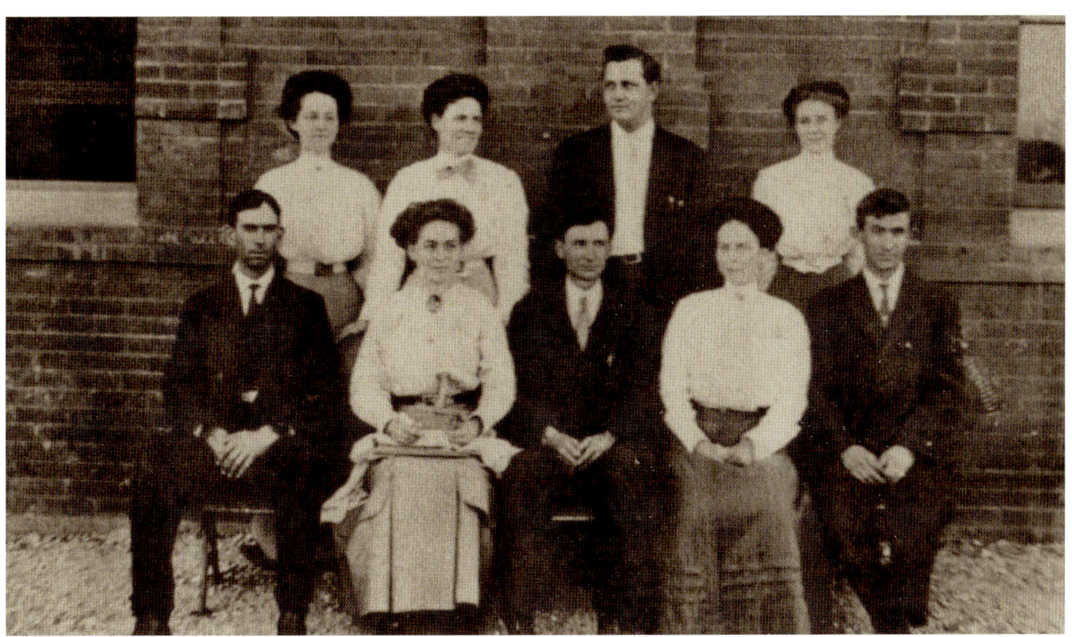

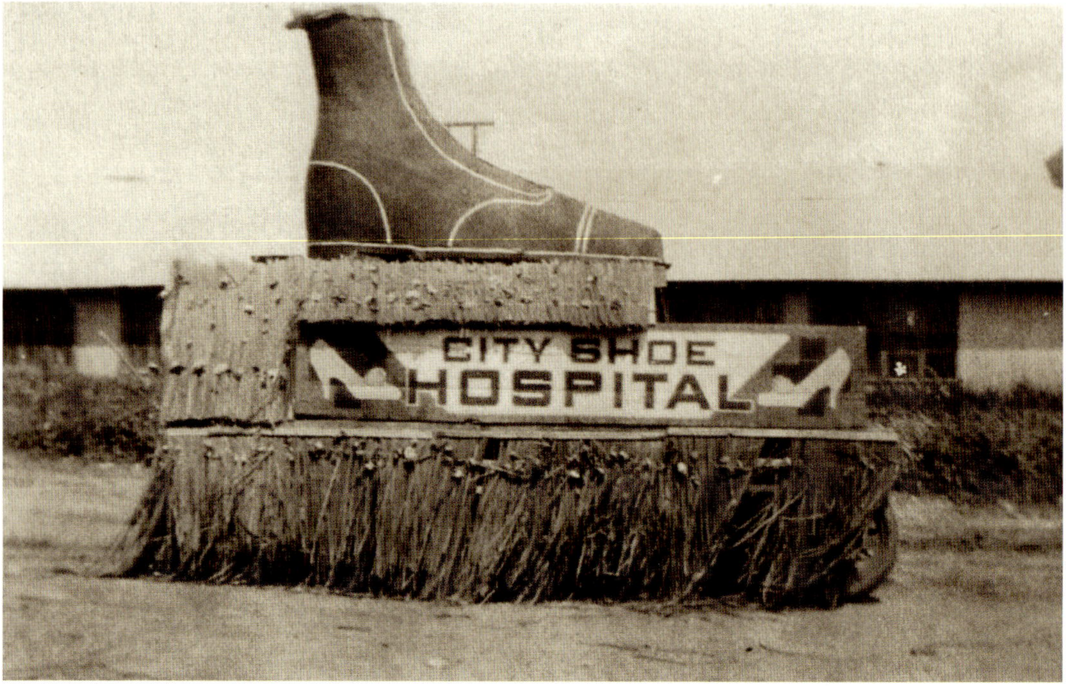

PARADE FLOATS: Floats have always been an important part of Homecoming Parades in Midlothian. In 1940, this giant shoe represented the City Shoe Hospital. Henry Spearman could fix any problem with one's shoes. In 2013, the parade tradition was still going strong, so the MHS class of 1963 decided to participate again. They met in the evenings to prepare their float, just as they had done in the "olden days."

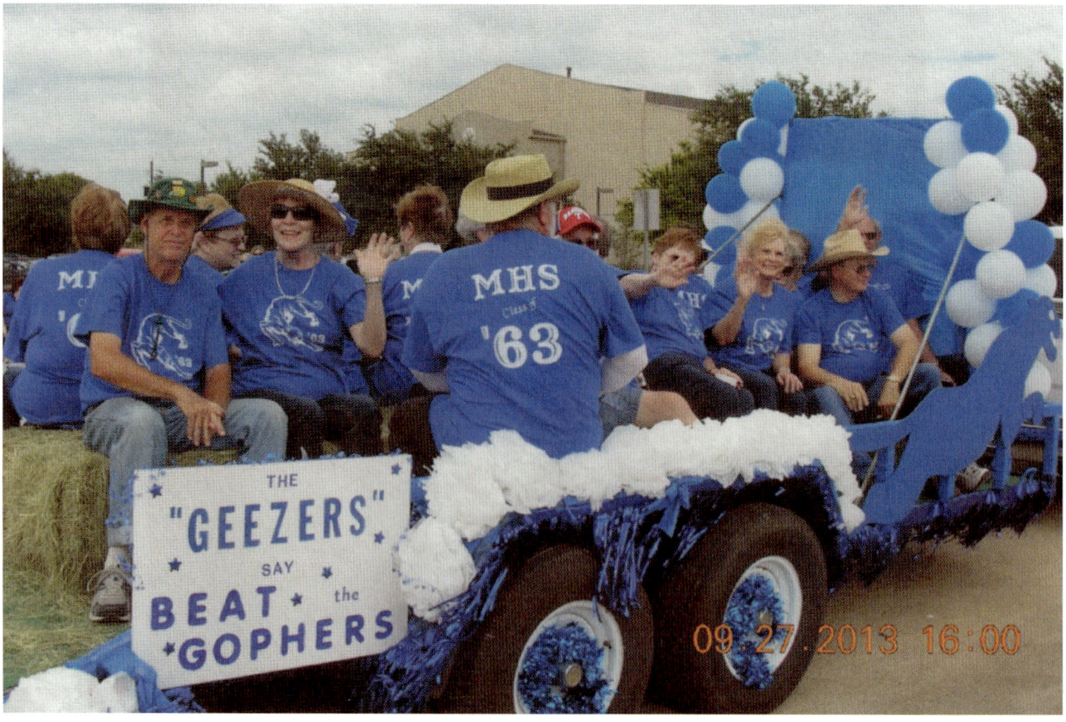

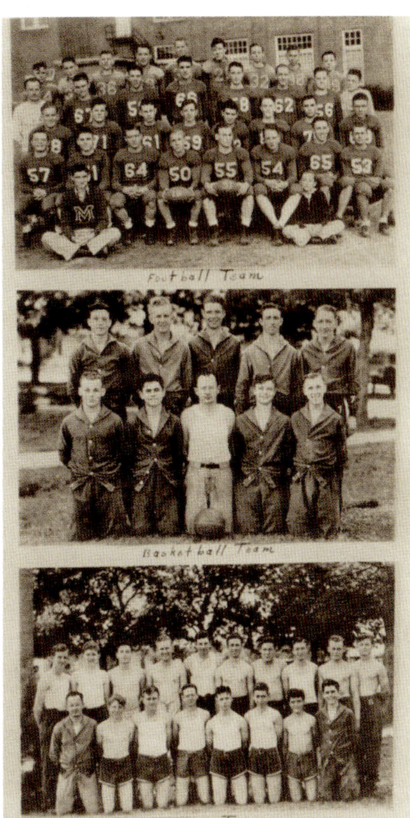

SCHOOL YEARBOOK: The first yearbook of Midlothian High School was published in 1938. The ball teams were shown on the same page, and there were no individual lists of boys' names. The band hall was in an old house across the street, where the 1950 gym would later be built. A. T. Baggett was the director; he was a very talented musician who also directed the 144th Infantry Band.

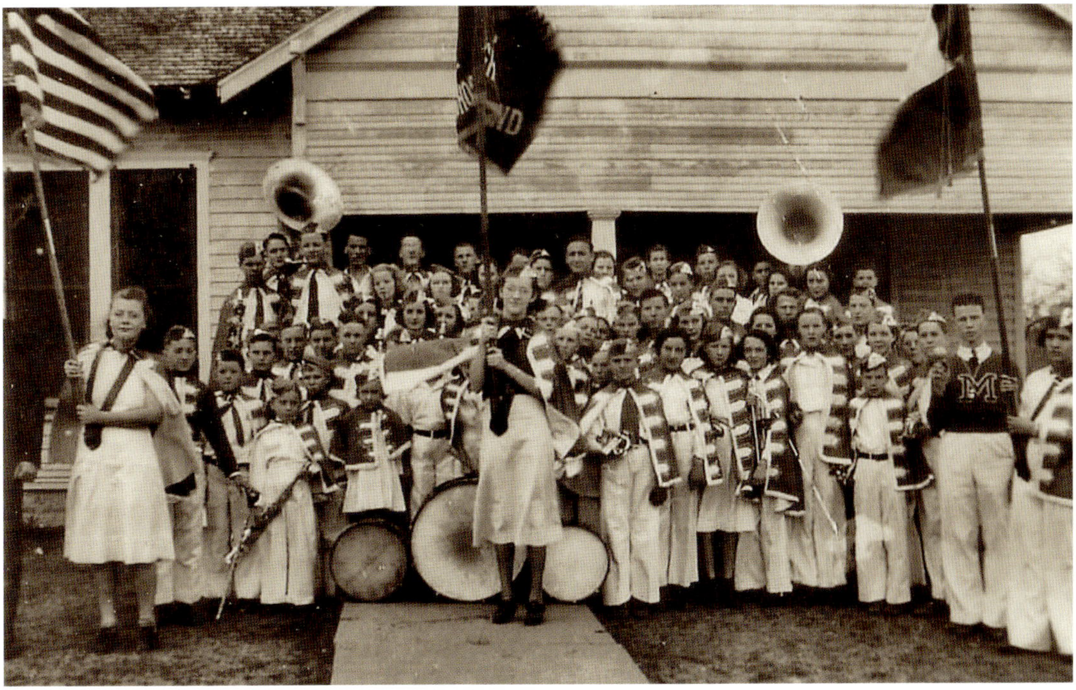

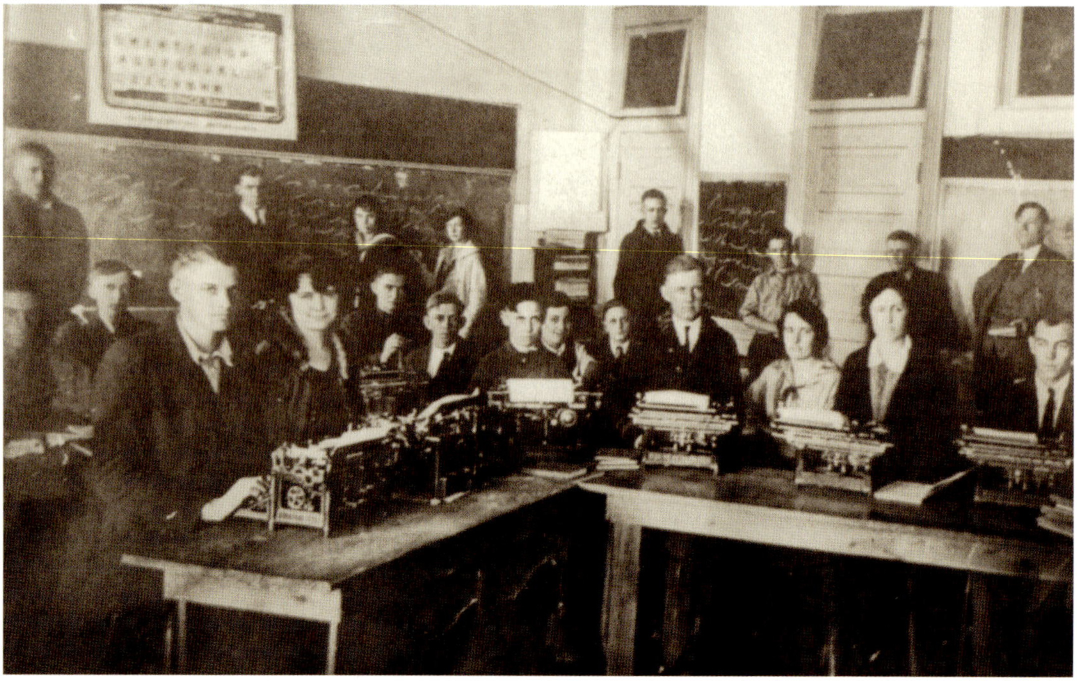

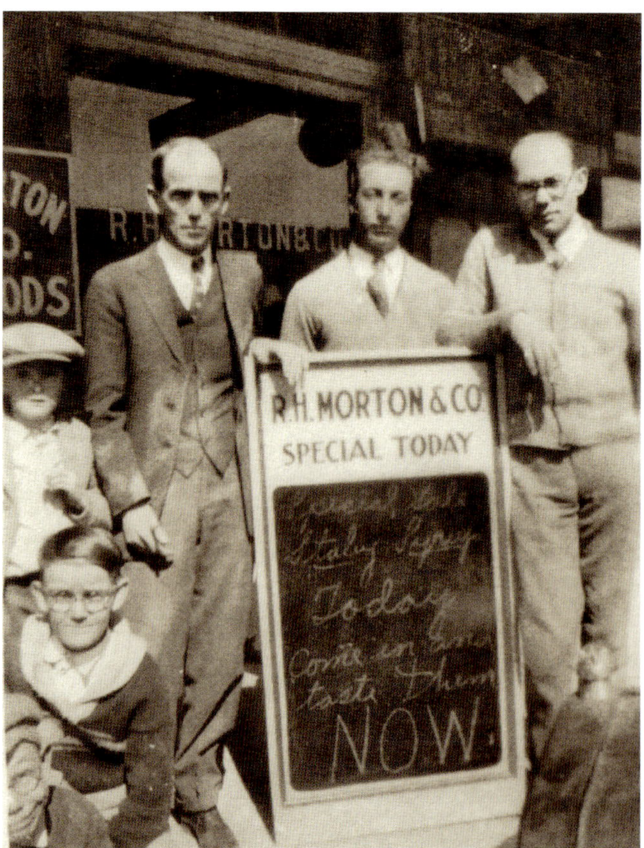

COMMERCIAL CLASS: The Midlothian High School Commercial class was photographed in 1923. *Students from left to right, standing*: Jack McClellan, Marcus Williams, Bulah McClendon, Pauline Philips, A. T. Baggett (later MHS band Director), Guy Atkins, and Leon Munden, and Principal J. R. Atkins. *From left to right, front*: Simon McElroy, Celvin Witherspoon, Frank Cornelius, Ruth Jean, Frank Reeves, Elwin Mason, Leon Curk, Tige Franks, Jack Crabtree, Frank Naile, Julia Hightower, Bernice Dodson, and Maurice Davenport. About 1928, Maurice Davenport is pictured (below) as an employee of R. H. Morton & Co. *From left to right*: Page sons, Hugh Page (partner of Rufus Morton), unknown, and Maurice Davenport.

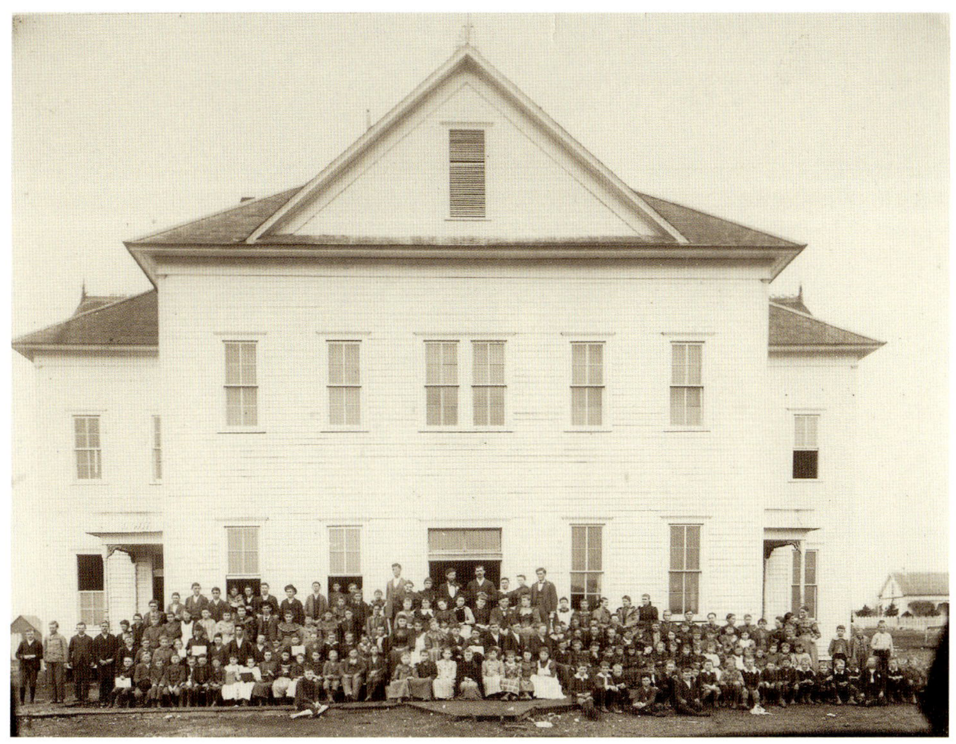

PUBLIC SCHOOL BUILDINGS: After an older, smaller building burned, this wooden building (above) was erected on the block given to Midlothian Public Schools by GC&SF in 1883. This building was built about 1895 and auctioned off in 1907.

The Midlothian Independent School District (MISD) was established in 1903, and the Trustees decided, in 1907, to build a new brick building for MHS. It is shown during a rare snow and ice event, in the winter of 1941–1942. It was razed and replaced in 1954.

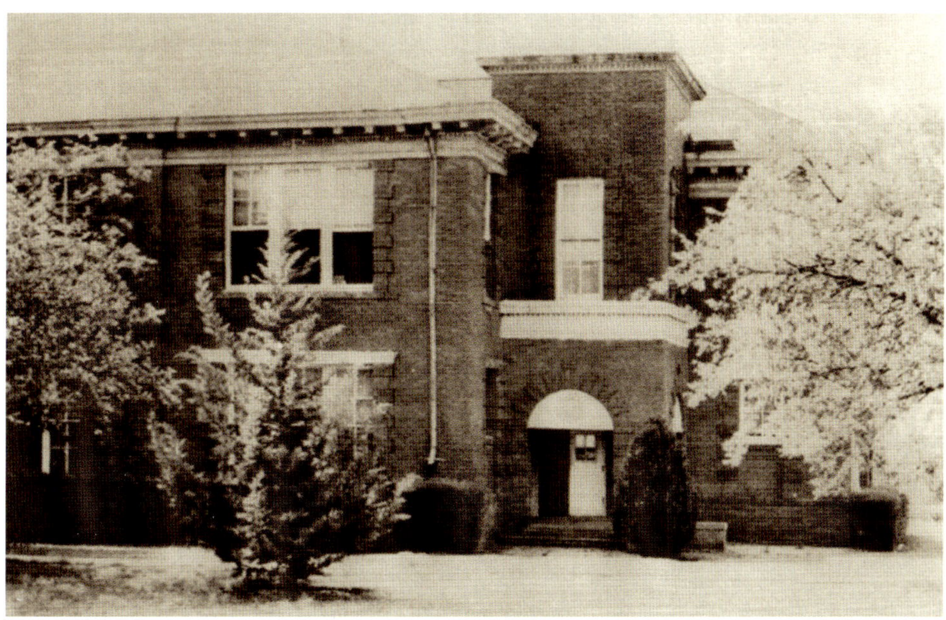

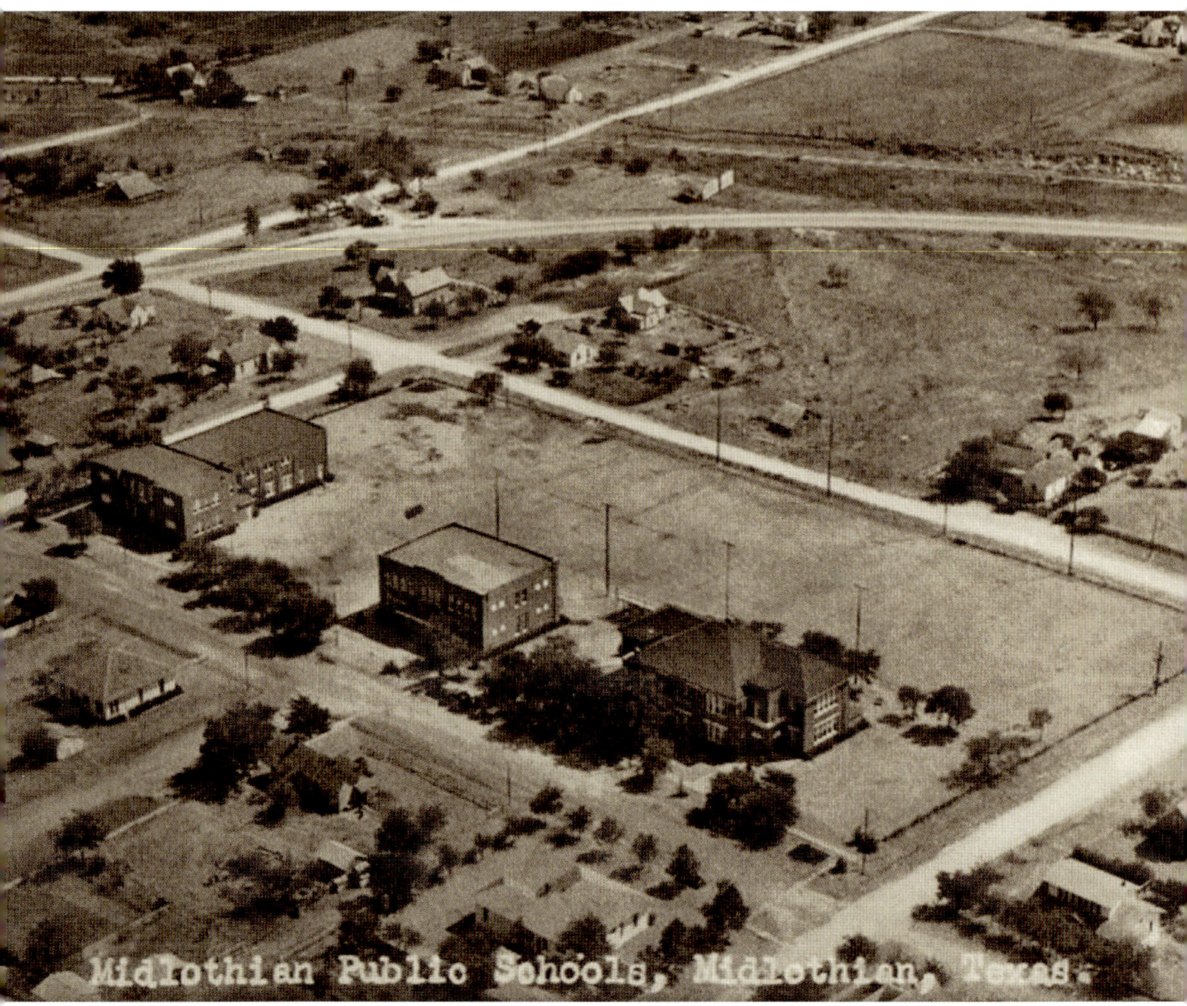

Barnes Aerial Photography photographed the Midlothian school district in the 1940s. At this time, all three of the two-story, red brick buildings were functioning on a very attractive campus. The T-shaped building on the left was built in 1920, opening in 1921 for primary age children, grades 1–4. It was named for Dell Mason Dees, whose parents donated money for the classrooms in her memory. She died of measles at age three. The Trustees obtained a loan to be able include the large auditorium at its rear. As late as 1964, all the MISD students, grades 1–12, could gather there for assemblies. This was also the site of Baccalaureate, Commencement, etc.

The middle building was known as the Grammar School, grades 5–8. It opened in 1915, having an auditorium on the second floor. South 3rd Street was deliberately closed in order for it to be built. Notice lights for the football field behind the Grammar and High Schools. Elementary students could play outside behind the Dees building.

The building on the right is the oldest of these three, built in 1907. This was the high school and the most ornate of the three buildings in its original form. It had undergone several changes in its thirty-eight years before this photo.

The High and Grammar Schools were razed, and a long, narrow, modern building replaced them, opening for class in 1955. Bricks from the Grammar School were used to build the Civic Center. The new school building was connected to Dees by a breezeway until the early 1980s when Dees, too, was razed and replaced.

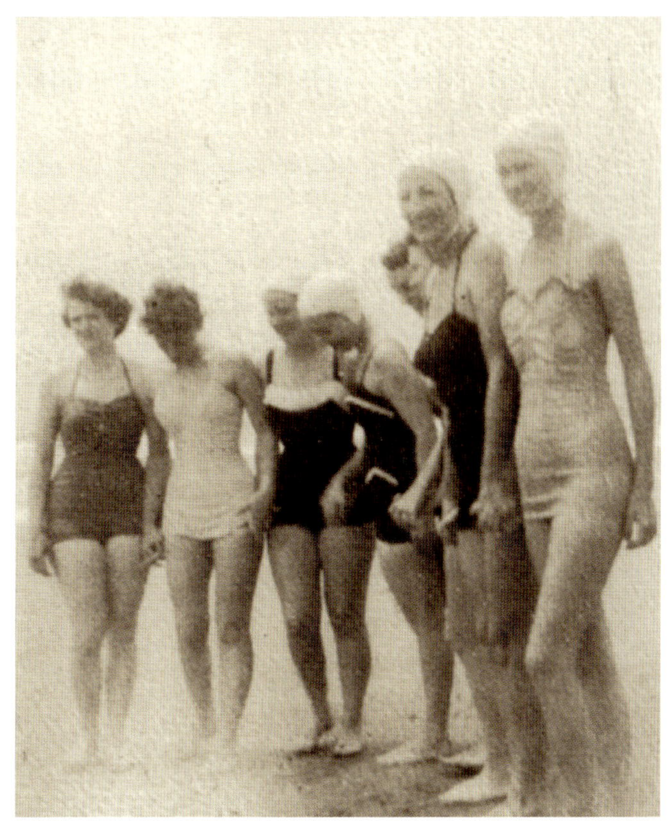

School Social Activities: In the 1950s and 1960s, the seniors enjoyed a "senior trip" to some tourist spot in Texas, usually a dude ranch or Galveston. They traveled via school bus, with no air conditioning or seatbelts. The class visited Galveston in 1957 where these girls, including a female sponsor, prepared for a swim.

The elementary students are dressed for a Thanksgiving feast in the late 1980s. Even some of the teachers and mothers have on Native American headpieces and Pilgrim caps. "Room Mothers" helped give class parties for all the major holidays.

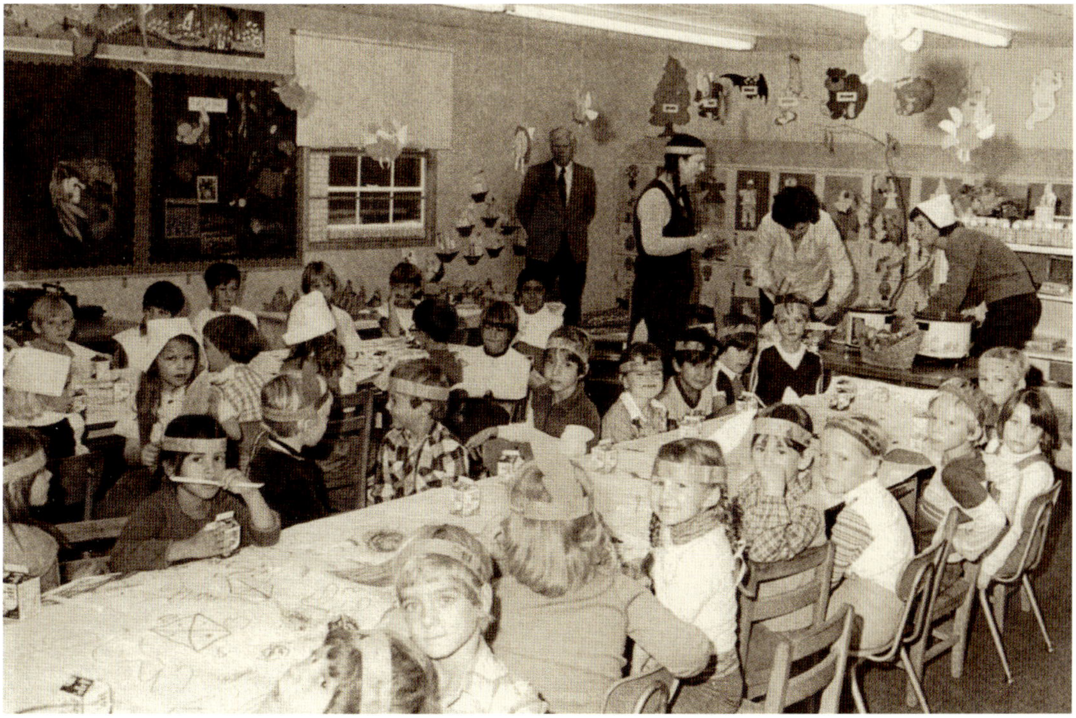

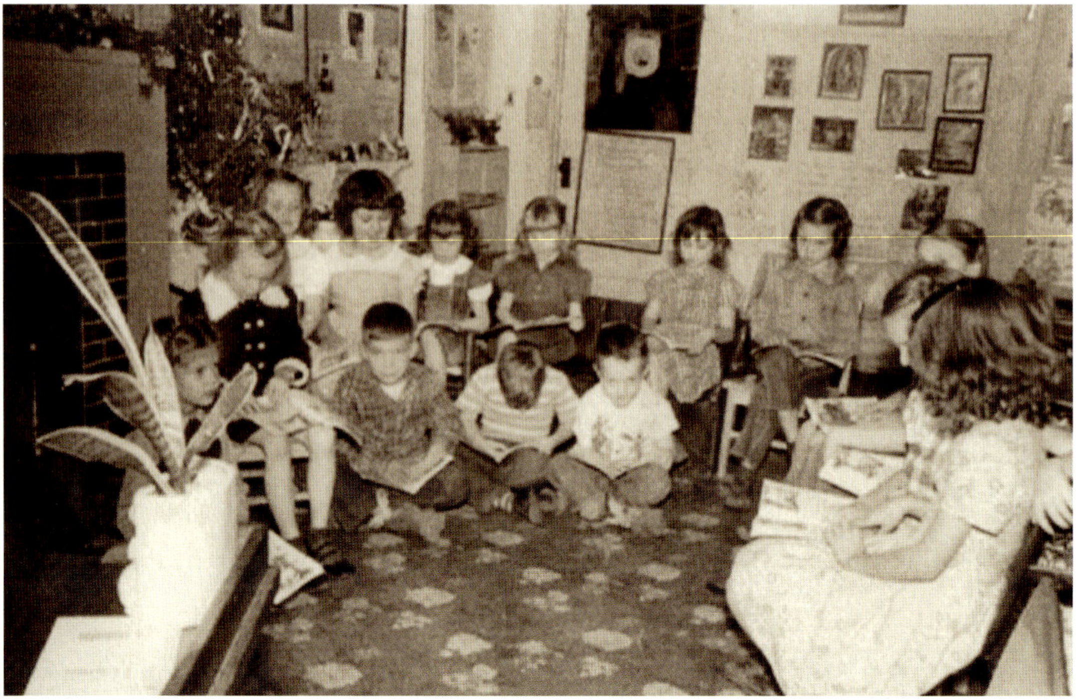

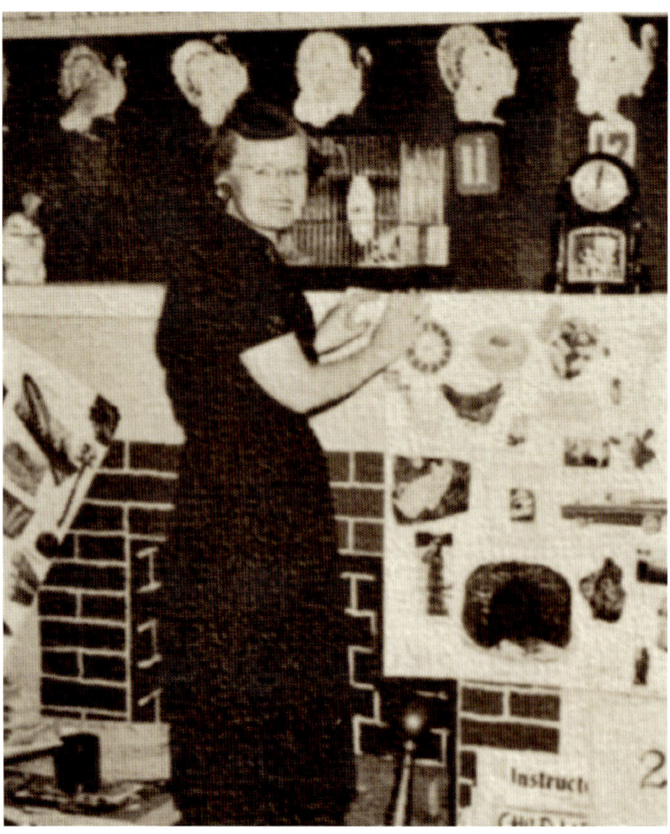

FIRST GRADE: In 1951, first graders in Laura Jenkins's class sat in a reading circle. Students loved her, as well as her room, because it was decorated so much like home. It did not matter that the fireplace was fake! In the late 1950s, Mrs. Jenkins, the Elementary Principal, was putting up Thanksgiving decorations. The clock on the mantle was a favorite because the little boy's and girl's swings actually swung when the hour struck.

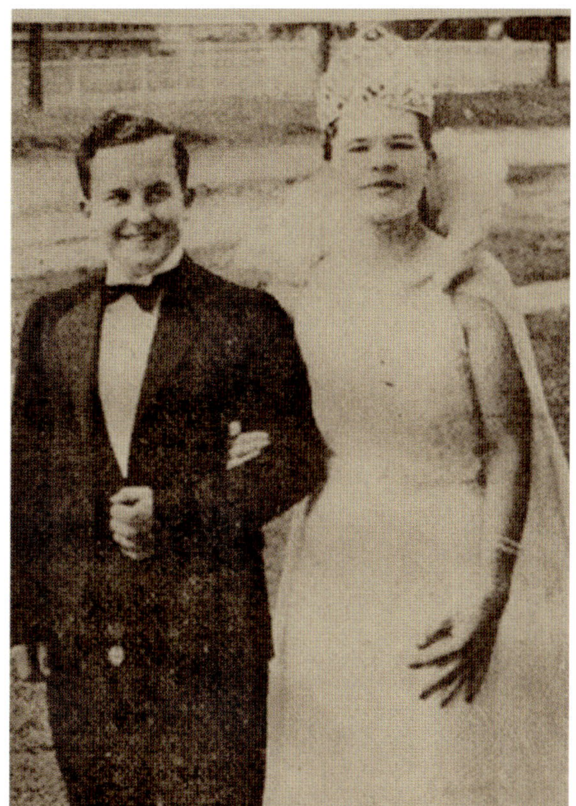

May Fete, 1920–1969: The May Fete was an annual coronation sponsored by the Parent-Teacher Association. In the early years, a Queen was elected, but no King. It began as a full day celebration. The King and Queen of 1935 were Keith Pryor (Warren) and Elizabeth Sewell. By 1950, the program had moved into the new gym where the Royal Party were seated on one end, and the other end was the site of entertainment for them and the audience.

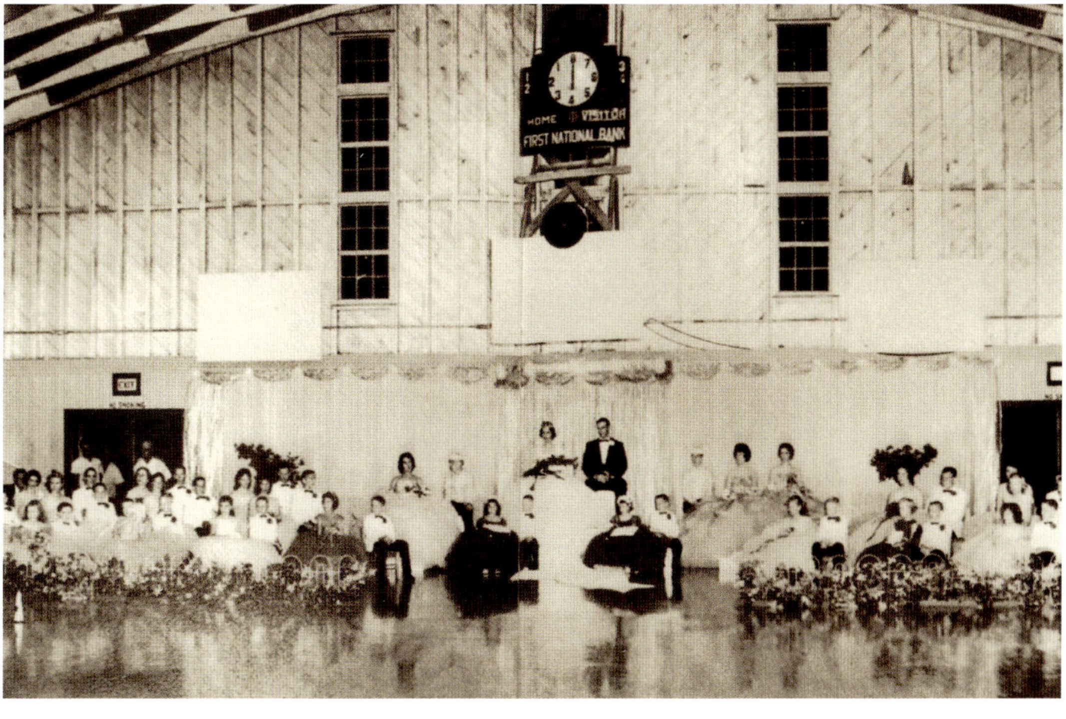

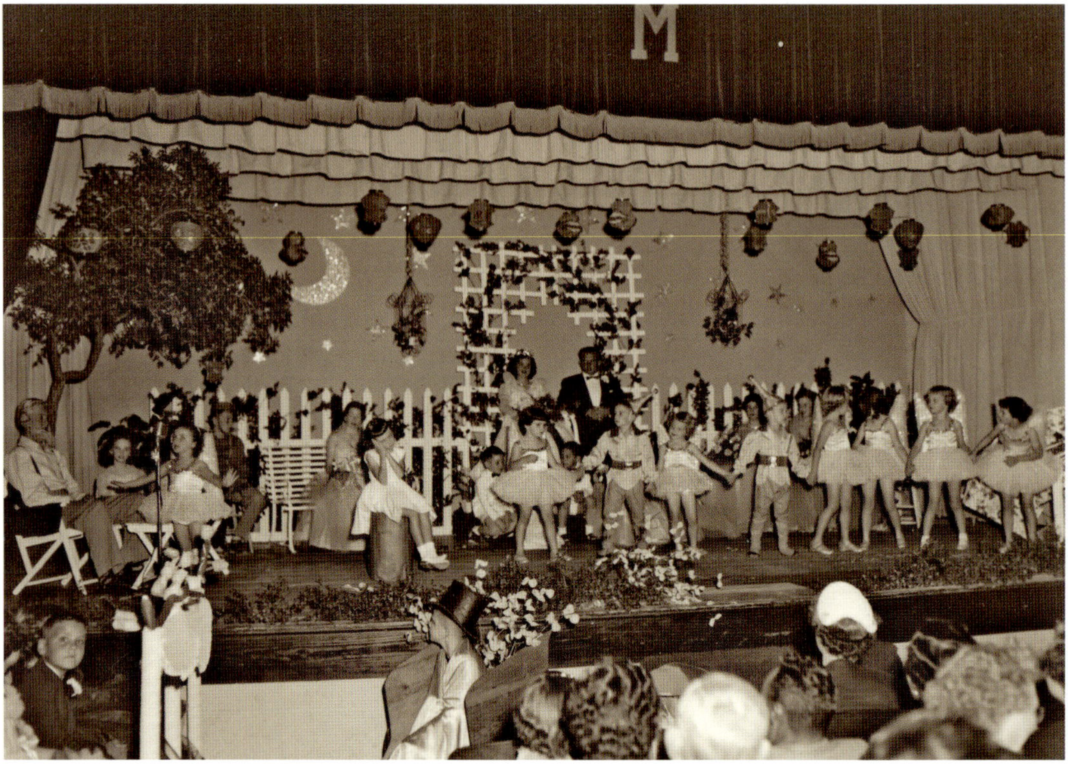

MAY FETE, 1954: The 1954 May Fete was held in the Dell Mason Dees Auditorium. The kindergartners performed as fairies and elves while one of their classmates sang "Beautiful Dreamer." The third graders performed a Mexican dance scene.

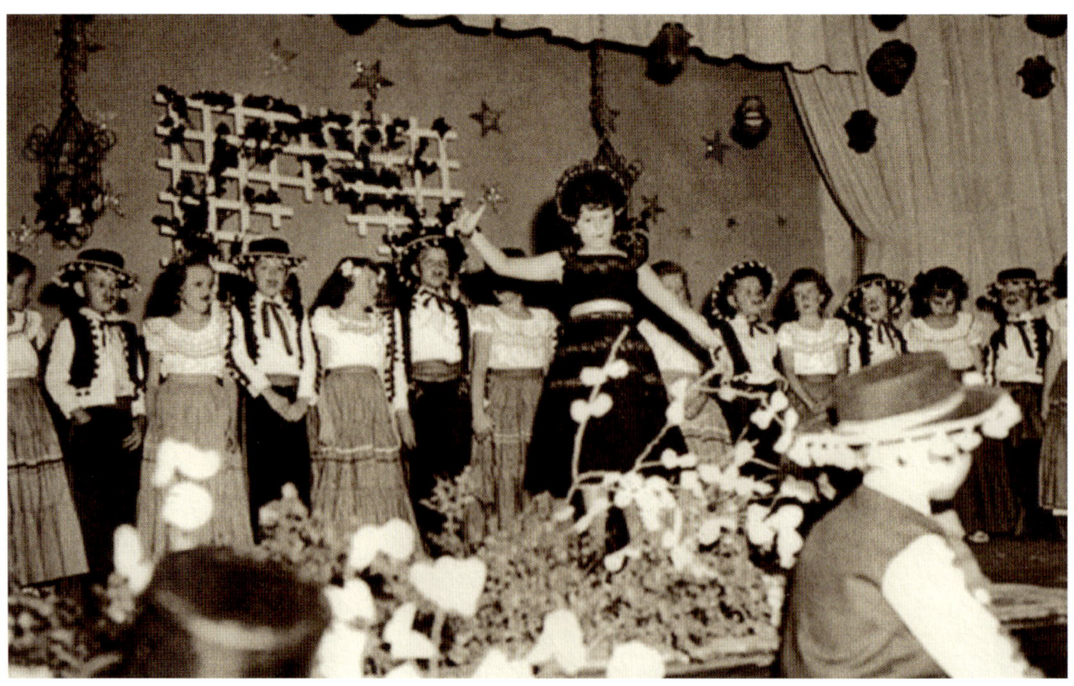

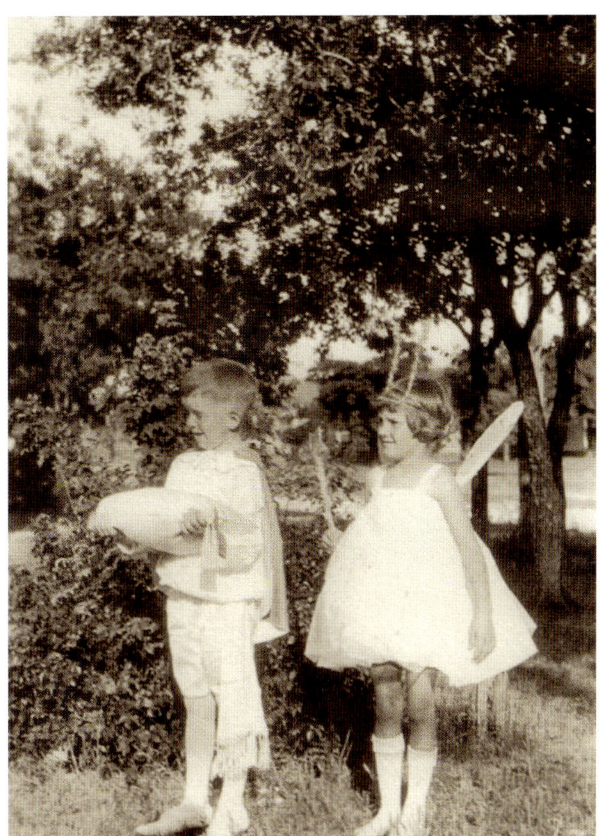

MAY FETE PARTICIPANTS: Neighbors Edward Harris and Charlene Morton were dressed for the May Fete, 1927. Edward was to be "Pillow Bearer" to Her Majesty Queen Phama Duke. Below, the two unidentified boys were "train bearers" in 1963.

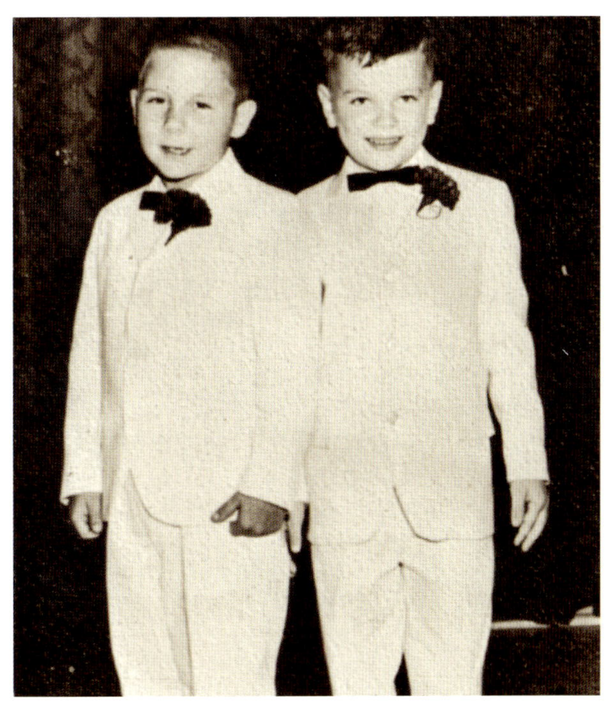

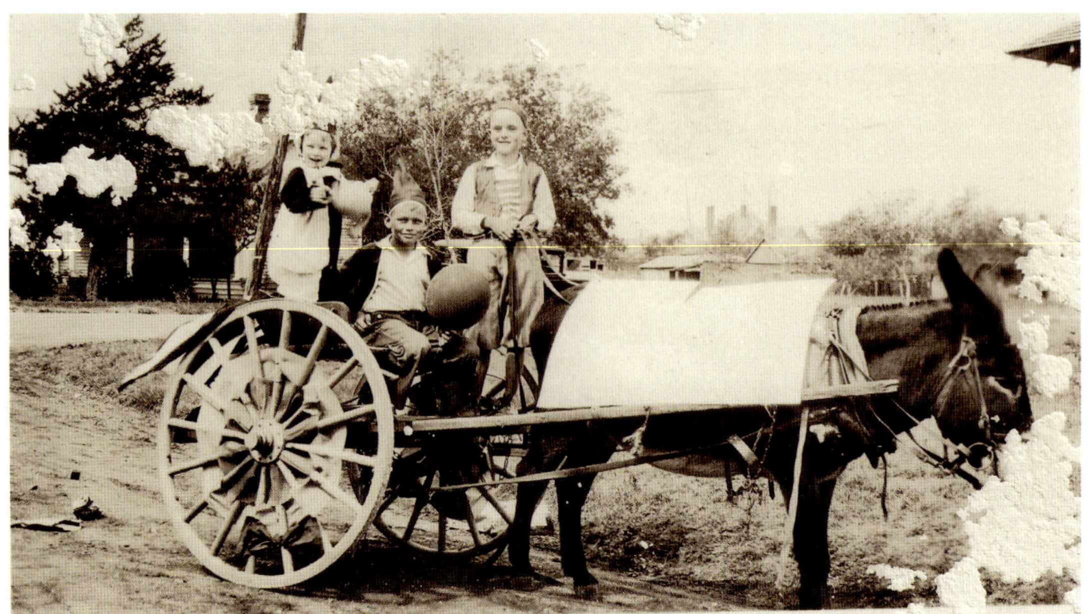

MAY FETE PARADES: When May Fetes began back in 1920, community parades were held in the afternoon before the coronation. These friends were ready to ride their cart in the May Fete parade, about 1928, above. They were Charlene Morton, her brother, Hubert "Buddy" Morton, and William Harris.

Below, Wilbur Lee Stephenson is riding "Spot" beside the float which his sister, Edith, is riding. She is the girl standing up on the float.

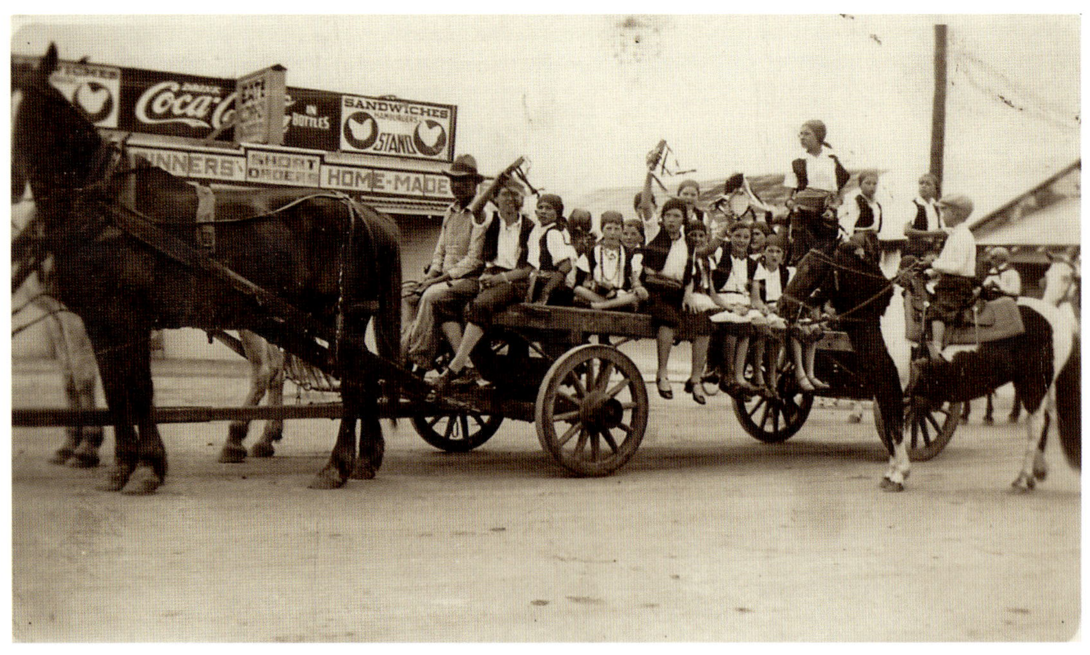

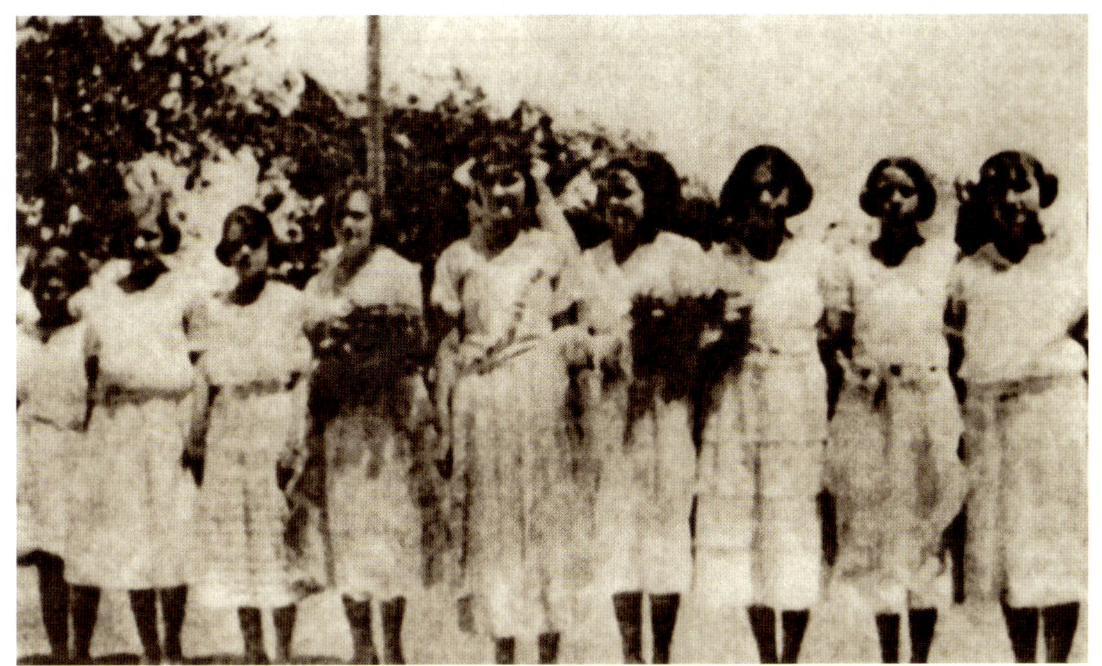

May Fete Courts of 1921 and 1963: The oldest extant photo of the Royal Party dates from 1921, the second May Fete. *From left to right*: Alice Franks, unidentified, Alice Lehrer, Letha Armstrong, Queen Alta Sherrill, Polly Below, Bernice Dodson, unidentified, and Geneva English. In 1963, Linda Kay Smith was Queen, escorted by King Acie Woodard, below.

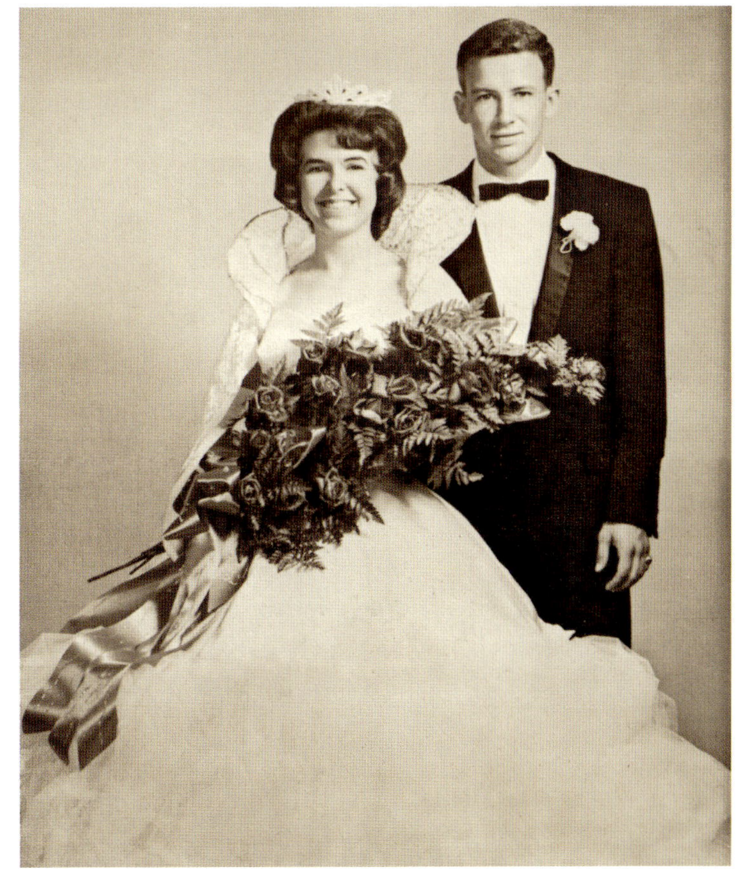

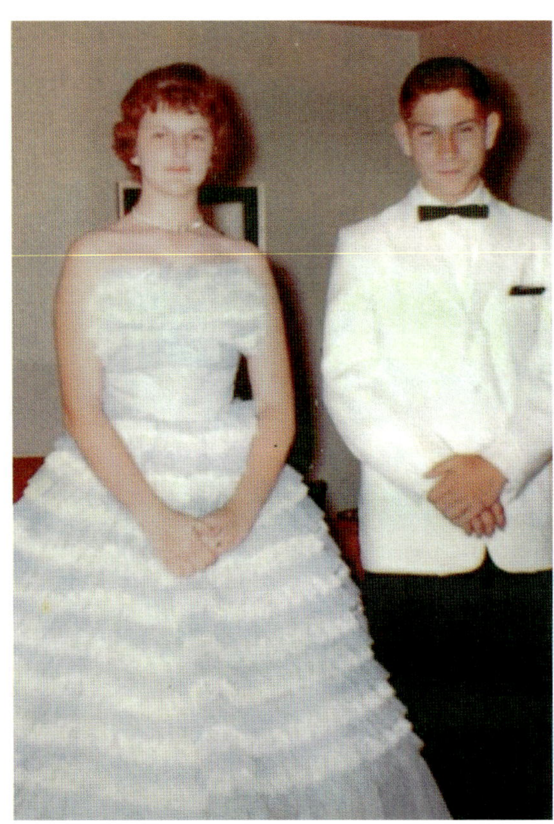

DUKES AND DUCHESSES: Besides the queen wearing white every year, the duchesses wore various pastels. A few of the colored photos from later years have been preserved. Beverly King and Larry Brim were Duke and Duchess for the eighth grade in 1960. Below, Betty Blevins and Bob Massey represented the first grade, 1963.

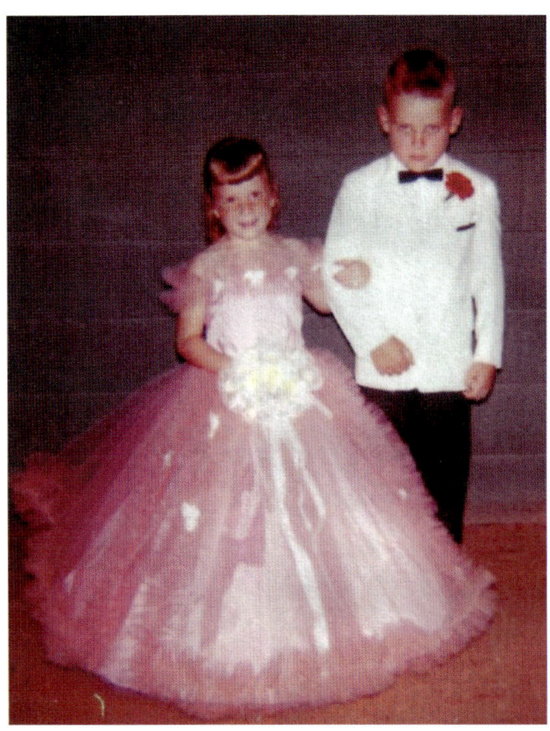

6

HOUSES

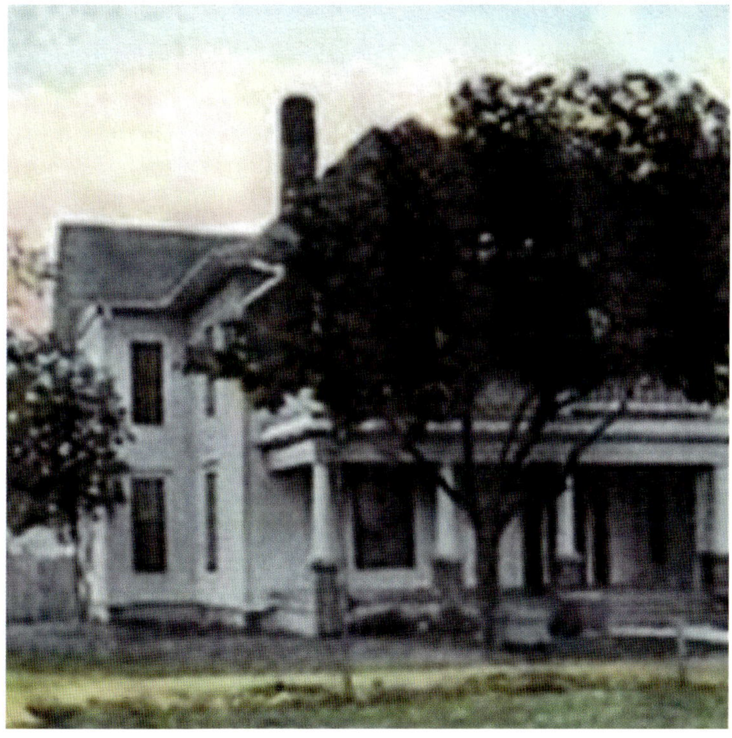

Known as the Stanberry Hotel, the house was actually built by Zilpha Newton Stiles Mullin. Her niece, Mrs. Linnie Stanberry, managed it. There were ten rooms available for patrons. The hotel was torn down in 1962, and the lot is now occupied by a warehouse.

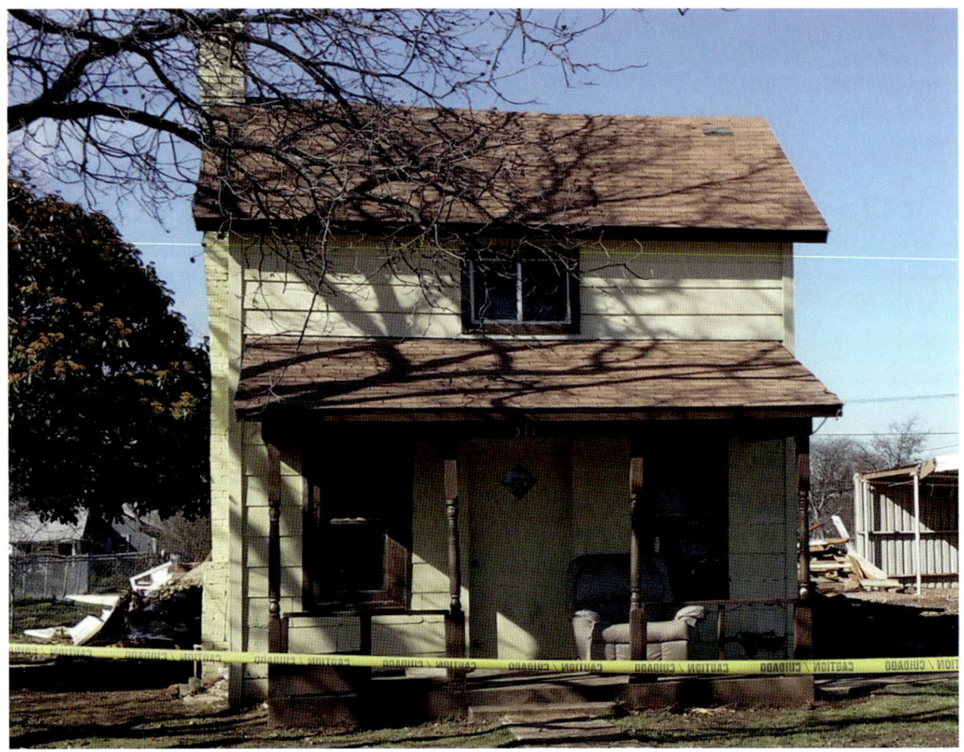

Old One-Room House: Per the Ellis County Appraisal District, this little yellow house was built in 1890. The present owner found an 1888 newspaper in it when remodeling began. Apparently, local developer W. R. Bentley had purchased the land from GC&SF when Midlothian was founded. It then went through several sales until reaching the present owner in 2005. When all the houses around it were razed, this one was repainted and moved to the western edge of the lot where, in 2018, it bears flags for Founders Row being developed there.

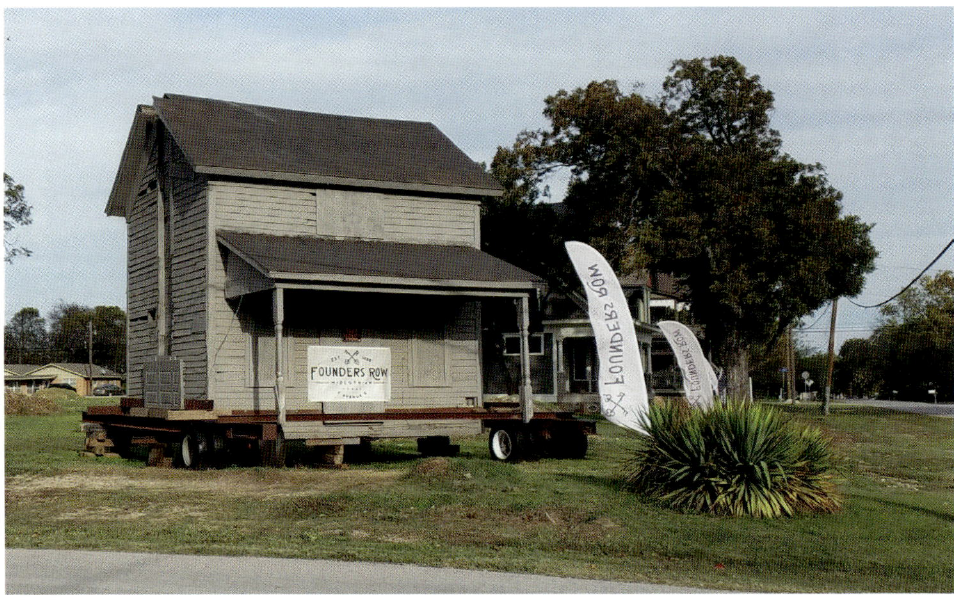

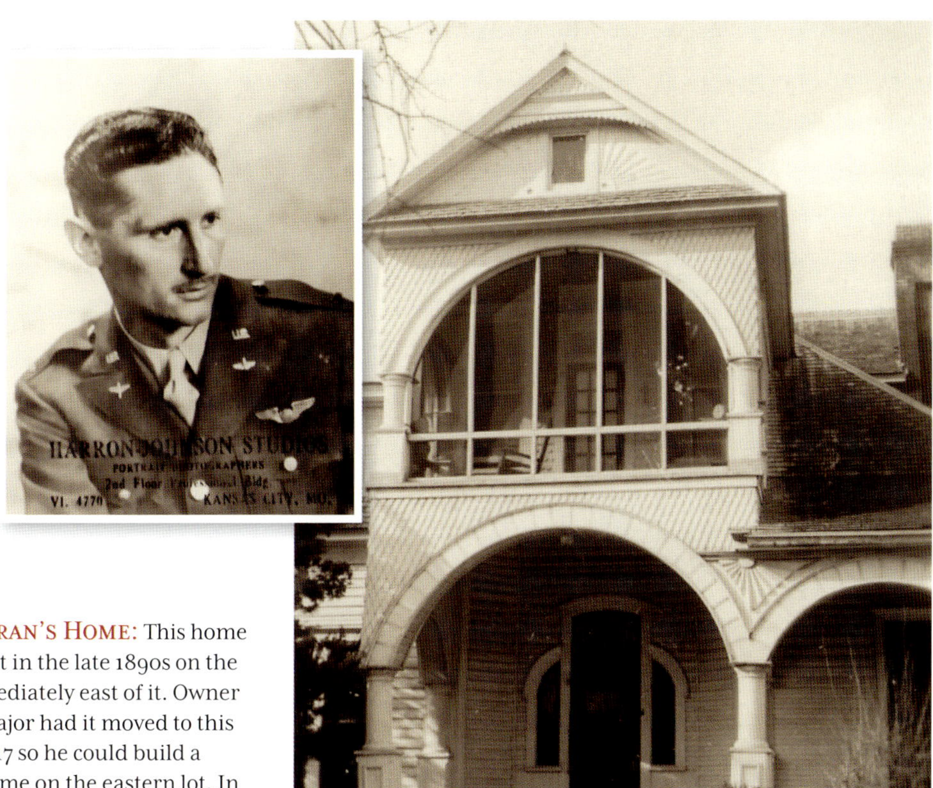

A Veteran's Home: This home was built in the late 1890s on the lot immediately east of it. Owner W. W. Major had it moved to this lot in 1917 so he could build a brick home on the eastern lot. In 1946, this house was purchased by Arthur Hagen, Sr., who had just been discharged from the U.S. Air Force. He is pictured in the inset, which shows the house at the time he lived there. It has been painted many different colors by 2018.

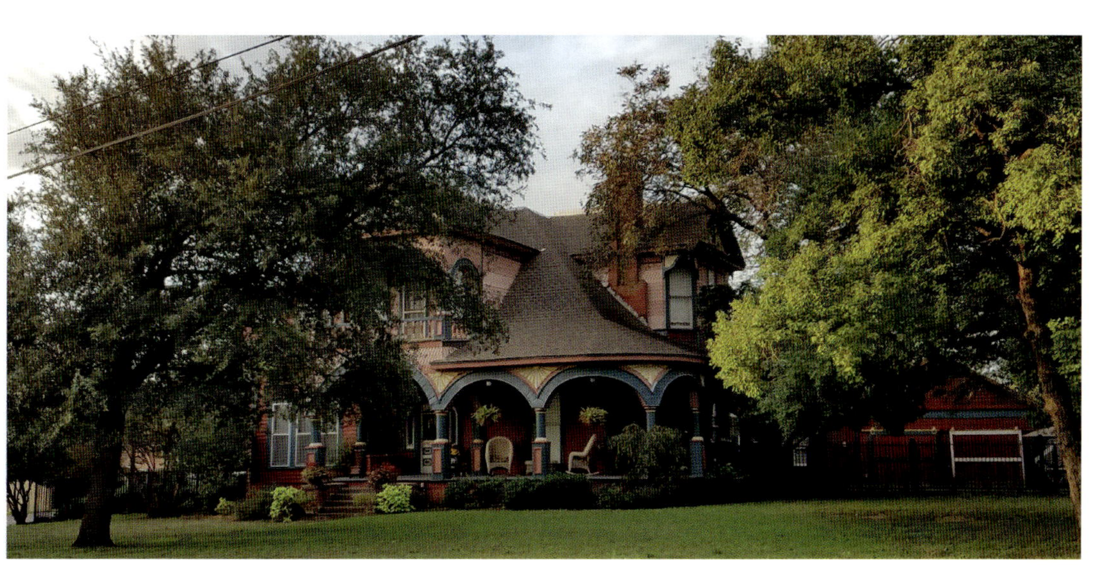

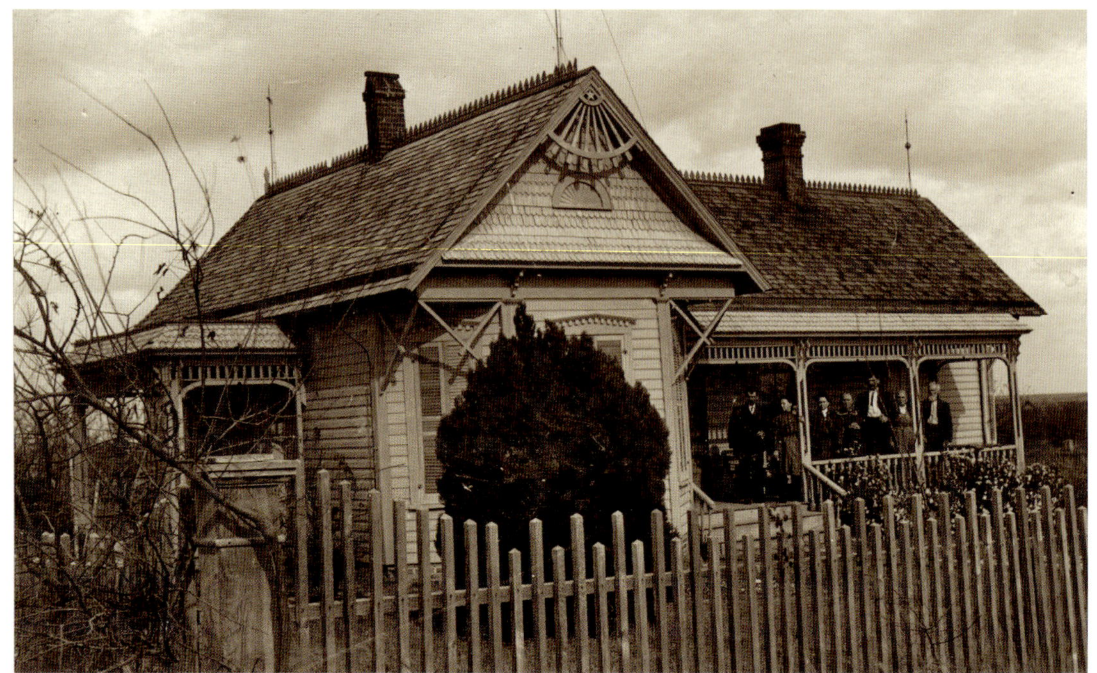

HOME OF McDANIEL, GIBSON, MORTON EXTENDED FAMILY: William Jay and Sarah Elizabeth McDaniel Gibson purchased this lot in1894 and had this home built the same year. Her parents, Benjamin Berryman and Anna McDaniel, lived with them. Ben had served the Confederacy in the 16th Texas Cavalry. The Gibsons had two children, Hubert and Ann Pauline. The home descended to Ann who married Charles Austin Morton. They, also, had two children, but the home was eventually sold out of the family. In 2018, the home shows major changes.

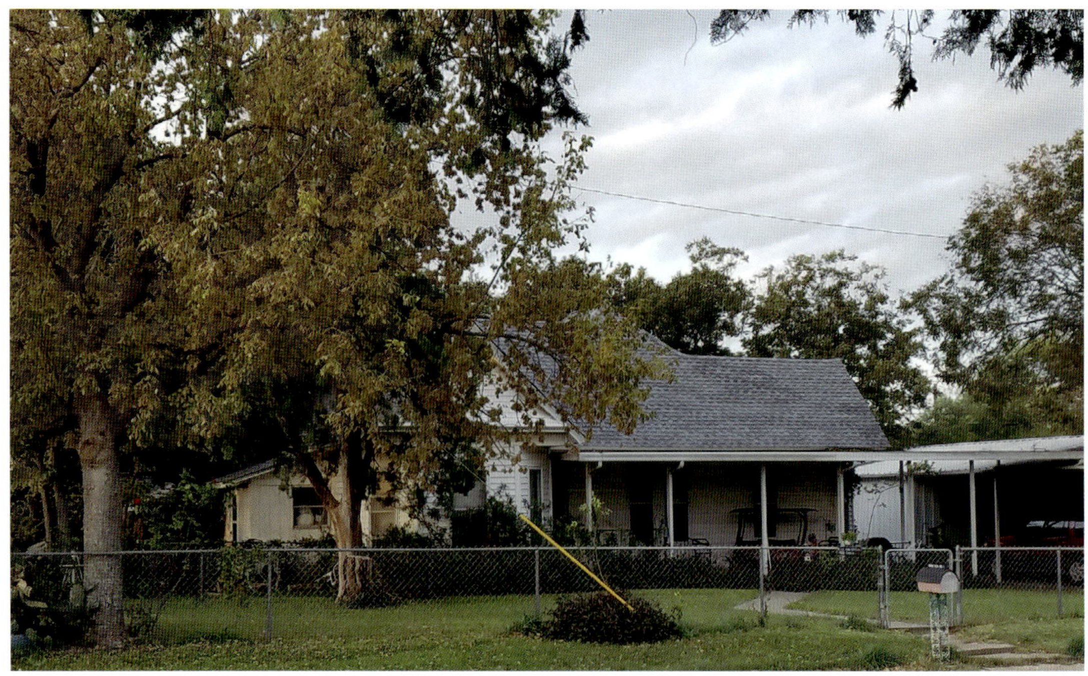

REESE HOMES: The home above was built by Samuel Livingston Reese in 1879 when he brought his family from Louisiana. He had served the Confederacy in Co. "H," 3rd Louisiana Infantry. This home eventually fell to his son, Sam Reese, while the land was divided among several children. Samuel's daughter, Mary Reese Hendricks, received land in the western part of the old homeplace. She and her husband built this home, somewhat reminiscent of her parents' home, a gothic-revival style.

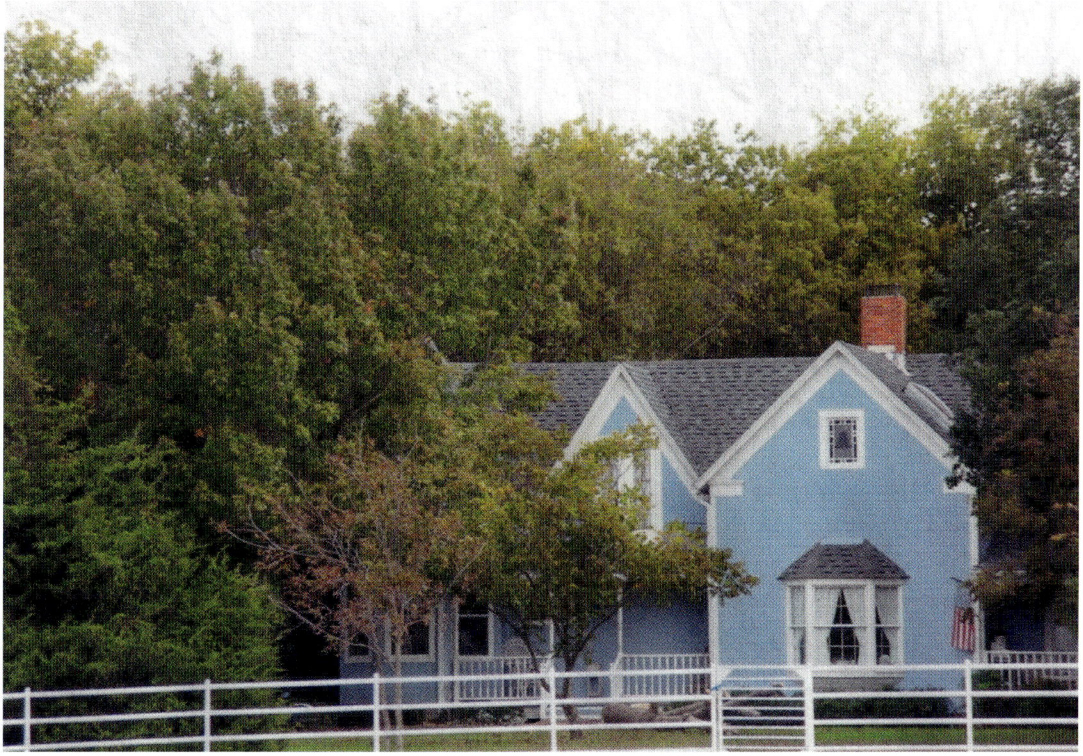

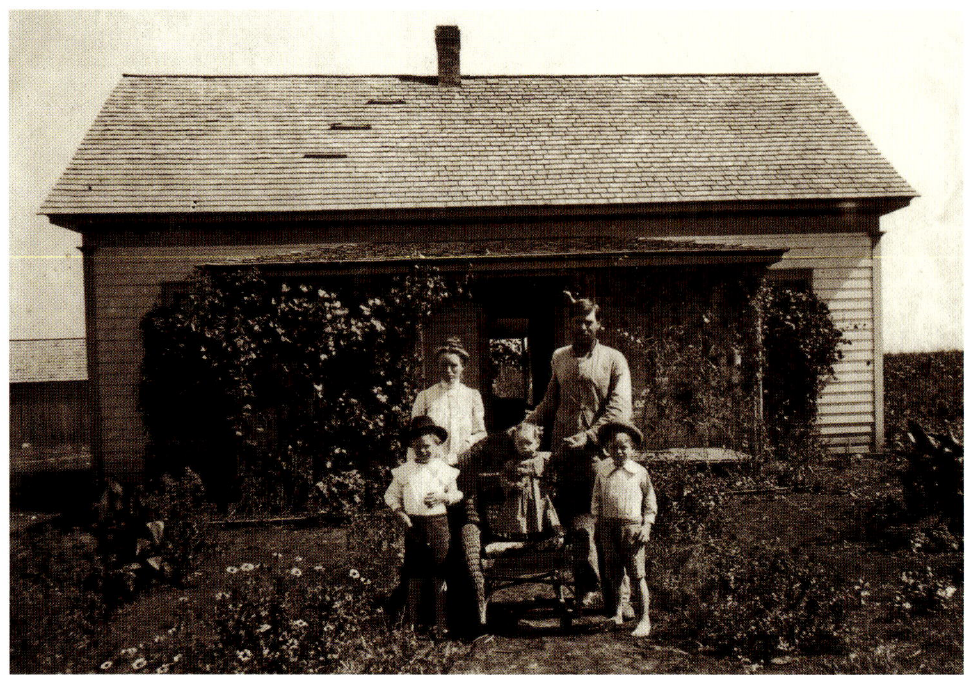

W. A. FEW HOME: William Allen Few married Laura Etta Ward in Ellis County, 1896. About 1903, they and their three oldest surviving children lived in this farm home, eventually moving onto South 9th Street, below. Their children were Curtis Wave, William Ward, Wilna, Joseph Weldon, Royal Windell, Winetta, and Wastell. Besides farming, Will was a merchant, selling groceries, gas, kerosene, oils, tires, tubes, etc. Most of these tied in with his being an agent for Magnolia products. He represented Ellis County in the 1933–1934 Texas Legislature.

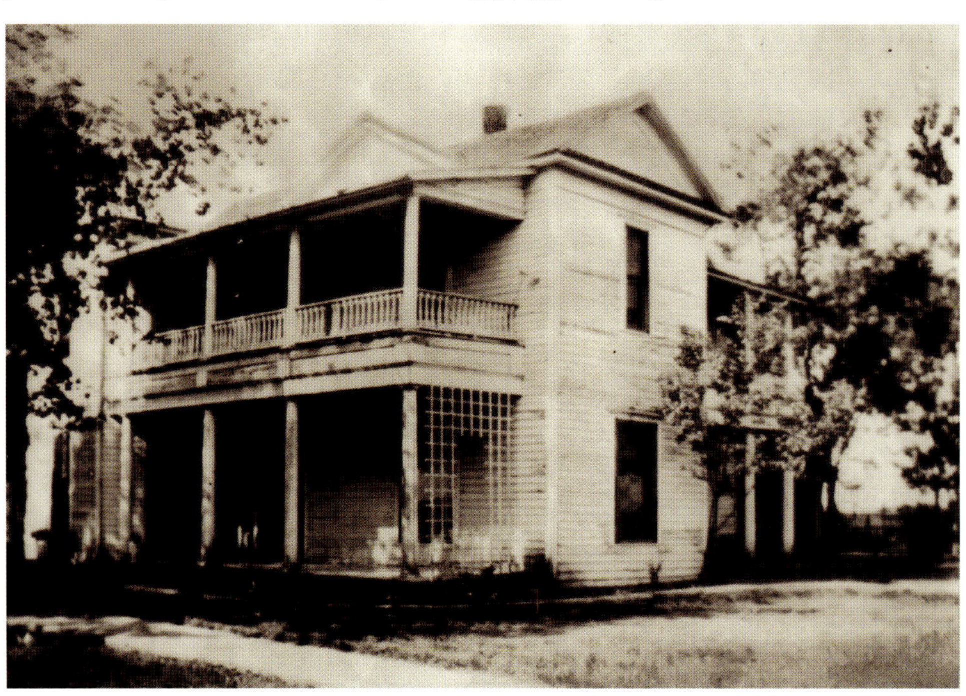

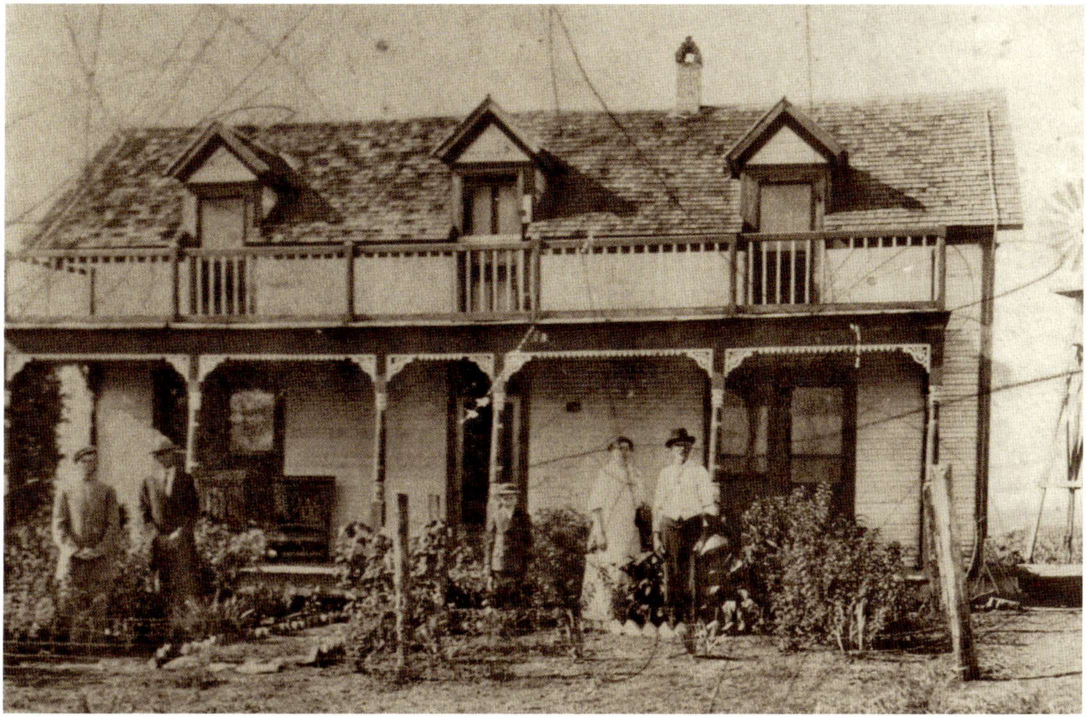

HENDRICKS HOME: Chalmers and Opal Hendricks lived in this home, above, located east of Midlothian on FM 1387. The people standing on the porch and yard are unknown. A housing addition was begun in that area in the late 1970s, and there is no longer any sign of the home in 2018.

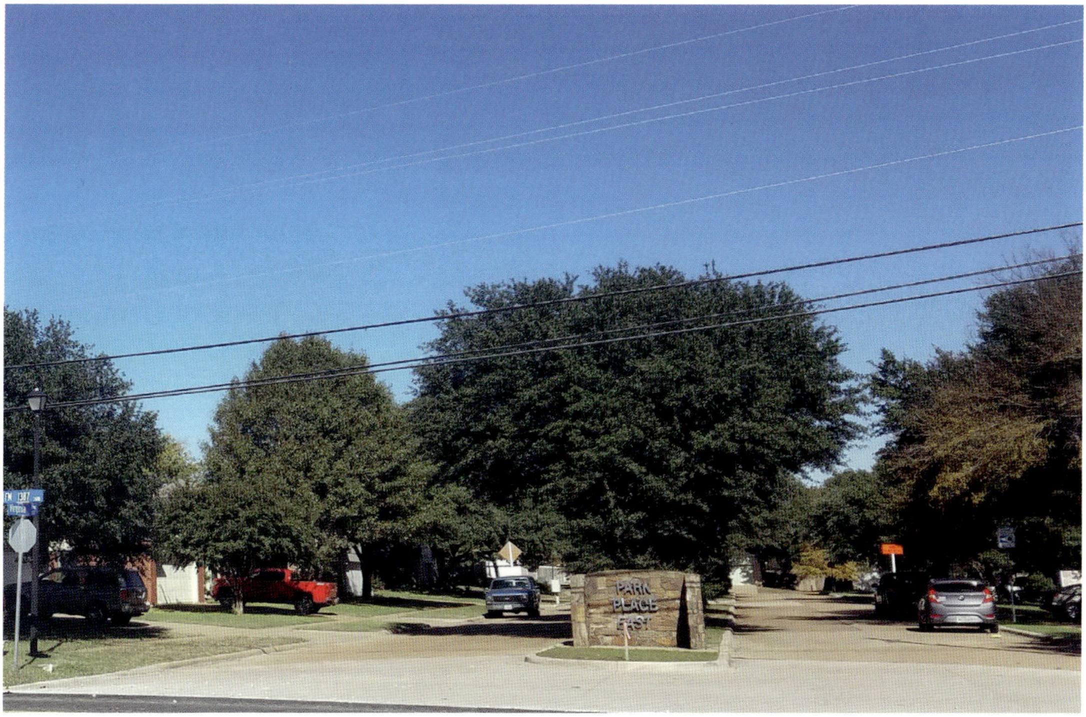

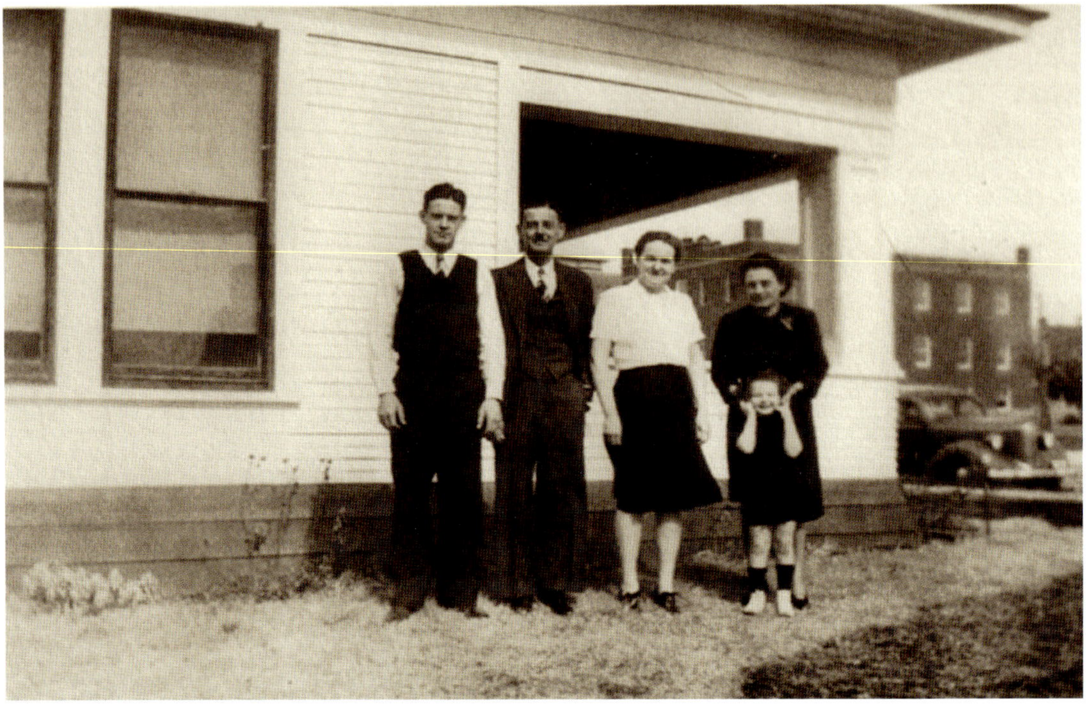

DeGrand Home: Chesley C. "Curly" DeGrand, son of Italian immigrants, came to Midlothian around 1920. He and wife Susie Cornelius owned this home across from the 1901 Methodist Church after the Education Building was added. They had two children, Suzanne and Charles Cornelius DeGrand. Charles is shown with his parents, wife, and daughter about 1957. The home had major changes by 2018.

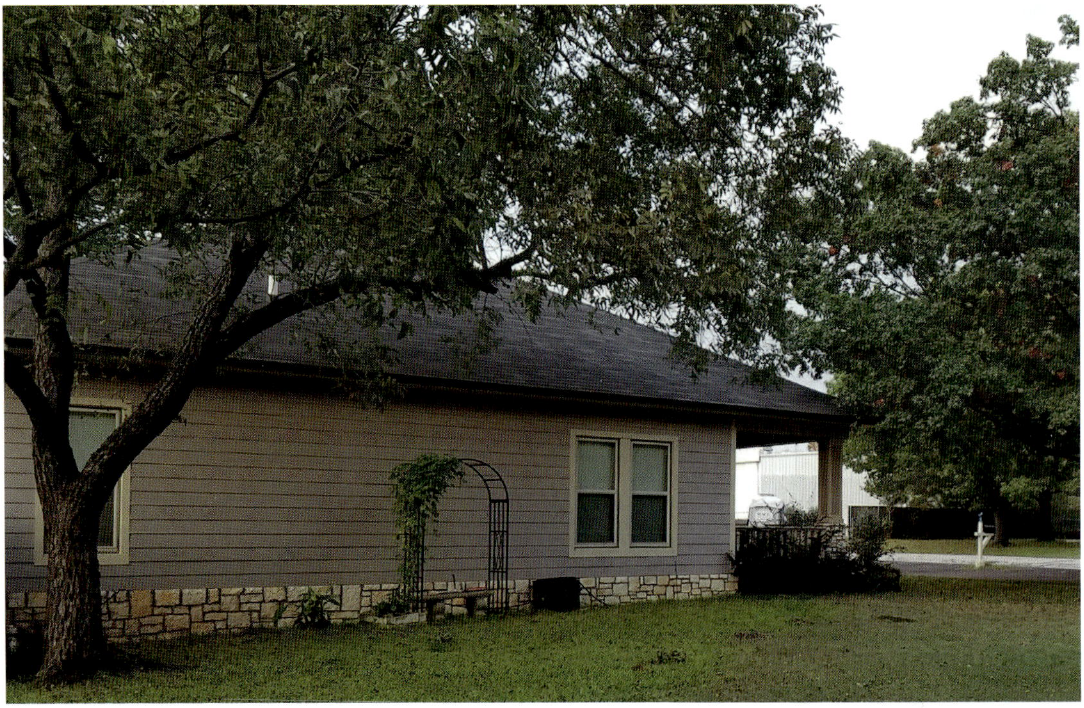